FOR TODA ...

Whether you're _____ work, GETTING YO _____ hard-hitting, commonsense answers to the work problems women face in today's job market. The system *can* work for you, if you know how to:

- **enter the job market** (here are invaluable "psyching" techniques and skill-sharpeners for the novice, plus solid information on making employment agencies work *for* you—not against you) . . .
- **beat sex discrimination** (a detailed, concise breakdown of what your rights are, when to fight, how to organize, and what legal remedies are most suitable) . . .
- **handle job-related hassles** (interviews, personality conflicts, resumés, sexuality traps, and more) . . .

PLUS: How to spot the "dead-end job"—*before* you get stuck with it; how to make an ally of your boss, male *or* female; how to find and *use* such vital career-helpers as childcare facilities, career counselors, employment services, and talent banks.

"**GETTING YOURS** is the next best thing to having an intelligent, compassionate, and totally understanding friend whose sole purpose is helping you re-make your life—exactly the way you want it!"

GLORIA STEINEM

getting yours

HOW TO MAKE THE SYSTEM WORK FOR THE WORKING WOMAN

LETTY COTTIN POGREBIN

 AVON
PUBLISHERS OF BARD, CAMELOT, DISCUS, EQUINOX AND FLARE BOOKS

AVON BOOKS
A division of
The Hearst Corporation
959 Eighth Avenue
New York, New York 10019

ISBN: 0-380-00600-6

First Avon Printing, March, 1976

AVON TRADEMARK REG. U.S. PAT. OFF. AND
FOREIGN COUNTRIES, REGISTERED TRADEMARK—
MARCA REGISTRADA, HECHO EN CHICAGO, U.S.A.

Printed in the U.S.A.

For my marvelous children
Abigail, Robin and David
who understand how to live with a working mother

and always for Bert
who understands everything

Contents

SECTION
I

Work, Home and Family:
The Personal Is Political

---

*Let the truth be known: there are no perfect,
private solutions. It is not the woman who
has failed but the system that has failed her.*

1

Requiem for a Queen Bee

"The true Queen Bee has made it in the 'man's world' of work, while running a house and family with her left hand. 'If I can do it without a whole movement to help me,' runs her attitude, 'so can all those other women.'

"Many successful women relish the fact that they are 'special,' that they have unique qualifications that allow them to get high-ranking positions normally denied to women.

"The Queen Bee has typically worked very hard to get where she is; she doesn't want younger women to have it any easier than she did.

"By insisting that the present system is open and fair to all, and that success is a direct result of personal talent and striving, the Queen Bee allows herself the luxury of self-congratulation. She is not at the top because of favoritism or fortune, but because she deserves to be there.

"Queen Bees are highly rewarded for being special, for 'looking so feminine' yet 'thinking like a man.'

"The Queen Bee tries to be a superwoman, and is as eager to 'win' in the traditional feminine role of wife and mother as in her career. She may strive to succeed in the wife-mother role as a way of reassuring herself about her femininity, to resolve conflict over success in a masculine world."

—from "The Queen Bee Syndrome"
by Graham Staines, Carol Tavris
and Toby Epstein Jayaratne

Guilty as charged! Now that social psychologists have defined the Queen Bee phenomenon in full detail, I recognize my former self as a dead ringer for that personality type.

In 1970, when my book *How to Make It in a Man's World* was published, I had never heard the phrase, Queen Bee. But I believed myself well-equipped to advise women on the perfect melding of marriage and career.

After all, I was happily married to a lawyer, I was the energetic mother of three young children and the director of three departments in a book publishing company. I cooked the family meals, did all the marketing and occasionally mounted a gourmet extravaganza known as a dinner party for ten. I waltzed from executive meetings to parent-teacher conferences with grace and aplomb. In the office, I planned $50,000 promotion campaigns to make best sellers out of unknown books. With equal attention and efficiency at home, I knitted ponchos for the children, embroidered samplers for the walls, planted a garden and never let the seeds of self-doubt take root.

I was determined to prove that any woman could have it *all*. Moreover, she could carry off this balancing act without shortchanging anyone in her life. My house was orderly, my husband's shirts were always fresh, his five-course meals piping hot (though I had to race home from work in order to perform this nightly miracle before he arrived). The children had their mother for papier-mâché projects, for bedtime storytelling, for company on class trips, for quiet talks and noisy games. My boss was similarly well-served. I took work home, made friends for the company, supervised my departments with a strong hand and was a living monument to company loyalty.

In reviewing my book, *The New York Times* called me "supergirl"—and I accepted the encomium with thanks. In fact, I was grateful to *everyone*. My husband *let* me work; my boss *let* me juggle business commitments when my homelife required it; other businessmen *let* me enjoy my triumphs. Hadn't men always been kind and helpful? What were woman complaining about, anyway? It was only a question of good management and organization, I counselled. If a woman worked hard at both her roles, she too could achieve career success "without sacrificing her femininity."

In those days I was big on femininity. And had anyone asked me to define it, I wouldn't have been in the least bit embarrassed to reel off the myths I lived by: be assertive but not aggressive (men are threatened by pushy women); protect the male ego at all costs (you can take him to lunch on your expense account but let him order the meal and don't pay the bill ostentatiously); look delicate, if not slightly sexy. You get the picture.

And while I'm confessing, I may as well admit the tremendous ambivalence I felt about other women. Psychologist Philip Goldberg has measured anti-female bias and reported on it in an essay entitled "Are Women Prejudiced Against Women?" It seems the answer is a resounding yes. Women don't believe in other women or their abilities. We don't trust one another, admire one another, defend, respect or support one another.

In my case, as with many Queen Bee types, being the exception—the youngest, smartest or only woman in the board room—was compensation for the strain of balancing "femininity" and professionalism. To be an exception one had to be different from most women and therefore more like men. The token woman is expected to feel flattered when told she "thinks like a man." Such praise was a form of initiation into the company of "the first sex." In return the token owes it to her male benefactors to share their disregard for "most women" who, according to the popular wisdom, are "scatter-brained," overly emotional, incapable of intellectual feats, irrational, undependable and unsuited to decision-making or high finance.

Given such a dismal profile of her sex, what aspiring woman in her right mind would want to identify with other women. So we Queen Bees cast our lot with the ruling class, never recognizing the self-loathing inherent in our disavowal of womankind.

What a colossal neurosis: defend to the death your "normal femininity" so that you may be allowed to function as a non-emasculating businesswoman. At the same time, dissociate yourself from your pitiful sisters so that you don't get tarred by the same brush that sweeps women out of sight. (If the Women's Movement hadn't come along, I might have become a card-carrying schizophrenic.)

It was the old divide-and-conquer game refined to subtle perfection. As girls, we had learned to compete with one another for dates and later for husbands. (Having a man *choose* you was the only way to affirm your worth.) As working women, we continued the pattern, competing not for promotions or recognition but for the few crumbs of male approval that led to the even fewer token top jobs that a woman might be permitted to hold.

While black people were alert to the ploy of tokenism—hiring one visible black executive could draw attention away from the lily white rank-and-file—it took awhile for most women to see that racism and sexism operate with the same nefarious machinery.

I was one of those who learned later than I should have. I began to notice the double-bind in all its workaday variations. If a woman was attractive and successful, it was assumed she had used her looks to seduce vulnerable men in high places. If a woman was plain-looking, her success was attributed to her "masculine drive" or worse yet, her sublimated sexual frustrations. (What that woman needs is a good lay, etc.)

In the hiring and promotion process, women were also damned if they do and damned if they don't. The single woman was a poor employment risk because she might get married, or because she might turn into a life-long spinster—and you know how intolerable those old battle-axes can be.

But the married woman was nobody's favorite employee, either. She might get pregnant and quit to raise her kids. If she stays on, her absenteeism rate is sure to rise when she takes days off to nurse a sick child. Or she'll up and leave us to follow her husband to a new job in another town. Married or single, the working woman can't win.

I began to understand that individual solutions are pointless, selfish and often counterproductive. If I have pressured my boss into a six-weeks maternity leave with pay, that's fine for me. But until it becomes company policy, paid leave is no more than a royal dispensation, granted by the reigning regent in return for satisfaction of one of his future whims or demands.

Eventually, I came to realize that I had more in common with the secretaries in their dead-end jobs than with the male colleagues who were presumably my equals. Women executives could be found in relatively few departments in the publishing industry. Even with graduate degrees, we were hired as clerical workers to start, and there was an unspoken limit in every firm as to how far up the hierarchy a woman could ever go.

There were industry-wide stag picnics at which good spirits and much deal-making took place—no doe allowed. There were assignments and clients that a woman "just couldn't handle." There was a larger office that was kept empty for weeks "in case a new man was hired."

I may have been at a higher salary level than those secretaries but as women we were in the same place. Man's attitudes toward Woman would determine how each of us fared—and the difference between my ill-treatment and their "oppression" was simply a matter of degree or flagrancy.

These insights came after I put in thirteen years in the business world and five years playing "supergirl" and supermom. To the outside world I seemed to have it together, but inside myself was a growing need to slow down, to share my overwhelming burdens, to be publicly imperfect, to work beside, with and for women.

Finally, I understood as so many feminists had before me, that a woman could never really beat the system. I had only played the game well by men's rules. In return I had been allowed to sit on the bench (so that everyone could see there was a woman on the team), and when the men racked up a comfortable lead against our opponents, I might be called in to try for a few baskets of my own. It became clear that none of the "successful" women I knew were anything more than second string players too, and that there could be no women captains and no women coaches as long as all the players—including myself—believed that it's a man's world.

That's my rather long-winded way of telling you that I've changed—and I believe no woman is too far along, too old or too entrenched to make similar changes happen for herself. The following chapters are guaranteed *not* to make you a superwoman. But they may help you reorder priorities, join with other women to eliminate the sexism to which none of us are immune, reassess both your personal and professional values, understand your rights as a working American female, reject the constraints of traditional sex roles and sacrosanct femininity, renegotiate the marriage contract, demand equal treatment in the workplace and take control of your own life.

This book reflects an entirely new perspective on "How To Make It"—not in a man's world, but in a world you create for yourself, a world that serves your needs as well as you have always been asked to serve the needs of others.

Whoever you are now—whether a Queen Bee exhausted by the burden of being exemplary, or a female drone with no sting who gathers no honey for herself—I hope you find in these pages a great many reasons to leave the hive and find a field of flowers of your own.

2

Housewife: The Ultimate Working Woman

You received no formal training for your life's work. You are all things to all the people you care for, but you're often taken for granted. You have no negotiable status on the job market. You work for love and satisfaction. You don't go on strike, punch out at five o'clock, demand sick leave or ever really retire. Who are you?

You're "just a housewife"—the woman who cares for a home and family for twelve to sixteen hours a day. You know that homemaking can be a physically exhausting, mentally stressful full-time job. So how come people are always asking: "Are you a housewife—or do you work?"

It makes no sense to blame the Women's Movement. Feminists don't demean homemaking. On the contrary, feminists want all so-called "women's work" to be upgraded and valued. Housewifery was an invisible profession long before the new feminists came along, and it's about time for our society to pay it some attention, respect—and even money.

In a newspaper interview, the editors of several major dictionaries admitted receiving pressure from women to change the word housewife to a more upgraded title, such as domestic economist, household executive or home manager. The greatest objection was lodged against the Funk & Wagnalls definition of the housewife as one "who doesn't work for a living."

Whatever you call yourself if you have chosen to work inside the home rather than outside it in the labor market, that choice is your absolute right. One can only hope that your decision has been made freely—without family or social pressure and without guilty feelings. If you have chosen this option you should still be able to alter the way you live within it. You *can* be critical of the housewife's role and of your personal image as a housewife. You can change the conditions of your job once you recognize that it *is* a job and that housework is *real* work by anyone's honest definition.

Perhaps the only one who can fully assess the value of the housewife and mother is a man who is widowed. After his wife dies he must replace the concrete services that she provided. Then he begins to get some tangible idea of what she was worth—not of course as a companion, lover, inspiration—but in her role as a working woman in his home and with his children. If he were to make a list of her job functions, it might look like this:

Mother: The nurturing force, spiritual and moral guide, comforter, wardrobe mistress, seamstress, caretaker, nurse, social director, problem-solver, lullaby-singer, educator, advisor. To replace her completely is impossible. But the responsible father will want to hire a surrogate who is a child-development specialist, not just a watchdog. Cost for a qualified substitute: $10,500 a year.

Cook/Dietician/Nutritionist: Plans balanced meals, varies creative menus, goes marketing, oversees children's snacks, organizes and replenishes the pantry, freezer and refrigerator, cooks and serves. Cost for cook: about $125 a week.

Cleaning Woman: Washes, dries, dusts, launders, irons, waxes, polishes, vacuums, sweeps, scrubs, makes beds, maintains order in drawers, closets, cabinets and shelves. Weekly salary for cleaning woman: $100.

Social and Financial Secretary/Hostess: Juggles children's play schedules, medical appointments, scout meetings, piano lessons. Serves as chauffeur. Maintains the family calendar of vacations, dinner parties, theatre tickets, club meetings. Sorts mail, sends greeting cards, invitations. Pays or organizes bills, mortgages, insurance premiums. Budgets, economizes, scrimps and saves. Cost: a bargain at $3 an hour; minimum ten hours: $30 weekly.

Interior Decorator: Periodically rejuvenates the house

with new curtains, green plants, a changed color scheme. Creates a warm atmosphere, chooses carpeting, purchases and coordinates furniture, organizes an efficient kitchen, decorates a charming and practical children's room. Cost for decorator when needed: $100 per day.

Wife: A very individual specialty. Not duplicated by all the above. Qualities such as love, understanding, intimacy, compassion, support, communication, excitement and deep sexual partnership are not to be found on a resumé. The widower can attempt to fill the void by dating or even by buying sex. The monetary cost will vary according to the degree of his loneliness and his libido. But the emotional cost will be immeasurable and the widower thus understands that a wife is essentially irreplaceable.

Naturally our fictional widower cannot afford $24,060 a year to hire the specialists described here. (That figure is the total of their salaries according to 1974 employment listings in *The New York Times.*) Moreover, few trained specialists are willing to work in private homes. So the widower must compromise. He hires a domestic. He pays her the going rate (in New York City it's about $95 a week for live-in help) and he hopes she'll keep things clean and be kind to his children.

Now here's the rub. The domestic worker comes from a labor pool at the bottom of the economic sea. Because she's poor, black or foreign-born, her minority status or her educational disadvantages prevent her from competing in the labor market. With few options available to her, she ends up a household worker—and no matter how competent and responsible she is, she commands no more than a rock bottom wage.

Our society devalues the work of the domestic for three reasons. First, because cleaning, mopping and scrubbing are obviously unpleasant, unrewarding and unskilled chores. Second, in a trick of circular logic, it is thought that domestic work *couldn't* be important because only the poor and uneducated do it for wages. And finally (and most relevant to this discussion), household work is demeaned because the housewife does it all for nothing anyway.

The domestic worker has begun to solve her problems through unionization and training programs which will upgrade the status of her labor by training and licensing her as a specialist.

But the housewife's exploitation remains because her role is considered to be socially ordained. She may lack personal esteem, but her *role* is exalted. It is part of the cultural mythology. No matter what her talent and temperament, every woman is expected to fulfill the role of housewife at some point in her life. (Imagine a world in which *every* man had to be a carpenter or physicist.)

Motherhood is similarly extolled; though the individual mother is dismissed for her parochial concerns—if not caricatured for her "smother love" or "Jewish mother" devotion. It is difficult to explode and examine these still pervasive myths—especially when many men have a psychological and economic investment in keeping things just as they are.

That's why the widower's experience is such a valuable key to enlightenment. It helps answer the question women have begun to put to one another and to the economists: What is a housewife worth?

She does her job for nothing, but she can't really be duplicated for any amount of money. She is priceless—but her only counterpart in the labor force is a domestic, whose price is at the lowest end of the wage spectrum.

A.C. Pigou's classic example says it best: A bachelor employs a housekeeper and pays her a salary. Then he marries her. Assuming her wifely roles, she forfeits her salary. In other words, the services continue but the value disappears.

Several years ago the Chase Manhattan Bank did a careful calculation of the average housewife's tasks, the number of hours she spends on each and the wage rate for these jobs in the labor market. The results showed that Harriet Housewife performs twelve specialized tasks for 99.6 hours a week (an equivalent of more than two full-time jobs!). The bank found the most modest counterparts for each task in the general labor market (instead of checking classified ads and choosing the most *qualified* specialists as I did for the fictional widower). Nevertheless, in the pre-inflation days when the Chase study was published, the housewife's combined tasks and long hours were worth $159.34 weekly, or $8,285.68 annually. Anyway you look at it, housewifery is a formidable occupation.

You can use this information to remake your image in several styles: you can feel martyred and silently continue the grind; you can declare yourself an unsung heroine and insist your praises be sung loudly and often; you can go out to work at a paid job; or you can take this hard-headed assessment of your worth and use it to institute vital changes in your working conditions.

Righting the balance: share the labor, spread the leisure

If your husband has a desk job or does basically sedentary brain tasks or paper work for forty hours a week, he is working less than half as long as your 99.6 hours and it's a safe bet that his work is far less fatiguing.

Equalize the situation. Add twenty-five to thirty hours of housework and child care onto his schedule and subtract it from yours. Instead of coming home to a can of beer, TV and the evening paper (with the assumption that his day is over and yours is just beginning), perhaps he should take over the kids' baths, supervise their homework or dinner, read them stories and get them to bed. He can do the weekly marketing on Saturday. Or the vacuuming. Or change the linens on all the beds. Perhaps he'll want to be in charge of the whole works on the weekends (thirty hours credit) in return for having weeknights to himself. Why not let you sleep later every morning while he gets breakfast and prepares the children for school? If he comes home from work to a hot dinner and calm, bathed, pyjamaed children, then the dinner dishes and general evening clean-up can be his duties.

The possibilities are limitless. Try out several shared work plans and see which works best for you both.

(In all fairness, if your man does manual labor, puts in a lot of overtime, stands on his feet all day, works over a steel furnace or in a coal mine, you'll want to decrease his share of housework accordingly.)

A day's work for a day's pay

If he's an incorrigible male chauvinist who wouldn't be caught dead with a dishrag in his hand, then the new balance must be achieved financially.

Without you (if you have children), he couldn't hold his job. (If there are no kids, what are you doing at home all day, anyway?) Without you, he would have to stay home with the children, quit his job, file for public assistance funds or spend money to hire someone so that he

can work. He needs you as much as you need him. And if
he won't share the load, he should pay you what you're
worth. Can he afford the Chase Manhattan figure of
$159.34 a week? If not, surely he can pay you the $95 he
would have to pay a domestic if you didn't exist. Still too
much? Then how about $50 a week on top of your allot-
ment for food and other household expenses: Even $25 a
week would provide a sense of your personal worth and
freedom—money that you don't have to *ask* for; *your*
money that you can spend as you choose.

What about benefits?

Individual solutions are not enough. We must integrate the
working housewife within minimum wage laws, social security, disability insurance and worker's compensation.
Such innovations require complex programs that must be
devised by national legislative and social policy makers.
They can't be instituted within the family unit.

There are some policy changes that *can* be made at
home. Consider adding a few fringe benefits to the new
deal you and your husband settle upon. As a working
housewife, you deserve sick leave, vacations and humane
working hours. If you plod through your tasks with a 102
degree fever; if your "vacation" means cooking and cleaning in a camper, tent or beach house instead of at home; if
you find yourself folding laundry at midnight—then it's
time to put pencil to paper and establish a benefit policy,
whether or not the federal government ever gets around to
it.

Retirement: now, ever or never?

Is there an end in sight? As I see it, every women who
works in or outside the home should have the right to quit.
Indentured servitude is illegal. Perhaps you and your husband should agree on a date when you hop off the treadmill and launch a new life. It could be when the youngest
child is five; or when you find the routine too stultifying;
when a job opportunity is too tempting to refuse; or when
you just plain want to quit and move onward and upward.

Two cautions: If you leave housewifery while the children are young and you have to hire a household worker,
don't continue the vicious cycle of exploitation. Pay her a
generous wage. *You,* of all people, know what she's worth.

And secondly, if you remain a housewife for the rest of your days, establish the fact that half your husband's savings, retirement funds, stocks, bonds and property is rightfully yours. It is not a money-grubbing request; it's the time-tested, fairminded community property concept. You've given up a career and a personal income to devote yourself to him, his career, home and children. According to a government study, the typical woman could have earned $58,437 if she had worked instead of staying home until the youngest child is fourteen years old. Not only did you sacrifice your career, it was because of your dedication and solidity at home that your man was free to seek and accumulate his fortune. You earned your half as truly as he earned his.

Thinking the unthinkable for your own good

Suppose the happy couple doesn't survive together into a ripe old age. Then the issue of a cheerful, shared retirement becomes a moot point. In the light of current divorce statistics (nearly half of all marriages fail), the housewife has no business comforting herself in a blanket of security. Likewise, since most men insist on being the *macho* sole provider, and thereby drive themselves to death 6.8 years before the average woman, the chances are that death will deprive the housewife of her husband if divorce doesn't do it first.

In plain words, you're only one man away from welfare.

Without marketable skills, a reliable income or experience in sophisticated financial matters, the full-time, dependent housewife is a babe-in-the-woods. If you're going to run that risk, the least you can do is protect yourself by being completely informed.

Do some straight talking right now. No matter how much you and your husband love each other; no matter how young and healthy you are today, these questions must be asked and answered:

Where are the bank accounts, shares, leases, deeds, installment contracts, insurance policies, etc.? Have you read them?

Are accounts and other documents held jointly? If not, what are your rights in connection with them?

Can you withdraw money from some account in an emergency?

How much life insurance does your husband have and who are the carriers? Are you the beneficiary on all of them?

Do you know your husband's accountant, lawyer and stockbroker?

What provisions has your husband made for you and the children in his will?

If something happens to him, how long can you support yourself and the children on the money he leaves behind? Will you have time to train yourself for a good job when you *do* have to bring in money?

These are disturbing subjects to contemplate. But once the "what ifs" are articulated and the economic facts clarified, the housewife's imagined sense of security is replaced by an adult responsibility toward the future.

The split schedule

Rather than let a spouse's premature death force a change of lifestyle under tragic conditions, you might join the small band of vanguard couples who are reordering the whole concept of support while both parties are still alive and well.

Instead of the husband bearing the entire wage-earning burden and the wife carrying all the house and child care responsibilities, you can split both roles down the middle. It's a great compromise if both partners can find jobs to accommodate it. He might work from 8:30 to 12:30 and you would find a job with a 1 to 5 shift. He devotes afternoons to the house and kids and you cover the scene in the mornings.

By 5:30 both you and he have functioned in two capacities: as income-producers and as homemaker-parents. It's an immensely humanizing alternative. Your children get an equal dosage of Dad and Mom and a more healthy balance of male/female influence in their upbringing. (The family will likely suffer a decrease in overall income because your work will probably be underpaid. But that's another battle in another war.)

The two-family commune

Two couples in a large city have devised a four-way cooperative that works beautifully for them. The wives are housewives-teachers; the husbands are househusbands-law students. They live across the hall from one another in an apartment house. Each couple has two young children. Through pooled efforts each of the adults is "on duty" for three consecutive hours every day (which amounts to the total twelve hours of waking time of the kids). An intercom system keeps both apartments in touch. Each adult does the weekly marketing for both families once a month. Babysitting is cooperative. Meals, laundry and housecleaning chores are pooled and shared. In this way the adults each have nine hours of free time per day—time to work, study, read or relax. It sounds like heaven.

If the temperament of your neighbors and all of your work schedules allow it, such an experiment might be worth a try. But remember to divide the tasks four ways evenly—and not by sex-typed jobs. No cop-outs ("that's women's work") permitted.

Whether in a communal situation or in the privacy of a nuclear household, the challenge is the same: to share domestic roles, to enrich women's lives and to give dignity and value to Home Work. Admittedly, the "man-of-the-house" is being asked to give up age-old power and privilege. We know that privilege is habit-forming and power is not easily relinquished. As wives, we sympathize with our husbands' period of adjustment. But as women we must agitate and insist that working housewives get their share of justice, fairness and tangible rewards out of life.

3

Is a Job the Answer?

Women who have always worked, brides who used their annual two-weeks vacation for their honeymoon, working mothers who didn't hesitate to dash back to the office as soon as the baby slept through the night—all you committed careerists may find the following discussion academic.

Is a job the answer? can only be a pressing question for those of you who checked out of the labor market upon graduation from school, as soon as you married, or the minute the obstetrician smilingly told you what happened to the rabbit.

Since then your husband and children have become your job and you've been persuaded that instead of a weekly paycheck, your rewards are measured in daily satisfactions. If you're a busy homemaker with demanding small children, going to work may be the furthest thing from your mind. And that's fine, if family life provides all the stimuli and satisfaction you want for the time being.

For some women—perfectly average, healthy females—there has to be something more. Gratification from a loving husband, bright children and a gracious home may be essential and precious, but it just isn't enough for everyone.

Staying home may no longer make sense. Perhaps your children are gone most of the day. Or your husband may be slaving at two jobs to keep the family off welfare, while you're feeling useless. The need may be emotional, intellectual, economic or a combination of the three. Similarly,

18

the malaise may take the form of boredom, depression or hunger for change.

How do you know that a job is the answer?

You don't. But if the evidence is convincing, you may be avoiding taking that step because of some complicated but common inhibitions.

Are you afraid that going to work will suggest that you couldn't find fulfillment in the classic womanly pursuits of house and family? Rubbish! Nobody *fails* at femaleness. We each mold our highly individual ideal of what is womanly. You may simply want to succeed in more than one arena. Growth and change are admirable in all people, regardless of their sex. Trying to enlarge your interests and experiences doesn't imply that you are cancelling or betraying what you did before. New values and forms of self-expression may be added without relinquishing the old.

The fear of failure may be an even more concrete inhibition. Why take a job and risk being proven incompetent? One answer is direct: because you'll never know if you don't try—and you'll always be curious. The other answer is more cynical. If men were to shrink from the job market because of *their* potential incompetence and proven mediocrity, there would immediately be enough job vacancies for all the unemployed women, minorities, teenagers and immigrants put together!

Will you recognize when you're really ready to go to work? Perhaps you're ready now. Try watching for symptoms such as these; they may indicate that a job is your answer:

● You read novels and newspapers but you still feel insulated. You want to meet a more diverse group of adults than are available in the immediate neighborhood.

● Your housework has shrunk to the point where your chores are finished in an hour or two. You have time on your hands.

● Whenever you think of the time and money that went into your education, it seems criminal not to use your training.

● You've heard yourself introduced as Bob's wife or Sally's mother once too often. You want your own identity.

● The kids make constant demands. You try not to

spoil them but they take your services for granted. You suspect it's because they have a life of their own—and your only life is them.

• Arguments with your husband about money have become more frequent and bitter. If you worked there would be enough to make ends meet, and then some.

• A full diet of housework and children is making a shrew of you. When you're tired and understimulated you take it out on the kids.

• There are so many things that need to be done in our society and you want to contribute to its improvement—for a salary.

• You feel inferior to your husband but you didn't use to. You wonder whether he's outgrowing you—or whether you've just blurred yourself into his world.

• No matter how or why—you just want to direct traffic, sell advertising, paint signs, teach, drive a bus, open a craft shop, take dictation, become an architect or get any job that offers a nice environment and a decent wage.

Whichever symptoms are present, it must be *you* who diagnoses them and *you* who prescribes the tonic—a full-time, part-time or temporary job—if it seems called for.

Once you've decided to get a job you can involve the whole family in a sensible, fair reorganization of the household. It may only be a matter of simplifying and reassigning routine tasks but even the slightest changes fare best with a husband's support and cooperation. Loving you, he should welcome anything that renews your enthusiasm for life. He must also be aware that so-called male and female roles are entirely arbitrary and thousands of couples are revising their family habits in a great variety of ways. With two working parents in the house, accommodation and compromise are absolutely essential.

The children too, may require an orientation period before they can accept that mother, like father, will have a life of her own, away from them. Reducing the quantity of time at home doesn't necessarily lessen the quality of mothering. But children need help understanding what may strike them as abandonment. They also take time to adjust to the redistribution of household responsibilities.

I've found that even the smallest toddler can be reasoned with if the logic is simplified. One mother was overheard addressing a three-year-old in this way: "Mommy likes her job the way you like games and adventures. But when I come home, and when Daddy comes home from his work, we can't get everything done by ourselves. We need help. Otherwise, we get tired and cranky. So please pick up your toys and put them on the shelf."

Having two working parents often results in a child's increased self-sufficiency and greater sense of importance to the family unit.

Employment isn't a panacea. It won't cure overweight, nail-biting or a faulty sex-life. But, by altering your life pattern in a constructive way, a new job might brighten your self-perception enough to take the edge off even those conditions.

Women have been known to overeat (and drink) out of boredom. Neurotic behavior is often the result of disappointment or rage at one's personal inertia. Work can get you out of the tedium, away from the familiar and into a world larger than yourself. If you feel worthwhile, appreciated and competent in your work, your new confidence may carry new energy into your lovemaking. It's been known to happen.

No one should dupe you into believing that a job brings automatic paradise. It just might lead to a worse rut than the one you left behind—as thousands of those plodding through miserable jobs will testify. Nevertheless, you should have the choice and the chance to find out what a job outside the home can do for you.

Self-actualization, usefulness, financial security and fun may only be as far away as your first paycheck. Rather than detracting from your pleasures as a wife and mother, you may be surprised to find that a job complements and enhances them.

4

The Working Mother: She'll Get By with a Little Help from Her Friends

You have decided to go out to work.

You hire a governess who combines the nurturing qualities of Florence Nightingale with the diverting antics of the Flying Nun. You land a housekeeper who used to work in Buckingham Palace. Then one fine morning your husband and children kiss you good-bye and you glide to your office, where David Rockefeller invites you to join the Board of Directors.

And then you wake up.

Dreams are fun but they don't often solve problems. And you probably feel overwhelmed by problems: What will happen to the house? Who will market, mend and cook? What about babysitters or after-school supervision? Will the kids be traumatized? Will your husband adjust or explode? And how about *your* adjustment?

Such problems are not limited to the woman who has chosen to take a job after years at home. Those who have been trapped by the Superwoman syndrome—doing two full-time jobs, household and career, and doing them all alone—will also want to start at ground zero and renegotiate the family contract.

If it's your first solo flight outside the nest the logistics problems may be additionally complicated by the family's emotional and psychological resistance. Are they losing you to the world? Will they become less important to you?

Will you become less available to them? Will a job change the woman they love?

Without lapsing into melodrama, I think one can say that the woman who succeeds in deconditioning herself and her family to orthodox sex roles, has authored a revolution—a creative, humane revolution with never a shot being fired. There is a redistribution of wealth, power and responsibility; a blending of strengths; a household support system that operates on behalf of *every* member of the family. But like most revolutions, it doesn't happen overnight.

Even the dearest, most enlightened husband may feel uneasy about a drastic change in family routine. While you have every right to his respect and understanding, he deserves your honesty, directness and reassurance. All of which means that discussions must precede decisions. Under all our superficial differences, working mothers often suffer guilt about the same things: about not being selfless and yet also about not fulfilling our youthful promise. The conflict leaves us ragged and confused. We are unable to live up to expectations—our own and everyone else's. It's time now to change or eradicate the expectations.

For example, whether we work by choice or necessity, many of us compensate for our guilt feelings by tiptoeing around our husbands' egos and overcompensating for spending less time with the children.

"I'm afraid my husband and kids will feel neglected because of my job," says one mother of three. "So I make the beds, prepare breakfast, sit with the kids while they eat, and even get in a load of laundry before I leave for work." While she does her whirling dervish number, her husband lingers over coffee. He's a fair-minded man who doesn't object to his wife's working—as long as it doesn't inconvenience anybody. There are millions like him and therefore there are millions of working mothers who become compulsive about their "I can do it all" perfectionism. No wonder so many of these women are not only defensive and guilt-ridden but also exhausted and defeated.

Obviously, the opening salvo of your peaceful household revolution must be honesty. Your husband and you should level with one another about hostility, fears and problems you both anticipate. Share your mutual and separate goals. Accept the fact that certain of your aspirations have nothing to do with "our" or "us" but only with "me" and "mine." Talk about the poetic aphorism that told us men's lives were full and varied but women need nothing more than love to sustain them. Ask your husband if he believes that. Ask yourself if you're ready to demand more out of life than love—despite a lifetime of romantic programming.

In these consciousness-raising sessions both you and your husband might vow to swear off sarcasm and put-downs. If money is the reason you're job hunting, you needn't discredit your husband's earning power. If it's personal gratification you seek in outside work, don't blame him for tying you down until now. "If it weren't for you I'd be rich and famous" is the monologue to avoid. Recriminations form a shoddy foundation for a new life. It's more productive to exchange feelings rather than to find fault with one another.

Tell him how you feel about your decision and what kind of work you hope to get. Ask him how he feels about your motivation, or about your growing independence, or about your being the only woman among his friends' wives who has chosen to get a paying job.

When you discuss new arrangements for care of the children, ask your husband to visit prospective day care centers or interview babysitters with you. Making these kinds of plans together sets the stage for cooperative parenting. Whatever your chosen child care arrangement, it's likely to be imperfect and frequently unreliable. As a result, even if you're not "doing it all," you can end up *worrying* about it all unless both parents acknowledge equal concern and responsibility for the children.

Are we paying the sitter enough? Can we really afford nursery school? Can we trust that the day care staff is well-trained? If the sitter becomes ill, where will we get a replacement? Which parent will stay home from work in an emergency? Who will remember to leave a note about Tommy's iron pills or Jennifer's art class? What will we do about the children during school vacations?

These are the kinds of questions that the working mother usually has to grapple with alone. No matter how egalitarian the marriage, when it comes to the kids, mothers get the feeling that the buck stops with them. And this is indeed the case for millions of single mothers who have no choice but to cope with such problems without help. But for two-parent working families it is a continuing organic process to change the old assumptions about Mother's primary responsibility for the children.

As far as the household chores are concerned, you can ask your husband point blank which of your usual duties he feels *best equipped* to take over. Put in those terms, he might be too embarrassed to claim that he can't handle a sinkload of dishes or a twenty pound vacuum cleaner. If he's been through the armed forces remind him that he once knew how to make a bed spiffy enough to bounce a quarter on. Reassure him that a few hours polishing the silver can't possibly tarnish his shining armor. Or as psychiatrist Lee Salk once put it: "Seeing my father cleaning up the kitchen in an apron didn't have the slightest adverse affect on his male potency, or mine."

Some couples have found it useful to make a written worklist or contract, dividing household duties according to the days of the week. In our house it seems to work out better on the casual understanding that "whoever can, does." You and your husband might want to review a few basics such as who cooks which meals when (you assume he's willing to learn to follow a recipe), and how the two of you plan to split the cleaning and child supervision.

What does a husband get in return for his renouncement of male prerogatives? Well, besides a clear conscience, he gets the knowledge that his virility is not dependent on his wife's servility. And he may also enjoy knowing that he has given his wife the gift all brides are promised but rarely receive—a full partnership in marriage.

Preparing the children for life with a mother who works

Your intimate understanding of your own child's maturity, sensitivity and level of comprehension will determine how you treat the transition period. At almost any age children have intense reactions to major changes in familiar routine. Compassion and empathy for children's responses open the communication lines and allow you to alleviate their anxiety before it escalates. For very young children maternal separation can be a very real terror. They need firm reassurance that you will return after work. Older children may perceive your new activities as an abdication of your motherly role and consequently, a loss of interest in them. Family rap sessions (ideally including their father) should clarify all the positive dimensions of your new job as well as reaffirm the enduring and invincible love you feel for you children.

The following suggestions and opinions come to you courtesy of the voice of experience—not expertise.

• If you really want to (or must) work then it's the right decision for you *and* your children. Staying home because of a mythical motherhood ideal leads inevitably to increased self-effacement, frustration and inertia. Children need a mother not a martyr. And women need self-actualization, not self-sacrifice. Has anyone ever proved that a full day spent with a bitter housewife is healthier for a child than a few hours with a contented careerist mother?

• Motherhood should be a mother-made concept, not a man-made fantasy. Baking brownies and sewing up a prom dress may be television's brand of mothering. You and I probably see it differently. Rather than service our children we might prefer to come home from the office and take everyone out for a bike ride or a jog through the park. Nothing beats a game of Scrabble before supper—unless it's calisthenics on the living room rug.

• Fatherhood becomes as meaningful as motherhood—and this startling discovery is as rewarding to the children as to their emotionally repressed dads. I can't think of a single child who wouldn't benefit from a little less Mama and a little more Papa in the home.

• Time becomes more wisely spent and more highly valued. With everyone sharing the housework, chores are finished sooner leaving more leisure for all. Evenings are savored and lengthened. Parents and children understand that weekends are the end of a *work* week and a time for pleasure and family activities.

• Children's attitudes become positive, not just tolerant of having a working mother. They take their cue from you and their father. When you're both cheerful about your decision to work and the time you spend away from home, it becomes plain to the children that you're working *for* yourself, not *against* them. If you can take them to your workplace, explain your job and introduce them to your colleagues or co-workers, so much the better. Then they can visualize where you are when you aren't with them. At some point you may even detect a note of pride when they tell friends what their mother's job is all about.

(If you need some extra help explaining things to your littlest ones get a few picture books like *Mommies At Work* by Eve Merriam or *All Kinds of Mothers* by Joe Lasher. There you'll find illustrated reinforcement of your new lifestyle. Your children will see that lots of mommies who do other things—like design bridges or answer telephones—still have "laps to snuggle in.")

Older children should also be encouraged to read biographies of women achievers. However, they can best adapt themselves to your new situation when all their questions receive honest answers. A teenager can understand the need for a second income; and a nine-year-old can identify with the boredom that idleness brings. Let them know that you're happy at your job and *want* to be working. "Want" is something every child understands.

I've also found that the logic of precedent proves the point: If children think of their father as a loving daddy *and* a grocer (steamfitter, doctor, etc.), it's not too hard to see that their mother can be a mommy and a speechwriter (nurse, horticulturist, etc.)—and still remain just as adoring and adored as ever.

How about you?

While considering all the people affected by your decision, don't neglect the character on center stage: You.

When I returned to work after maternity "retirement" my feet hurt. I hadn't worn high heels in six months. And that was the least of it. From the shoes on your feet to the ideas in your head, you are going to be a changed person. You've been basically a *consumer* of goods and services; now you'll be a *producer* as well. You've been procreative; now (hopefully) you're going to be creative. Up until now you've been your own taskmaster, setting your own schedule. Soon an employer will hold you to an established set of standards.

Well before your first day on the job, a crash course in self-discipline could facilitate the transition. Put yourself on a tight schedule at home so that the pace of the business world doesn't bowl you over. Set deadlines for various tasks. Practice bookkeeping chores at home if you're going to take a clerical job. You can set up a filing system for household bills, catalogue your books, tabulate income tax items or plan a new budget based on two incomes. Get used to having lunch at the same hour each day, instead of snacking and nibbling. Get all your projects done by five o'clock and take a few trial runs out in the rush-hour traffic. Try a joy ride on the commuter bus or train—you may as well know the sordid truth, if you don't already. Rehearse quick recipes to use on the nights when it's your turn to cook. And ask your husband to take over several dinners while you're still at home. It's disgraceful how many men can't find the can opener in their own kitchens.

Give a thought or two to your appearance, but don't panic about your skin, hair, weight or wardrobe—and *don't* get desperate about masking your age. Many employers equate maturity with stability. Simplify your hair style, perhaps. It will save precious time and money formerly spent at the hairdresser's. Forget about buying new clothes unless you own nothing but torn blue jeans. Today's workday fashions include shoulder pads, knickers, plaid skirts and bell-bottoms. You can't possibly be out of style because virtually any garment from any of the past four decades is "In."

I think the best possible advice I can offer is Leave Yourself Alone! You're going to compete for a job, not a beauty prize.

Does your decision to work spell Utopia for you and the family? Not quite. But with loving cooperation it won't be Armageddon either. Millions of working mothers are in the same boat and somehow it floats. Welcome aboard, but don't expect smooth sailing. There are plenty of shoals and storms that interfere with the voyage whether or not you and your husband run a tight ship. Beyond your household is a world that seems determined to make it tough for you. In fact it sometimes seems as though the working mother is the most beleaguered, misunderstood member of American society.

From the President of the United States to the Madison Avenue adman to the man-in-the-street, everyone has an opinion about mothers who work—and hardly anyone asks us for our first-hand testimony.

Former President Nixon vetoed the Comprehensive Child Development Act (see Chapter 6), which would have provided quality child care facilities for millions of youngsters. He said he believed family life was eroded when mothers worked outside the home. Yet he demanded that poor women take jobs in return for welfare assistance, even if it meant *their* family lives were disrupted.

The folks on Madison Avenue tell us that a new detergent or snack food is all a working mother needs to manage her busy life.

The man-in-the-street—otherwise known as occasional husbands, boyfriends, co-workers or legislators—insists on perpetuating old accusations: that mothers only work for "pin money;" and that working mothers are slightly deviate because they don't find total contentment in the domestic sphere.

All this may be expected. What is surprising is our own persistent defensiveness. Perhaps, if we knew more about the company we keep, we each might feel less freakish, abnormal and isolated.

Who are the working mothers?

According to the Women's Bureau of the U.S. Department of Labor, in 1973 half of all American mothers with children from six to seventeen years old, work outside the home. One-third of all women with kids under age six hold outside jobs. Another way of looking at the figures is—26.2 million American children have mothers who work.

(This is as good a place as any to ask where are the children's books about working mothers? Where are the TV comedies that reflect daily reality for these 26.2 million children whose mothers are *not* serving fresh-perked coffee to an afternoon bridge group? By perpetuating this fairy tale, the media renders millions of women *invisible*.)

Of this country's 51 million families, nearly six million are headed by women, and 53 per cent of these women are working mothers. They do not work for "pin money;" they work to feed, clothe and house their children because there's no one else to do it.

For a multitude of reasons, about seven million husbands are not in the labor force. They may be students or aged and infirm men whose wives must become sole support of their families. These women also lack the prerogative of believing that their jobs might "erode" family life.

In the large remaining group, over ten million working mothers have husbands present in the family and about two million are widowed, divorced or separated. The

Women's Bureau has the last word on why these mothers work:

"Because they or their families need the money they can earn. Some work to raise family living standards above the level of poverty or deprivation; others, to help meet the rising cost of food, education for their children, medical care and the like. *The majority of women do not have the option of working solely for personal fulfillment.*"

Once this reality is stated, we see how absurd it is to criticize the working mother or to deny her child care centers on the theory that without a place to "leave" her children she will renounce her evil ways and return to the home and hearth. The point is that most working mothers have no choice.

But what about those of us who work not because we must but because we want to? Are we prodigal women because we dare to pursue a life of our own? If there is no economic hardship does that mean we are selfish ingrates because we choose to work anyway?

Women have been painstakingly trained to be maternal, self-sacrificing and supportive. No matter how extensive our education, we've been schooled to become wives and mothers above all. Whenever we've whispered "What about me?" we've been made to feel insubordinate and ungrateful. But no more. The Women's Movement has given strong voice to our whispers and we've discovered there are millions of us with the same needs, wishes and dreams. If we seek diversity, if we refuse a derivative identity, if we demand personhood, we are simply exercising our rights as human beings. After all, we pass this way only once.

5

Out of the Mouths of Babes ...

A friend of mine who used to be a newspaper reporter is now on a leave of absence to spend full-time with her three-year-old. One day, when her son expressed interest in a TV story about a crime reporter, my friend decided to tell the child about her career:

"Before you were born, Mommy used to have a job like that," she said, building up to an exciting description. "I went to fires or to the police station and the stories I wrote were printed in the newspaper with my name on them."

After listening attentively, the boy said: "Mommy, when you had this job before I was born, did you used to be a man?"

Not all children equate work with maleness. Most kids—even three-year-olds—can understand that millions of women hold jobs outside the home. However, there are fascinating variations in the ways in which children relate to this fact of life—especially when the working woman also happens to be one's mother.

I remember another little boy whose mother was a lawyer and whose grandmother was a judge. When I asked him if he also wanted to be a lawyer when he grew up, he giggled. "Only *girls* can be lawyers," he answered, looking at me as if I were out of touch with reality. As John Stuart Mill wrote: "Everything which is usual appears natural."

Children's perceptions of various aspects of life are a favorite subject of psychologists. But surprisingly little is known about the effect of maternal employment on child development.

We do know that Dr. Benjamin Spock now believes he was wrong in counseling two generations of mothers to sacrifice their own interests and aspirations for their children. Since 1971, Dr. Spock has been recanting, regretting the guilt he aroused in working mothers, and reassuring his followers that children do not necessarily suffer if their mother works.

We also have some research evidence to guide us. A 1970 paper by Ruth E. Hartley states that "data have indicated that a mother's working seems to have some very desirable effects on her children; daughters have more of the self-determination and spunk needed for modern living, take a less passive approach to the world outside the home, and assume a more positive attitude toward the woman's role."

Several researchers from the Columbia University School of Public Health found that the mental health of both daughters and sons is not so much influenced by a mother's work status as by the extent to which she is satisfied with her role—whether that role be working-mother or homemaker-mother. This finding suggests that our children care more about how we feel about what we do, than what we actually do. Accordingly, the contented working mother is likely to be perceived more favorably by her children than the dissatisfied but available stay-home mother.

In another study, Elizabeth Douvan noted that mothers who work part-time had better relationships with their adolescent children than either non-working mothers or those who held full-time jobs. This conclusion helps buttress the argument for more diverse and flexible work schedules. (See Chapter 14.)

We also know, thanks to data gathered by the Women's Bureau of the U.S. Department of Labor, that juvenile delinquency is not determined by whether or not a mother is employed. "Studies indicate that it is the quality of a mother's care rather than the time consumed in such care, which is of major significance."

On the totally positive side, Kagan and Moss discovered that women who are "aggressive and competitive" raised daughters who tended to achieve intellectually. Robert Blood sampled a Detroit population group and found that "Daughters of working mothers are more independent, more self-reliant, more aggressive, more dominant. . . . Because their mothers have set an example, the daughters get up the courage and the desire to earn money as well."

While we may debate and analyze such results, the fact remains that in 1973, of approximately 64 million American children under the age of eighteen, over 26 million had working mothers. Six million of these children were preschool age. Moreover, the Census Bureau tells us that 14 per cent of all children are being raised by mothers alone. For these children there is no room for debate or analysis. There is only the reality of their working mother—and perhaps the alternative of the welfare lines.

Kids seem to understand what motivates their mothers to work outside the home. They know whether the needs are emotional or economic or a combination of the two. If they haven't been told directly, they have absorbed the information osmotically.

To learn more about the child's view of the working mother, I spoke with several youngsters about their daily lives, their feelings and opinions.

• None of the children said they resent their mothers' jobs and not one felt envious of friends whose mothers are at home.

• Each of the girls, from kindergartners to high school seniors, said she plans to combine family life with a career when she matures.

• All of the boys said they would not object if their own wives *insisted* on working, though most preferred that the woman stay home while the children are young.

• None of the boys would be willing to be a full-time, stay-home father, even if they could afford not to work. They all agreed that a steady routine of cleaning and child care was unthinkable.

• Empathy for the mother was matched by ambivalence for the enlarged area of the child's responsibility. They understood their mothers' fatigue at the end of the day, but expressed some resentment for having to carry a larger share of household chores themselves. On the other hand there was unanimous enthusiasm for the added independence this entailed. Several youngsters described themselves as more "grown-up."

• While they may miss having Mom home after school, the children said they've learned to solve problems and to discipline themselves in homework. Of the few children who actively wished that someone was home after school, only one child actually preferred that the "someone" be the mother rather than the father. The rest felt that finding *either* parent in the house would provide the desired welcome.

• A great many children were critical of their *fathers*. They said they wished their dads would spend more time with the family, be more helpful in the house and more sensitive to their mothers' needs.

• When asked about working women in society at large, all the girls in my random sampling said that women should be able to compete for *any* job. The boys were not willing to go that far. Many of them expressed discomfort at the idea of a woman truck driver, construction worker or professional athlete, no matter how competent the individual woman might be. The young women were unruffled by questions of "femininity:" it was the young men who were zealously protective of "the feminine ideal."

• In an adolescent group session, all the girls said they would vote for a qualified woman to be President of the United States but only one boy felt he could even *consider* voting for a woman leader and then only "in a dire emergency."

The children speak for themselves

Do kids understand why their parents work or what they do on their jobs? Do children differentiate between male and female job commitment? Are they planning to follow in Mom's or Dad's career footsteps?

Francesca R., age 6, did not know the names for her mother's job (hatcheck attendant), or her father's (waiter). This was how she sized up the situation: "Mommy and Daddy work to get dollars. We give Mommy kisses when she makes a lot of money. Once she got a dollar for one coat. Daddy works at a restaurant. Mommy makes more money than Daddy."

Albert B., age 9, was proud that he babysits for himself while his mother, a secretary, and his father, a police officer, are at work: "When my Mom comes home we have dinner together. Daddy comes home at 10 P.M. and makes his own dinner. He can cook steak and chicken okay."

Seventeen-year-old Bruce S. was quite articulate about his salesman father and his mother, a market researcher: "I think my parents have more to talk about since my Mom has been out working in the world all day. I understand her need for diversity; when I'm home sick, I go buggy in the house all day.

"My Dad had some hang-ups about her taking away from his role as breadwinner but I want my wife to work to help with the income and to satisfy herself. If she became a big success, I'd be proud of her as I'd expect her to be proud of me."

Two daughters of a mother who is a bookkeeper and a father who edits a magazine, had different views of the same parents. Nancy K., age 10, said: "My Mom adds. My Daddy brings home papers and changes some words and crosses out other words. Mommy isn't tired when she comes home; she's more pleasant than she used to be. I don't know what she did all day when she stayed home. It must have been boring 'cause we were in school.

"When I grow up I'm going to work too, and if my husband doesn't like it—tough potato chips on him."

Nancy's sister, Susan, age 14, admitted: "At first I resented my mother working. I was used to finding the meal ready and the chores done when I got home. Lately I don't mind pitching in, although she doesn't think any of us help enough—including my father. We're all trying to change.

"I can see that Mom is much happier working and I think she has the right to do what she wants as much as the rest of us."

James F., 6, lives with his divorced mother, who is a credit information clerk. When she comes home from work, his mother picks him up from a babysitter's apartment in the same building. Here's how James fills in the details: "My Mommy wears dresses or pants to the office and she eats lunch there. She goes to work because she doesn't have a husband."

Rocio N., 13, is one of five children of parents who work together in a nightclub flamenco act. She said of the arrangement: "On weekend nights I babysit while my parents work until three in the morning. The next day, my father always tells my mother what she did wrong in the act, but he thinks he was perfect.

"I cook breakfasts; my mother does all the other cooking and cleaning, plus she goes to dance classes all week.

When I get married, my husband and I will split the house jobs for sure."

Timothy M., 16, also cast a critical eye on his father, a transit worker. Tim's mother is an investment assistant: "Since I'm an only child there's not much mess. Still my Dad helps only slightly. I often wonder if my Mom minds coming home and then fixing dinner every single night. After all, she works all day just as hard as my father."

Cheryl Ann, 10, was grateful that her mother is a legal secretary, especially since her father, an export manager was unemployed. "We used to have a housekeeper," Cheryl Ann recalled. "Now my sister and brother and I keep our rooms clean and make our own breakfasts. I think it's good that my Mom makes enough money to support us while my Dad is looking for a job. I think if a woman puts her mind to it she can do anything."

Anthony M., 14, remembers: "My parents haven't lived together since I was eight. My Mom has been working since I was ten. (She's a tax accountant.) It had to be done. My father gives her money to support me and my brother but we still need her income. We help her too. Sometimes, if she gets real nervous about being fired or something, I give her advice and calm her down. She knows she can count on my brother and me."

James C., 13, said thoughtfully: "At times I resent having to clean or put dishes away. Then I realize that if us four kids didn't help, my Mom would have to do it all alone.

"My father talks a lot about his job (he's a tube tester)—like he complains about the union. My mother never talks about herself (she's a school aide), and my father doesn't seem interested in her job. Maybe nothing interesting ever happens to her."

Six-year-old Alexandra H. wasn't too clear about the duties of her father, a travel agent, or her mother, a coat checker: "My Daddy goes to an airport and gets money there. My Mommy cleans and washes dishes and goes to work. I like my babysitter; he's an old man but he plays ball with me. I wish my Daddy would be home more because he smells nice—like shaving lotion—and I wish he played with me."

The mother is a travel agent, the father, a commercial artist, and two of their children chose to comment on their parents' relationship. Elizabeth G., 15, said: "My Mom and Dad have a lot of arguments about male chauvinism because he still considers himself the head of the family. If she wants to know about something important—like the insurance policy—he says 'Don't worry, I'll take care of it,' and she gets mad."

Elizabeth's brother, Allan, 9, hypothesized: "I think my Dad would be jealous if my Mom made more money than he does. I'm for the Women's Movement. To tell you the truth, men usually get better jobs than women and some men take advantage of women. I think men shouldn't boss women around."

Her mother is a bank teller, her father is a policeman and Tamara H., 17, works as a salesperson seven hours every day after school: "My mother got bored staying home after her four kids were in school but she was afraid of what my father would say if she worked. Then she got a job and he just accepted it. I've been working ever since I was fourteen because I hate asking anyone for money."

Howard N., 11, complained that his father (an unemployed letter carrier) "just doesn't listen. When Mom comes home from work (she's a school clerk) and wants to tell him something, she has to keep repeating it. He just doesn't pay attention.

"If I get married and my wife is more successful than me, I wouldn't tell my friends about it," Howard added. "I'd be too embarrassed."

Emily F., 17, comes from a professional family. Her mother, an editor, never *had* to work to supplement the family income because her father is a doctor. "The one thing I remember consciously feeling when I was little was that my mother always looked so elegant and beautiful when she went to the office. But more than that, I've always been proud that she had important work of her own. I think her life is at least as exciting as my father's."

By themselves these young people's comments are enlightening and occasionally amusing. But in synthesis, their responses are overwhelmingly provocative and much more disturbing than amusing.

The children do not seem upset about their mothers' jobs but they are deeply affected by the conflicts these jobs arouse between both parents. The father who objects to his wife's working or who shows his resentment by studied indifference, may believe he is motivated by a desire for his wife to be a full-time mother. Actually, it is the father who may be hurting his child far more by his unfeeling attitude toward the mother.

The interviews were noteworthy too for the patchwork child care arrangements that they revealed. Young children fend for themselves—obviously because there is no spare money for a babysitter. Those who had sitters were in the hands of fate. Some children were happy to be in the care of a relative or neighbor; less fortunate children were bitter about babysitters who never played with them or who put them in front of a television set until a parent picked them up.

, Any eavesdropper on these poignant conversations would have been struck by the absence of a community support system; there were no child care centers, no after-school programs, no communal arrangements or neighborhood cooperatives, no systematic utilization of the services of senior citizens as child companions.

Communication between parents and children ran the gamut from nonexistent to lively. Some kids understood and respected their parents' work, related to it or contrasted it with their own aspirations, discussed parents' positive and negative experiences openly. Other youngsters seemed to feel excluded from everyday adult reality; their parents' jobs were remote, dull or mysterious. There was no sex-determined difference in this phenomenon. The children were interested or disinterested regardless of their sex or the sex of each parent. An organic, relaxed interchange on the subject of work seemed to be a function of individual style rather than sex, class or race.

Child development specialists Sarah M. Shoffner and Richard H. Klemer have written extensively about parental influence on job choices, and it is a staggeringly potent influence indeed: "Parents serve as role models, affectors of children's self-concept, motivators of children's interest and achievement, providers of the developmental environment, and job information givers."

With open channels of communication we can share our work experiences with our children. Through the microcosm of our own jobs they can begin to understand about trade and commerce and art and economics and accomplishment and disappointment and human relations. Through us, they can graduate from the school of hard knocks without any bruises. And perhaps, through us, they can glimpse their futures.

6

But What About the Children?

Congresswomen Bella Abzug and Shirley Chisholm believe that nothing short of a $23 billion child care program will do the trick.

Anthropologist Margaret Mead suggests that government and industry allow working mothers to bring their small children to work.

Germaine Greer, author of *The Female Eunuch,* writes that the solution is a housewives' cooperative with an open-house policy for neighborhood children who have two working parents.

Elizabeth Barrett, who sued the Internal Revenue Service, and thousands of less litigious women, insist that a full business deduction for child care expenses is the answer.

Richard Farson, psychologist and children's rights advocate, says that allowing kids to live together and govern themselves in children's residences is the way of the future.

The question that inspires these proposals is: What should we do about the children? It is the most complex, worrisome and urgent of all the problems facing working parents.

Since the mass culture has made the working mother an invisible citizen, policy-makers in both the public and the private sector can continue to behave as though all workers are men or single women. Working mothers are not yet a cohesive constituency with the capacity to boycott products or remove politicians from office. Without such sabre-rattling there is no real pressure on government or business to devise viable child care systems.

The relatively few child care facilities that are available suffer from inadequate funding, short staffs and long waiting lists. As long as government continues to think of child care as a hand-out for the poor, this sorry situation is likely to continue and worsen. Child care must be seen as every child's right—not as a parking lot for disadvantaged children or as a custodial dumping ground for children of irresponsible mothers. Child care must be viewed as a downward extension of the educational system; an opportunity to enliven and enrich the very young; a twenty-four-hour resource center replete with learning and play materials, caring adults and a great variety of other children to play with.

Thinking of the child care center in this way transforms it from a welfare orphanage to a positive alternative to the home. If such an alternative were available for your children, would you avail yourself of its quality services?

Many women can't shake the formidable shadows of Dr. Freud and Dr. Spock and their awesome pronouncements about the irreplaceable mother. Yet recent research has indicated that there may be *more* harm done by an overinvolved mother who invests so much in her kids that she stifles them and bankrupts herself. Statistics show too, that there is no direct correlation between juvenile delinquency and whether or not the child's mother works. Maybe hallowed Momism is a myth altogether. The work of Bruno Bettelheim and others would seem to suggest that children raised communally feel greater social responsibility, suffer few psychoses and enjoy as much parental affection as do children raised in the nuclear family. In American communities (as opposed to Israeli kibbutzim), communes are unusual and difficult to sustain. However, on its small scale, the child care center can provide the kind of integration that is good for a growing child in our polyglot society. Middle class as well as poor children, white as well as black, benefit from daily exposure to a rich environment outside the home and to a variety of adult influences aside from the mother.

Intellectually, you may accept these findings. Emotionally, you, like many mothers, must first overcome that conditioned reflex that says a mother's place is within shouting distance of her child.

In her book, *Natural Parenthood*, child psychologist Eda LeShan tells of the mother who was ready to quit working because her four-year-old had nightmares. In the classic female guilt reaction, the mother assumed it was *her* fault—until she learned that nearly 70 per cent of any given nursery school population have some nightmares, working Mom or not!

I have always been struck by how pristinely guiltless fathers are. When their children fall out of trees during working hours and father doesn't reach his afflicted offspring until two hours after the accident, no mea culpas are called for. A father's love isn't measured in time or constant proximity (though more of both would be appreciated by most children).

So take the nightmares in stride, take a cue from the guiltless father and plunge right into the morass of making arrangements for someone else to mind the kids.

Child care arrangements: who, which, how and how much?

Do you and your husband want the children to be "watched" or "taught" while you're at work? Babysitters with degrees in child development are hard to come by. But if you believe that your child's waking hours are for learning, creative play and programmed physical exercise, be prepared to search long and hard for a graduate student or professional person and expect to pay premium fees for such optimum care.

On the other hand, if you feel that your toddler learns enough at home, and your school child gets sufficient stimulation in the classroom, then you may only ask that your babysitter be literate, loving, good-spirited and alert to hazards.

Determine which hours coverage is needed. Overlap the time rather than cut corners. No child should have to return from school to an empty house. Figure out the most you can afford to pay, without eroding your income totally and making a mockery of your plan to become a two-income family. (Some women however, justify working outside the home for emotional reasons, even if baby-sitting fees consume nearly all *their* income.) After both parents interview several prospective sitters, you might engage the best applicants for one or two trial evenings just to see how well they assume responsibility and whether the children take easily to them.

When you've hired the best sitter available, be scrupulous in preparing her or him for your high expectations. Review the games, toys and art supplies that your child enjoys most. Discuss appropriate lunch menus, post emergency phone numbers, establish rules that matter most to you (no in-between meal snacks; no TV besides Sesame Street), clarify that you and your husband should be notified at the first sign of fever or other serious symptoms in the child. To a large extent you will have to trust the sitter's judgment when the unforeseen arises. But under normal circumstances the child's everyday routine can follow guidelines that you and your husband set out in advance for the sitter to follow in your absence.

If a housekeeper or babysitter is beyond your means, your child care options begin to narrow. Only the very poor can qualify for the few free or low-cost day care centers. For the rest of us quality child care remains an elusive dream. Yet we know a comprehensive federal program was once within reach. Passed by both houses of Congress, the Child Development Act would have cost this country the price of a few extra fighter bombers. But in December 1971, the will of Congress was ignored and President Nixon put his veto on the bill, in name of his quaint fears for family unity. Since that veto, neither the Senate nor the House has acted upon newly proposed child care legislation.

One gets a heady glimpse of the possibility for responsive federalism by reading Congresswoman Bella S. Abzug's child-care bill which would authorize $2 billion in development monies in the first year and go up to $4 billion in the third year.

The Abzug bill calls for comprehensive health services to be available through the individual child care centers so that *every* American child, regardless of family income or sophistication, would have regular medical, dental and psychological attention as well as periodic check-ups. Other provisions in the legislation would ensure community control so that parents can oversee the caliber of programs and personnel. Where the income falls below the standard of living budget established by the Bureau of Labor Statistics, parents would send their children to the center at no cost. Families above this income level would pay fees on a sliding scale according to their financial status.

This is not nirvana. This kind of full-scale program

could be as American as apple pie and kindergarten. The question is can we give up the extra fighter bombers and get Congress moving again?

A Department of Labor/University of Michigan study reveals that one-fifth of working mothers with preschool children would work more hours if decent child care centers were readily available. But without major federal support of such centers, women's work patterns will continue to break down according to economic extremes and their children will be treated accordingly. The very rich will afford help and private schools, the very poor will qualify for inadequate day care centers, and the great working class and middle class will be lost in the squeeze—except for small favors from the Internal Revenue Service.

Taxing our energies

In 1973, the income tax law was changed to allow a new deduction for child care expenses. Though the rules are complex, basically if husband and wife (or a single parent) earn a total of $18,000 or less annually, they can take a deduction of up to $400 per month for at-home care of all children under age fifteen. Obviously there are several strings attached to the IRS's prize package.

To discourage use of day care centers, the deduction for *out-of-home care* is limited to $200 per month for one child, $300 for two and $400 for three or more children.

To eliminate the most common solution in working parents' homes, the IRS won't accept claims for babysitting fees paid to *relatives*.

And to deter the most practical step—part-time jobs for mothers of young children—the IRS disallows any deduction for child care expenses unless you have worked *at least three quarters of a full-time work schedule*.

After checking out these ifs, ands, and buts, if your household still brings in $18,000 or less, you may be eligible for the full deduction of $4,800 per year for child care. For each dollar you earn over $18,000, you deduct fifty cents off the allowable deduction. Thus, at a total combined income of $27,600, you may deduct nothing.

This income limitation and the penalty for part-time and out-of-home care indicate that the Internal Revenue Service is not ready to accept the phenomenon of the working mother. It should be noted that there is *no* income limitation on the business expenses an executive can deduct. If he earns $100,000 he can still take off the cost of a business lunch. Clearly, we have a long way to go before child care costs are seen to be as valid employment-related expenses as the two-martini lunch.

Beyond these major inequities, there are countless minor flaws in the current system. Hassle-free living is virtually impossible, for example, if schools offer no lunch program. When the child must come home at noontime we must provide supervision and a meal. If a child is sick or our sitter doesn't show up, there is no back-up person, no social network to plug into. In this affluent society, we are each alone with our crises.

Making the best of a bad set of options

With all their imperfections, here are the six basic arrangements you can make for the care of your children:

1. *Depend on relatives.* Nearly half of all children of working mothers are tended in their own homes, most frequently by the father (when he is working a different shift than his wife), but often by another relative. Older brothers and sisters are a fine source of babysitting talent if they are mature and responsible—and if they are not deprived of their own childhood freedoms altogether.

Even though babysitting may be viewed as a family duty, the older sibling will greatly appreciate a small wage for doing the job. Other relatives will probably expect a regular salary (remember it's non-deductible for kin), though grandparents generally mind their grandchildren gladly and gratis.

Asking a grandparent to fill the post may not be the imposition you think it is. Older people often complain of feeling unwanted and useless. In their senior years they may have acquired patience and gentleness that they didn't exhibit when they were *your* parents. These two factors may combine to make Grandpa or Grandma the ideal babysitter while giving them the sense of being needed.

2. *Hired sitters.* These may be hired through an agency, newspaper ad or community grapevine. They may vary from sleep-in housekeepers (who clean, cook, mind the children and charge up to $125 a week), to live-in college students who babysit in return for room and board to nurses or trainees from nearby hospitals ($1.50 to $3.00 an hour, depending on the area's going rate), to local high

school kids (50 cents to $1 an hour for afternoon and evening coverage), to retired people in the neighborhood who have no families or responsibilities of their own (negotiable weekly rates), to foreigners who come over on work or student visas for a limited time.

3. *Family Day Care.* Thousands of children are cared for in family homes other than their own. Under this system you or your husband drop off the children in the morning and pick them up after work. Though not licensed in most states, these informal group day care setups can be satisfactory, especially if your child is under three. When a warm, affectionate person runs such a program in a spacious home or apartment, four or more infants can thrive when gathered together for parallel play, meals and naps. But there are all too many family day care homes that are bankrupt of stimulating activities and caring caretakers. (Four crib-confined children propped in front of television sets all day is nothing short of criminal neglect—and this has happened more than once.) Choose your family day care home only after serious research and reliable references. Fees should run from $10 to $35 weekly.

4. *Nursery 'schools.* For three- to six-year-olds, the private nursery school probably offers the best child care in terms of trained professional staff, enriched environment, learning equipment and play facilities. Because of astronomical costs (up to $2,500 a year) and limited programs (9 A.M. to 1 P.M. is a long day, and during vacations school is closed), only the privileged few can avail themselves of this possibility.

5. *Cooperatives.* If you can mobilize other mothers and fathers with similar needs and standards who work at home or on staggered schedules, the round-robin cooperative is a practical method costing little to operate. With five participating children you would have the group at your house one day each week. Your contribution is your time, food and imagination. In return your child gets four days a week in four different home environments, with four new adults whose talents are different from your own—and you get four days a week in which to pursue your work, worry-free.

6. *The child care center.* As we've seen, the child care center is the rarest of all arrangements and the one with the greatest potential. While over five million preschool

children have working mothers, there are day care centers for only 640,000 of them. Waiting lists are more than ten times the capacity of most centers. It's probably easier to start a center of your own or pressure your company to do so.

Several financial set-ups already exist as models. Through a combination of federal grants and private fund-raising, the University of Oregon Day Care Center in Eugene has become a showcase project serving over a hundred children, ages six months to five years. A parent cooperative, the center charges anywhere from $85 a month to nothing at all, depending on need.

The latest Revenue Act allows a business to deduct over five years, the expenses of acquiring, constructing or rehabilitating property for use as a child care facility for employees' children. There are only eleven on-site industry-sponsored day care centers in America. One of them is at Joshua Tree Women's Sportswear in California where the center is open from 6:50 A.M. to 6 P.M. six days a week. Employees pay $2.60 per day. The company picks up the remaining cost which amounts to only $12,000 per year after taxes and the company president, Bernard Grenel, says, "It's not a burden; it's something we think is worthwhile."

If your company doesn't buy that attitude, try this alternative. The Ford Foundation gives $15 a week as a child care allowance for each child through age twelve if the staff member's family income is less than $10,000. An additional $5 per week is reimbursed if the child is enrolled in a licensed day care center. Families earning between $10,000 and $20,000 get two-thirds of the full benefits and part-timers get half benefits. With forty-two children enrolled during the first year, the program cost the Ford Foundation only $12,500 and management is "delighted" with the results.

We can't wait for the federal government; we need programs like the three mentioned and we need them *now*. For nearly one million "latchkey" children (who have no supervision), four per cent of them under age six, child care is a necessity. For mothers and fathers who spend up to one-third of their earnings on babysitters, it is an economic imperative. For all children, a totally safe, caring, educational alternative to the home is a *right* this great nation should be able to guarantee from birth.

7

The Dual-Career Family:
The Optimum Cooperative

She's a physician, he's a professor of chemistry. They have a two-year-old child. When the babysitter doesn't show up one morning, which parent stays home?

He's a New York lawyer, she's a book editor. He gets a fabulous job offer in Minneapolis. She can't find comparable work because there's no book publishing industry in Minneapolis. Do they move anyway?

He's a musician, she's an executive. Her company offers her a promotion with a hefty raise. Taking it means she would earn more money than her husband. Does she accept?

She has to prepare for her speech tomorrow. He's working against a deadline on his article. The kids are hungry. Who makes dinner?

These are just a few of the daily decisions faced by couples in an admittedly elite group known as the two-career families. What makes them different from other working couples is the professional nature of the wife's work. It is assumed that her career commitment is as great as her husband's, that the demands of her work are as important, and that she is motivated by intellectual rather than economic need.

The dual-career family is interesting to contrast with two other kinds of husband-wife-work relationships in traditional households. The first is the *two-person career* in

47

which both partners are devoted to the career advancement of the husband. The wife frequently works to put
her husband through school; then she stays home to care
for the house and children so that he is free to do the
world's work. She is also expected to entertain his clients,
shop for his business gifts, act the hostess and get along
well with other company wives. His side of the bargain is
to "support" her. Some say that such a division of labor is
fair, albeit sex-typed. But it should be emphasized that
when two persons focus on the enhancement of one person's worth, only the one person is storing away nuts for
winters ahead. In other words, if the upwardly mobile husband dies or the marriage ends in divorce, the wife's prospective employers don't tend to give much weight to the
skills she developed while working on *his* career.

The second traditional household is the *two-job family*.
Both partners work, usually full-time, and the wife's salary
is frequently the financial life-raft for a family drowning
in debts. Despite this dependence on her work, its value is
rarely acknowledged. Her work is for extras; his work is
his life-commitment. He "lets" her work, but she must also
manage her domestic duties and remain available to the
service of others. When the debts are paid and the family
is solvent, she is often elbowed back to the nest—no matter how much she may have liked her job. In the end, hers
is the dispensible occupation; his is the indispensible
career.

On the surface, these two models—the two-person career
and the two-job family—would seem completely different
from the non-traditional elite, *two-career family*. Here,
both partners are professionals. Shouldn't all things be
egalitarian in a partnership of equals?

Unfortunately, real life isn't that easy. Two-career
families also function within our culture and are therefore
subject to the same sex-role pressures and the same standards of marital "normality" as everyone else. Because of
this, the difficulties experienced by two-career families are
simply *intensified* examples of all couples' work-family adjustments.

In this time of radical change in women's roles, the
dual-career family can be a mirror on *your future* whether
or not you're a professional.

Mobility

In conventional families the wife is supposed to say, "whither thou goest I will go." If her husband is transferred to a better job, she packs and picks up stakes no matter how hard it may be to leave her job or her friends. However, for two-career couples, this rule can't be applied with biblical rigidity. Each professional person needs the freedom to move wherever opportunity beckons. He or she also needs the right to stay put in order to develop a career, rather than be uprooted by the spouse. These two provisos can easily clash. I've found that most two-career couples approach the problem from a practical standpoint, not according to "the man wears the pants" theory.

David Dretzin, an attorney, is married to Joanna Merlin, casting director and sometime actress. He speculates: "If she was unhappy here, I would think seriously about moving. We certainly would move for her physical health so why not for her mental and emotional well-being. Joanna isn't hooked on a specific job but she has to be working in some productive, creative capacity related to the theatre. Because I understand this, I can't say I have a calling and my wife just has a job. But any specific move would have to depend on whether I could find a good position in the new location, or else whether we could all live on her income."

Temporary career moves require different judgments. When actress Barbara Barrie won a role on a TV series, she had to live in California for several months during the shooting. Her husband, Jay Harnick, a theatrical director, has assignments in the East, so he remained in New York with their two children. Eventually, Jay and the children flew to the Coast to live with Barbara. Jay is no stranger to this mobile life-style. "Sure, there are momentary feelings of resentment when I'm managing the family alone. And I miss her a lot. But if it made sense to move wherever her career thrives best, we'd make out. I would work as a director in L.A. or we'd both commute cross-country, or we'd just maintain two homes."

Many couples justify short-term separations for long-term gains. Ray McGuire, a professor who teaches in Maine, cares for his two children all week while his wife, Judy, goes to graduate school in Massachusetts. The family reunites every weekend.

In contrast, Jan and Richard McLain of LaCrosse, Wisconsin, openly resolved that neither of them will entertain thoughts of moving just for career advancement. "He's a sales manager. I'm a newspaper reporter. We could do our kind of jobs anywhere but we love it here and it's a perfect place to raise our son, so why rock the boat," says Jan McLain.

Sometimes when one spouse is offered a good position, it's possible to negotiate with the company or university to get them to provide a good job for the other spouse too. Stanford, MIT, Oberlin and Hampshire College are among those institutions who hire married couples to share a single job. For example, Pat and Steve Brenner split one teaching job at Iowa's Grinnell College; other couples split jobs as university administrators. Such ideal situations are impossible to arrange if colleges have a nepotism rule that precludes hiring relatives onto the same staff. In most cases one job opportunity is offered to one member of the couple, and the other spouse is expected to come along and take the jobhunting risks. Usually, it's the woman who takes pot luck finding a suitable job in the wake of her husband's move. Her problems are compounded by widespread and generalized discrimination against women. Ironically, if the opposite happens and the man follows his wife's career moves, the family unit profits because he stands a better chance of finding a well-paid new job in our pro-male job market.

Money and status

If we weren't programmed from birth to believe that men must be superior to women in salary and status (as well as height, size, age and education) this subject would not arouse guilt and ego trauma. But we are, and it does—except for some.

Judith and Richard Newman, both architects, exhibit unusually relaxed attitudes about their relative earnings and work status. "We're comparably skilled," says Richard. "I design office buildings, Judith designs residences; but we both can design both. Because I'm confident about our separate talents, if she's making more money I can attribute it to circumstances, not to a deficit in me. And if in some circles, I'm known as Judith's husband, the only thing I feel is pride in my wife's good reputation."

Judith Newman describes their adjustment this way: "Richard is not interested in money. He's easygoing and his wants in life are simple. I'm assertive and hard-driving. For the two of us what matters is a meshing of these temperaments, not money or status comparisons."

On the subject of money, an enlightening point is made by Barbara Barrie: "Both of us measure our careers in terms of fulfillment rather than achievement. I don't feel guilty about making more money or having greater celebrity," she says. "I only worry when Jay doesn't feel personally elated about his own work."

"If I'm working up to my own potential, everything's fine," says Jay Harnick. "The only time I think about the salary difference is when we're contemplating a major purchase. Then something in my head says that Barbara should make the decision (about buying a car or apartment) because she brings in more money. It's more a result of the old work ethic than male chauvinism. I think of it as her money if she earns it—even though I think of it as *our* money if I earn it. But we end up making mutual decisions anyway because we want each other to be pleased with the final choice."

Over three million American wives earn more than their husbands but many professional women honestly confess that they can't allow that to happen to them. "I'm balancing my career and marriage on a tightrope as it is," says one advertising woman. "If I threatened his male ego in the financial area, the whole act might tumble down."

Competition—whether in money, honors or public recognition—is a major hazard. Ursula and Warren Farrell, both feminists, moved to Washington, D.C., when she won a White House Fellowship. Warren, a political scientist, gave up a teaching job at Rutgers University. In Washington, he was surprised at how hard it was to be introduced constantly as "the husband of." He felt the bite of being secondary—going to sherry parties while Ursula lunched with politicians and statesmen. He began to understand women's resentment about standing "behind" their men. "It can get to you after a while," he says.

To avoid the bitterness of competition, wives seem to do most of the accommodating—by consciously promoting their husband's brilliance, affecting a submissive role in their private life and curbing their own careers.

Integrating work/home/marriage/children

For professional couples, hired help seems a virtual necessity, especially when there are young children. Still, the happy, well-functioning two-career families find that balancing work schedules with the demands of the home requires the kind of sharing that ignores standard sex-role divisions of labor.

"Everybody does everything," says Gail Parker, president of Bennington College. Her husband, Thomas, vice president of the College shares the cooking and the care of their young child.

Architect Richard Newman makes breakfast and prepares his son's boxed lunch. Jay Harnick supervises bedtimes, reads stories, plays with the children in the park. Richard McLain irons and alternates cooking. David Dretzin says, "I do the grunt work and other jobs where lesser skills are required, like setting the table or doing dishes."

These men and several of those surveyed in Lynda Lytle Holmstrom's study "The Two-Career Family," commented not on the indignity of men doing housework but on the drudgery and tedium inherent in the work itself. While many women feel guilty "imposing" on their husbands' time, the men take their wives' work seriously enough to assume household responsibilities so that both partners have more time to work and to enjoy each other. "I suppose I could demand my male right to relax at the end of a long, hard day," says an engineer whose wife works in government. "But then I'd never get to spend time with her. Housework gets done in half the time when two people do it—then there are hours left over for both of us to enjoy together."

The New York Times interviewed several dual career couples and found that "fewer men expect to be waited on and more contribute to the daily chores." The article cited Jeremy Foster-Fell, who does the cooking and who wakes up at night in response to the baby's cries (his wife, Judy runs a model agency); Eugene McGuire, who cleans and prepares breakfast and boxed lunches for himself and his lawyer wife, Pamela; and other men who pitch in across the board with no specific assignments. "It's just that marriage is a partnership and neither partner should be over-burdened," said Janet Gosnell, a public relations consultant whose husband drives the kids to lessons and club meetings, does the dishes and cooks.

Professional marriages seem to thrive on an intellectual respect that spills over into other aspects of the couple's life. Several commented that their sexual relationships were best when each partner felt a strong personal identity and particularly when the wife felt valued for herself. A few couples also made the point that busy, tired professionals feel freer to skip sex without having it interpreted as a rejection of the partner.

When babysitting problems arise or a child is sick, these couples respond to each crisis according to who can most easily accommodate that day's work schedule to the needs of the children. This might mean missing a class, postponing a meeting or working at home that day. In most cases, the professional's high status or autonomous work set-up permits maximum flexibility. People on regular eight-hour jobs alternate absences from work during those rare emergencies. But in everyday situations, babysitters or other surrogates make more than adequate stand-ins. "I've learned I'm not so indispensable," says Joanna Merlin. "Someone else can take my kids to the dentist as well as I can. I'll count the fillings when I get home."

There was overwhelming agreement among the families I questioned, that it was good for children of both sexes to perceive each of their parents in worldly roles. The kids seem to get an extra measure of excitement out of life, too.

The Harnick children see their mother on the Broadway stage or on television; they can meet their favorite stars or wander around movie sets. They get a behind the scenes view when watching their father direct a play.

The Newman children see buildings designed by their parents rise from the ground up. They understand something about the process from blueprints to bricks-and-mortar. By admiring the work of both parents, children form life-long patterns of respect for both sexes.

Social lives of two-career families are generally less active than average because of the excessive career demands. But these families appear to gain great satisfaction from spending free hours with one another, their children and their professional colleagues. When they do entertain, the wives still do most of the cooking and planning. But the husbands recognize the toll on women's energies and they compensate by doing the shopping or clean-up or by planning restaurant celebrations instead of at-home parties. At social gatherings or during after-dinner discussions, these couples and their friends rarely split up according to sex. Men and women together seem as comfortable talking about their children as about their jobs, national politics or the economy.

The machinations of household routine in dual-career homes follow their own logic. Rather than have the children fed early, a surprising number of couples cherish having dinner together with their children. Even if it means a later mealtime and an even later bedtime, they consider this ritual inviolate. In our house, parents and children converge from all directions: we from our offices, the kids from drama class, the park or visits to friends' homes. Occasionally, there is a young sleep-over guest too. What with team table-setting, meal preparation (husband, wife and babysitter working in concert), bathtime, general end-of-day clean-up, phone calls, a quick cocktail or a glance at the television news, it may be seven or seven thirty before we all gather around the table. Creative chaos thereby leads to a warm, animated dinner hour, full of the day's news. For us and many other families, getting the children into bed at nine o'clock instead of an hour earlier, is no scandal. We've used our evening time to braid together the strands of our independent lives before we go our separate ways again tomorrow.

Dual career families also tend to consider vacations to be family affairs. Because so many professionals must travel for business reasons, they cherish getting together for trips at a second home in the country.

Judith Newman demurs. She favors taking an occasional pleasure tour on her own—and she makes separate vacations sound eminently reasonable. "Every five or six years, I go off to unwind, to talk to *nobody* and to see sights that only I care about." Perhaps other adults would also be more rejuvenated by utterly self-indulgent occasional flings. (Why are flings always thought to be sexual?) If you're an art lover, Disneyland is not going to do for you what the Sistine Chapel would. Maybe you're a tennis nut, and your husband revives with a steady diet of golf, golf and more golf. Think about splitting vacations:

take a week together with the kids, doing things in the same place at the same time, then take another week when you can zip off to a tennis camp while your husband takes to the links. The kids can choose to follow a parent (or a sport), or they can stay with their grandparents. There are always children's camps and children's hotels and friends to crash with for a few days.

Separate vacations may well be the last frontier for the dual-career couple. But most of their other adjustments are neither radical, nor out of reach for every working couple. They are accommodations based on an equal evaluation of the time and career commitment of both husband and wife. Ideally, none of us should have to be high-powered professionals to achieve this kind of harmony, consideration and respect.

8

Domestic Affairs

Every woman who ever has reason and budget enough to employ a housekeeper has the opportunity to become the kind of "boss" that she dreams of having herself. In this one-to-one relationship (between the working woman who goes outside the home to a job and the working woman who comes into the home for *her* job) is reflected all the elements of employer-employee relations, writ small and intimate.

I've known working women who carry such heavy burdens of white liberal guilt that they cannot bring themselves to employ a black woman in their homes. In their own way, these well-meaning liberals do as much damage to the position of black women as do the exploitative duchesses who blithely issue commands to their "maids" or "cleaning girls."

In her speeches, Eleanor Holmes Norton, Commissioner of Human Rights for New York City, frequently reassures white audiences that it is perfectly all right for them to hire a black domestic worker when they take jobs of their own. No one who pays a domestic worker a fair wage should suffer a moment's guilt, says Ms. Norton. Household labor is entirely respectable and useful labor. When compensated fairly a domestic worker can feel as much satisfaction and self-esteem as any other working woman. The problem is that working women who are themselves oppressed occasionally turn into oppressors of those working for them.

• "I made $26 per week working 9 to 4 and babysitting until 9 at least three nights a week for the same family. I got no benefits either."

• "I used to do everything—moving couches . . . cleaning garages, carrying groceries . . . and walking their stupid dog in all kinds of weather."

• "I get vacation every year. When they take vacation, I take my vacation the same time—only I don't get paid for mine."

• "I never worked on a job that paid sick benefits."

If you are a domestic worker, these complaints may ring a lot of bells. If you employ a housekeeper, listen hard. The household workers quoted above participated in a pilot project conducted in five Ohio cities by the National Committee on Household Employment (NCHE), a nonprofit group dedicated to the concerns of household workers. But Ohio doesn't have a corner on exploited domestics.

There are over 1.5 million household workers in the country, almost 97 per cent of them female and about two-thirds of them black. In 1972, their median annual income for full-time work was $2,365—on which many of these women must support themselves and their families. One in five black American women work as domestics. Because of educational and social disadvantages (only 21 per cent are high school graduates), these women have few job options. Even as domestic workers, they rarely enjoy benefits that most employees take for granted: sick leave, paid vacations, legal holidays, unemployment insurance and worker's compensation. Until May 1974, they weren't even covered by federal minimum wage laws.

Many employers discriminate deviously in hiring domestics. Ads that say "European preferred" may as well specify "No blacks need apply." Other Help Wanted notices call for "Jamaican" or "Caribbean preferred"—telltale euphemisms meant to hide the employer's intention to take advantage of workers whose immigrant status is tenuous or who are ignorant of American tax laws.

Low wages and lack of benefits are the most glaring and visible inequities. But on the job, behind closed doors, exists an infinite variety of daily indignities. "The day worker may be expected to clean eight rooms, get up on a ladder and do the outside of the windows, scrub the oven and clean out the refrigerator all in one day," says Carolyn Reed, coordinator of the Progressive Household Technicians of New York.

Each household has different demands and standards of performance. Some homes are disorganized as well as dirty; some employers are bossy, their children unruly or unkind. Employers may betray their disrespect for the household worker in several ways: by calling her "Mary" or "Honey" while insisting on being addressed as Mrs. Clark; by referring to her demeaningly as "the girl"; by asking her to eat her meals away from the family. Other employers still give cast-off clothes or leftover food in lieu of a deserved salary increase.

Domestic workers may be fired at will or on whim, often with no notice. Also, it isn't unusual for a job applicant to travel a long distance to a job interview, only to find that she can't negotiate a decent wage—and must pay her own carfare back and forth anyway.

Lacking a specific or standardized job description, a woman hired for certain duties may eventually find herself performing extra chores that weren't in the original bargain.

Carolyn Reed gives a typical example: "Let's say the day worker is supposed to clean, vacuum and do light washing. But the employer discovers that the worker is super-efficient; so little by little she's got her doing the mending, cooking dinner, minding the children, running errands, ironing and scrubbing floors. This is one business where the more competent you are the worse off you are."

Live-in housekeepers (11 percent of all domestics) have the same problems as day workers—and then some. Because they're giving free room and board, employers feel they can pay live-ins less salary. Ms. Reed's answer is: "You want someone to live in because you want them available for work at odd hours—not because you want to give them a home. Most household workers prefer to live with their own families, but with the scarcity of jobs for black female heads of households, they take what they can get. If you want them to start breakfast and they would have to get up at 5 A.M. to reach your house by 7, it makes sense for both of you if the worker lives in. That makes the room and board a condition of employment, not a bonus."

While most working people put in an eight-hour day, the live-in housekeeper commonly stays on call from early morning until well after dinner is cleared away. Even her time off is not her own. She may be expected to babysit, answer phones, water the lawn, or be home to receive deliveries or repair crews.

As paid jobs lure women out of the home—where they did *unpaid* housework—other women will take their place to do *paid* housework. We do our own dishes for nothing, but the work isn't *worth* nothing. Similarly, we do our own electrical repairs free, but when we call in an electrician we pay for the professional service. Domestic workers at their best, are also professionals. Rather than continue the chain of exploitation, those who employ other women should accord them the same respect as is given the electrician or any other technician for hire.

Household workers continue to professionalize themselves; they are entering training programs, organizing for economic advancement, and informing themselves of their employment rights. If they are not to become a vanishing species they must be supported in their efforts to upgrade themselves.

During the 1960s, the pool of household workers decreased by one million. Since the median age of domestics is fifty, the labor force will lose still more by attrition. To attract young women (who might otherwise become cashiers, clerks or saleswomen for the same wages), and to keep older women in the field, certain improvements are essential:

WAGES: The 1974 minimum wage law extended coverage to household workers for the first time. On January 1, 1975, the minimum hourly rate became $2. It rises to $2.20 on January 1, 1976, and $2.30 on January 1, 1977. The minimum wage, plus time and a half for overtime, applies to domestic workers who receive at least $50 per calendar quarter from one employer or who work more than eight hours a week in one or more households. Exempt from coverage are casual babysitters and caretakers of the old and infirm. Live-in housekeepers are included in the minimum wage but not the provision for overtime pay.

Carmen Maymi, Director of the Women's Bureau of the U.S. Department of Labor, reminds employers: "In those states where the minimum wage is higher than that established by federal law, the state minimum must be paid." A 40-hour work week paid for at the minimum wage would only yield $80 a week or $4,160 annually (with paid vacation)—hardly a subsistence income, especially for

heads of households who are trying to stave off welfare.
The Progressive Household Technicians recommend a fair
minimum of $3 an hour, while the United Church of
Christ asks churchwomen to pay $3.95 an hour or more.
In any case, wages should be reviewed at least once a year.

SOCIAL SECURITY: If a worker earns $50 or more
per quarter, her employer must pay a share of the Social
Security tax and take the remainder out of the domestic's
salary. (Many employers agree to pay the entire tax as a
fringe benefit to the employee.) The value of food, lodg-
ing, or clothing given to a household employee is not subject to the Social Security tax. In this labor market, perhaps the most unemployable person is the *older* black
female. It is imperative for this proud, hardworking wage-
earner to have Social Security benefits in her later years.

VACATIONS: A day worker should receive one day of
paid vacation per year for each day per week that she
works in a household. Live-in workers should get two
weeks vacation after one year full-time employment.
NCHE suggests that vacation time be renegotiated after
two years.

SICK DAYS: The employer should specify in the job
interview how many paid sick days will be allowed.
NCHE recommends one per year for the once-a-week day
worker and six paid sick days for the full-time or live-in
employee.

ACCIDENT INSURANCE: Homeowners' or tenants'
policies should include coverage for accidental injury to
domestic workers. Josephine Hulett, now Field Officer of
NCHE, formed an affiliate in Youngstown, Ohio, as a
result of angry reactions when a domestic worker who
broke her hip on the job received no medical payment—
although the employer's home was covered by personal liability insurance. Accident coverage is now mandatory in
Ohio.

HOLIDAYS: NCHE calls for eight paid legal holidays
per year for live-in workers; six holidays for full-time,
live-out employees and one legal holiday per year for day
workers when the holiday falls on the normal working day.

*WORKING CONDITIONS AND PERFORMANCE
STANDARDS:* Agree on these items in advance, ideally
in writing:

1. *Time schedule:* Hour of arrival, departure, rest periods, meal breaks, timing of vacation, willingness to work

overtime, probation period (two to three weeks is fair, says Ms. Hulett).

2. *Task list:* Uvelia S.A. Bower, founder director of Household Employment Association for Re-Evaluation and Training (HEART), says an outlined workload allows the employee to be thorough, creative and satisfied by her accomplishment when she's finished. HEART also counsels employers to plan the workday realistically; strenuous tasks come first, followed by a five-minute rest period; in a two-story house, all the morning tasks should be on one floor, the afternoon tasks on another; sitting jobs should alternate with reaching, lifting and standing jobs. Employers should be as detailed as they like on the task list, but they shouldn't work alongside the employee. A professional household worker wants to be trusted to do things her own way, within the bounds of the employer's instructions.

3. *Safety:* Appliances should be in A-1 condition and appropriate cleaning products and materials should be available. Workers should not be asked to perform chores that imperil their health and safety. Employer and employee together should read product or appliance instructions and warnings so that both parties are responsible for their safe use.

4. *Extras:* Discuss the employee's attitude toward cast-off clothes and food leftovers. If a uniform is required, the worker should know whether she is expected to pay for it and its laundering. (Some domestics object to certain uniforms because of the Hollywood stereotype of the fat black maid in a black costume.)

5. *Set policy regarding the household worker's children:* During her child's school vacations or babysitter emergencies, can she bring her kids with her? Decide *before* the emergencies arise—and keep in mind how *your* work responsibilities fall apart when you're hung up over child care arrangements. If anyone should understand such crises, it is women who employ other women!

6. *Work relationship:* Have a periodic job review; revise the written or spoken contract to accommodate changed duties; discuss timing of raises; air personal slights or misunderstandings on either side as soon as they happen.

The employer should give the day worker at least five days' notice if her services aren't needed, otherwise, compensate her for the lost day's pay. By the same token, the employee should give the earliest possible notice of illness so the employer can get a replacement. Two weeks' notice should be given by either party if live-in employment is to be terminated from either direction.

Housework can be a happy art

Jasmine Twyman, 54, of Peekskill, N.Y., is a day worker who is so pleased with her six employers that once a year she throws a lavish party for them (and for favorite past employers). She has worked for some families up to sixteen years. Ms. Twyman has always received Social Security contributions, paid vacations and paid sick leave. Her day rate is $25 plus carfare. Her hours are her own because her employers believe she knows how to manage their housecleaning better than they do.

"This has been my line of work since I was fourteen," says Ms. Twyman. "I'm a professional." She inspires respect, resents familiar imitations of black language and doesn't permit an employer to call her "Honey Chile" or to say "Hi y'all." She accepts cast-off clothes because "they're more beautiful than anything I can afford," but she feels the clothes are given in friendship, not charity.

Carolyn Reed also speaks of her profession with pride: "An experienced household worker can walk into your home and understand your values. She can tell if you care about your plants, if you're fanatic about your kitchen, but don't pay much attention to the bedrooms, if your books matter to you. She can quickly determine the best appliance or household product to use for every job. You don't have to tell her where things are kept or when the closets need cleaning or whether the floors are overwaxed. She knows what products are hazardous to use around small children. She enjoys preparing a party, presenting beautiful food, seeing the house sparkle."

To increase the number of household technicians who answer to Ms. Twyman's and Ms. Reed's description, household work must be upgraded and adequately compensated. Most important, that one-to-one relationship between employer and employee must be businesslike, and based on mutual respect and personal dignity.

A California court recently upheld domestic workers' right to picket in front of the private homes of their employers. Among the sisterhood of working women—whether we're called labor or management—it should never have to come to that.

SECTION
II

A Job Is a Job
—or is it?

We know that some people live to work, while others work to live. This is not merely an economic fact, it's an attitude.

9

Taking Control of Your Life: Career Counseling and Do-It-Yourself Shortcuts

"I just can't decide what I want to do."

"I'm 38 and I've never worked, so who'd hire me?"

"I'm really not very good at selling myself."

"All I know is that I want to work with people."

"If only I could understand what jobs are out there . . ."

Those are typical statements uttered in despair by the woman who longs for a *career* but ends up in just any job, by the clerical worker who feels trapped, by the college graduate who is brainy but unfocused, by the housewife who feels economically worthless—or by any one of us at a moment of confrontation with our future.

As women we often find ourselves in a hopeless bind. We're taught that the ideal woman is modest and self-effacing, but we know that people don't get good jobs by selling themselves short. We've learned that most men feel uncomfortable with high-powered, highly paid women, so we fear that success can spoil our social lives. Most important, because our youthful energies were directed toward getting married, we've never been encouraged to think in terms of total *life-planning*.

While boys grow up with the idea that they must chart their careers, make decisions and actively plan their futures, girls look ahead to who our husbands might be, where his job might lead us to live, or how many kids we might have. We women have rarely been encouraged to think about what *we* ourselves want to be doing twenty-five years from now; or how much we are capable of earning in a lifetime; or what would constitute real long-term personal fulfillment, beyond the joys of family life.

In recent years, self-actualization for *you,* the woman and the person that you are, has become a respectable pursuit. And for thousands of women, that's where career counseling comes in. If you can afford it—and if you live near a reputable counseling service—take a flyer and let professionals help you sort out your prospects in the job market. If career counseling is too expensive, inconvenient or inaccessible, you can borrow their methods and do-it-yourself. With rigorous self-analysis, you can follow the same principles, put yourself through the program and emerge a confident jobhunter, raring to go.

Whether they call themselves life-management courses or career development workshops, most of these programs speak the same language. They promise to change your life—and in many cases they seem to deliver. Their techniques, timetables and fee scales vary considerably. There are free consultation centers and costly programs that take many months to complete; crash courses offering vocational first aid and leisurely seminars with visiting experts and videotape replays to help you study your speaking style and body language. I've heard good and bad reports about nearly every method, so it's essential for you to find the one that serves your needs best.

Once you determine what fee is within reach, go and interview program directors to be sure that their teaching philosophy and course content strikes you right. Ask to talk with people who have finished the course, or sit in on a trial session. Find out what companies have hired "graduates" of the program. Ask for a few case histories. Watch out for fancy placement services who promise counseling but are actually employment agencies eager to find you a job and collect their commission.

If psychological methods are part of the counseling process, check that the staff has authentic professional credentials. Quiz the director about the program's expressed goals. Does it get to the root of your negative attitudes about yourself, or does it only teach you how to ask for a promotion or a raise? For simple practical help, you should not have to pay a fee more suited to in-depth life-planning counseling.

Before signing any contracts, check your findings against the following composite description of some of the most intensive, and expensive, programs I've researched. (And if it all sounds common-sensical, consider adapting this information to a do-it-yourself plan.)

Most of the programs have both male and female staff with diverse business and psychological counseling experience. The directors' attitudes reflect an approach that is, if not avowedly feminist, at least pro-women and realistic about the female's special problems. They begin with the basic premise that nearly *everyone* has developed key skills for dealing with life. The role of the career guru is to bring these skills into focus and help you apply them to your life plan.

Generally, the first phase of the program includes individual and group counseling sessions devoted to identifying your basic life skills by examining your patterns of interest. In other words, what have you enjoyed doing in the past in any aspect of your personal or employment history, and what have you done well?

Jim Gallagher of Career Management Associates believes that the successes of the past, however small, predict the successes of the future. He has all his clients rate their past successes whether or not they *seem* job-related. He asks you to look at your school performance, your factual accomplishments on former jobs (no matter how dull), your strengths in volunteer or club work, the highlights of your athletic or leisuretime pursuits.

Do you thrive on efficiency and order or is your best work done in an atmosphere of cheerful pandemonium? Do you need physical outlets for your energy? Are you good at detail work, using your hands, conceptualizing projects on a grand scale? Can you talk people into giving their money or time to something you believe in? Are you gifted with numbers, puzzles and challenging calculations or computations? Do you enjoy public speaking? Have you been happiest and most productive when you're involved with others on a team project; or are you an effective loner?

Isolating your strengths and preferences provides your first clues as to whether you're a leader, an organizer, an originator, a team-worker, or whatever. Later on, this pattern begins to overlap onto an existing trade or specialty. You begin to think of yourself as a potential job holder. You start describing yourself in positive terms: "I am a gregarious person; I would make a fine public relations woman." Or, "I have a keen talent for money management; I'm going into banking."

Carl Bielby, of Mainstream Associates, uses many of the same methods but his stress is on the concept of the "creative conversation"—the art of transmitting your best possible self-image to the outside world. He helps clients research who they are and what they are in order to create a new career objective, and then fit themselves into a prospective employer's "needs, problems and future plans." Bielby wants clients to sparkle and effuse when presenting themselves. But beyond the job candidate's personal style must be a solid grasp of what the company wants and how *you* can provide it.

Janice LaRouche of OPTIONS: Career Workshops for Women, a feminist counseling service, puts the accent on women and their common hang-ups. She dissects the sources of lost confidence and helps clients over "feminine role-playing" so that they can begin to assume power and take themselves seriously as working women. Her workshops are a blend of practical advice and intimate consciousness-raising. With a small group of similarly aspiring friends, you can duplicate this process, even without a leader.

During the self-assessment phase, counselors ask you to read the signals about yourself and consider which of your skills are transferable to the job market. Then you translate your talents and interests into the jargon of the business world. If you were once responsible for planning an ecology day or a testimonial dinner, consider yourself an experienced "administrator" or "coordinator." Count that senior citizens program you organized in the neighborhood. Give yourself job credit for making all the travel arrangements for your husband's sales force. If you set up the office procedures at the church school, call yourself a systems analyst.

A nun, for example, distilled her experience as a Maryknoll missionary in the Phillipines so that it read like an impressive work record: "developed slum improvement projects, organized children's camp, recruited and hired staff, obtained administrative support and budget." The nun's skills in one context translated readily to executive potential when she left her order. She had learned to analyze the parts to make a new whole. A teacher or homemaker can do the same.

Take the housewife who claimed she hadn't "worked" in twenty years. It turned out that in her "free time" she had coordinated a staff of seventy-five volunteers that had been raising $100,000 a year for the local symphony orchestra—first rate qualifications for a professional fundraiser.

A political campaign worker or the organizer of a community center has accumulated valuable skills and sophisticated knowledge that a foundation, university or city agency might consider ideal experience.

"Treat volunteer work as though it had been salaried," advises Gallagher. "You can use the phrase 'Contributed services worth $15,000,' once you've determined your market value."

All the career counselors remarked on most women's generally low salary expectations and attributed this to low self-image and ignorance about what good jobs really pay. Because many women have been isolated from the information-exchange network, they don't know what they're worth by their own standards or anyone else's. This is somewhat rectified during the self-assessment phase of the counseling program, which includes measurement or testing of personality, vocational interests, adaptability, motivation and goals. Afterward, there are reviews of specific occupational categories and their pay rates.

If you are giving yourself the counseling course, start collecting want ads and keep records of the salary range for those jobs that interest you. Ask close friends what they earned in their starting positions. Compare notes with other jobhunters. Get a feel for wage variations by asking your husband or friends about salaries for various jobs in their offices. People needn't tell you their own salary, but it's no skin off their egos to clue you about how much other jobs bring on the auction block.

Next comes the *job search phase* in which you're trained to locate organizations and persons, not necessarily to offer you THE job, but to extend your range of personal contacts. Their counsel may help you pinpoint a job target on the other side of town; word-of-mouth is the language of opportunity.

Carl Bielby describes the job market as an iceberg. Only 25 per cent is above water—those are the jobs advertised in newspapers or listed with agencies. The rest, he says, are known only to insiders. Since women have been sys-

tematically excluded from the circles of power and opportunity, asking for help is a way of getting on the inside.

Alene H. Moris of Individual Development Center, says
she always has to persuade women that it's okay to call an
authority figure for information. "Their immediate reaction is 'Oh, I wouldn't want to bother anyone.'"

Actually, most people like being bothered, in a nice
way. If those who have succeeded in business can give advice or pass along job leads, it's a way for them to reaffirm
their own success. You can make it clear at the outset that
you're looking for *help*, not a job.

I know this method works. I've seen it enlarge several
women's circle of contacts to the point where, by the time
they finished talking to the advisors they knew so much
about a given industry (and knew so many people in it)
that prospective employers were fighting to hire them.

Take a copywriter to lunch to learn how an advertising
agency operates—even if you think you want to end up in
the art department. If you have your heart set on working
for a garden shop, buy a shrub or two and chat with the
owner to find out how landscape designers are hired and
whether you might need specialized training for your
green thumb.

Some career centers have Big Sister programs that pair
an inexperienced woman with a veteran. The Big Sister becomes your vocational resource person throughout the
counseling process—she answers questions, makes referrals, helps with your resumé, and teaches you to track
down job leads in the business that she knows well from
her own experience in it.

In the job search portion of the counseling program,
one group dynamic works especially well. Getting together
with peers is most effective to practice interviews, role-
playing, designing a resumé, discussing job classifications
and doing task-oriented exercises to improve self-perception. Giving a five-minute presentation of your background and objectives will help you crystalize your
commitment while polishing your style. Try right now to
describe yourself glowingly, but without braggadocio.
Then ask an admiring friend to describe you. The comparison should be enlightening!

Carl Bielby sees this period as a rehearsal for the
"creative conversation" that you will eventually carry on
with an advice contact or a prospective boss. "I think 85

per cent of all hiring is based on good vibes," he says. "So you have to turn on enthusiasm about yourself."

You might organize a women's group for impromptu practice sessions. Let one woman play the interviewer while another is the job applicant. The trick is to "turn-on"—to emote and communicate enthusiasm about yourself without ever compromising your dignity as a person, and as a woman. If you're entering the job market for the first time, emphasize your potential, your enormous energy or your willingness to learn. If you want to change jobs, never be negative about where you're coming from; be positive about where you're going.

During one "creative conversation" workshop session, I watched one woman with downcast eyes apologize in a quiet voice for her shyness. She warned the group in advance that her work experience was fairly boring and unexceptional. She assured us that she could never behave confidently, no matter how she tried.

With the group leader's encouragement, the woman slowly unfolded an employment history that sounded like a spy novel. She had done (successfully) industrial surveillance; work with frauds and forgeries for American Express; she had tailed suspects, coordinated investigations with European police forces, covered Central Park, done fingerprinting, social work with welfare families and addicts, and was presently studying toward a Ph.D. in Public Administration.

The group listened in awesome silence, punctuated with questions and exclamations. We hung on her every word. When she finished speaking, she twisted her fingers and kept looking at the floor. Then she listened to us. Our enthusiasm for her was profuse. We thought she was a winner; we all coveted her unique experience. After a spirited exchange of questions, I watched the woman become remarkably animated about who she is and what she can do. Never before had she seen herself reflected in the eyes of others. It was a life-enhancing moment—and one that you should try to experience before you go out to sell yourself to a more judgmental listener.

Which brings us to the last step: Doing It. Going out into the marketplace, putting out feelers, being interviewed, asking for information, researching firms and the people who run them, and generally amassing evidence to help you make the final decision at the same time as a decision is being made about hiring you. This is not the wall-flower line at the spring prom. You don't have to wait to be asked and you don't have to take the first comer. A company must pass your rigorous inspection as well.

Find out the prospective employer's problems and plans for expansion; does the boss have a favorable reputation among co-workers; what is the company's present and past pattern of promoting women; are any lawsuits pending against them on the basis of sex discrimination complaints; do you feel comfortable about their benefit policy, the work atmosphere and the career ladder they're offering to you?

Your group can't be too helpful in the company research phase (unless a friend has inside information), but they can all benefit from a cooperative strategy session. Stage creative conversations to negotiate salary. To borrow a courtroom metaphor, you can think of your resumé as a written brief, but you still have to plead your case in oral argument. Prepare yourself for interviewers who claim "A single woman doesn't need such a big salary," or "We don't feel we have to start you at our top rates because you have a husband to support you." Practice being firm about what you're worth and what you know the job is supposed to pay.

Look to your group for support in contending with a sexist interviewer. ("Why does a pretty girl like you want to be a mechanic?") Work together making lists of your nonnegotiable demands like job security or how much travel you'll agree to. Discuss among friends what really makes you happy and what sort of work would compromise your integrity.

Jim Gallagher says that American society matches identity with utility. Therefore, what you do ought to be consistent with what you *are*. "And that can only be true if you're the one who makes things happen in your own life."

Ideally, women should be teaching other women the techniques of career planning and self-improvement. Then we would see more emphasis on preparing women to use legal remedies against sex discrimination. Then we would also have less authoritative posturing in group sessions and more of a sharing of common experience.

While dozens of new feminist counselors are setting up career programs, we still have relatively few female role models because of decades of bias and repression. Until more professional women are able to make careers of career counseling, we can take the helping hand wherever it is offered without condescension.

It doesn't matter how formal the counseling process, as long as the goal is personal growth and full utilization of your aptitudes. At the end of the program, you may not find the "right" job, but you will be a lot surer about who you are, where you're going and to what you should devote your working hours during the years to come.

10

The Employment Agency:
Ally or Saboteur?

"Gd jbs. Hi pa. No fee."

I have a warm spot in my heart for employment agencies and their funny advertising abbreviations. Many summers ago I sought several agencies' help in finding my first paid job. After questioning my interests and reviewing my meager skills, one agency placement counselor referred me to a "Gal Friday" position at a book publishing company. Though the job paid only $55 a week, it was exactly the work I wanted and it launched me on a satisfying business career.

In subsequent years, other personnel agencies helped me switch jobs to upgrade myself. And when I was in the position of hiring staff people myself, I found a few agencies that could always be counted upon to send suitable candidates.

Other women have had somewhat different experiences. Their complaints about private employment agencies range from outright sex discrimination (all female applicants get typing tests) to age discrimination (a key problem for women returning to the work force) to simple ineptness (sending applicants on wild goose chases, losing resumés, mismatching the person and the job).

Each year America's nearly ten thousand personnel agencies place about four million people in new jobs. Despite testimony about their occasional abuses, agencies can serve even more jobhunters—particularly the upward-bound working woman who knows what to expect from them.

How agencies operate

Instead of interviewing a lot of candidates, which takes company time and staff, a business establishment may list a job order with an employment agency—noting all the specifics as to salary, fringes, duties, experience and education required, travel, relocation and so forth.

If you have registered with the agency because it specializes in placements in your field or because you have answered the agency's ad for a specific job, your card is kept on file. If you are "marketable," you are sent out on as many interviews as it takes to land you the job you want. Usually, your card is kept active for thirty days after the date of your last contact with the agency.

Good agencies function as a two-way screening process: they review applicants to find the most likely prospects for a company's needs, and they comb through job orders to find the best position for your needs. They work best when they have adequate information about your experience, qualifications and personality. Tell them everything you consider important in a job. Do you prefer a small company? Must you take your vacation in summer? Do you work well under pressure? Are you willing to perform your kind of work in any industry? Can you work overtime if necessary?

Robert A. Marcus, of the Sloan Personnel Agency and president of the Association of Personnel Agencies of New York (APANY) estimates that an agency counselor spends about fifteen minutes interviewing an applicant who is interested in a clerical job, and from thirty to sixty minutes talking with a professional or middle-management person.

Rudy Schott, president of F-o-r-t-u-n-e Personnel Agency, makes the point that a complete and meaningful job order can't be taken down in a five-minute conversation with the company. "We help the employers widen their vision and keep the job description more flexible," says Mr. Schott. "That helps us enlarge the applicants' opportunities and choices."

If you consider using an agency's services, check whether the job you are interested in requires that you pay the agency's commission. Recently the trend has been toward "Fee Paid" services, where the employer pays the agency's finder's fee. The advertisement or the job order card must contain this information. In some cases fees are split between you and the employer while other jobs require you to pay the entire commission. Agency commissions are controlled and limited by the laws of your state. You should see the rates and sign a contract with the agency in advance so that your fee responsibility is clear from the start.

A University of Michigan study found that private employment agencies placed 45 per cent of the workers surveyed, and that 59 per cent of the agencies' applicants found the kinds of jobs they wanted. Nonetheless, things *do* go wrong.

What to watch for

In the best of all possible worlds, agencies acting as matchmakers would marry the right person to the right job and everyone would live happily ever after. Unfortunately, despite broad legislation to protect the applicant, discrimination may still threaten the perfect union between you and your chosen career. When dealing with an agency here are the potential problem areas.

1. *Job advertising.* Title VII of the Civil Rights Act of 1964 and most state laws prohibit employers, employment agencies and unions from classifying jobs by sex, unless the job has a bona fide occupational qualification (a legitimate BFOQ might be a size 8 dress model). Many newspapers have voluntarily discontinued the separate Male and Female columns in their job classified section. Other papers print a disclaimer stating that they have separate columns "for convenience" but that a person may apply for any job regardless of sex.

In the *Pittsburgh Press* case, the U.S. Supreme Court ruled constitutional a Pennsylvania state law that had been interpreted to prohibit separate columns. But future cases will have to decide whether newspapers can be prosecuted under Title VII where there is no such state prohibition.

Even though a newspaper is not an employer, agency or union as specified by Title VII coverage, the Equal Employment Opportunity Commission Guidelines recognize that its sex-specific job columns have the *effect* of discriminating. It is human nature to avoid places where we are not wanted.

If your newspaper lists jobs by Male and Female listings, *disregard* them. If an agency specializing in management jobs (or engineering, law, architecture, etc.) lists such jobs in the Male section, do not let this have a chilling effect on your aspirations. Register with whatever agency handles the category of work that you are trained to do, or interested in—and insist that you receive fair consideration for every opening, as decreed under the law.

While agencies are not responsible for a newspaper's policies, they do control the advertising copy in their own want ads. Most agencies are careful to ask for a "person" or "individual." However, in a recent Sunday paper I found several ads in direct violation of the laws against sex discrimination:

"Secy. #2 gal for #1 Man."

"Asst. Acct. Exec. Pharm agency needs detail man."

"Dental Technician. Head crown & Bridge man."

"Dictaphone. Vogue appearance a must."

"Exec. secy who wants to become involved in her work."

Any ad that requests candidates by sex or appearance is forbidden. Any ad that calls for a June grad, a beginner or a "junior" is in violation of the age discrimination laws. While asking for a man, boy or "gal" is flagrant, there are subtle, tricky uses of the language that hint at the desired sex just as forcefully. Ignore these too. Just as a man should feel free to apply when a job calls for someone "attractive," "charming," "poised," or "with a pleasant telephone voice," a woman should not be put off by traditional male code words like, "a real shirtsleeves position" or "must have dynamic, aggressive personality," or "military experience preferred."

According to A. Bernard Frechtman, general counsel to the National Employment Association, generic job titles like "salesman," "draftsman" or "cameraman" are acceptable under the law, except in New Jersey where desexed language is required. For New Jersey jobhunters, "sales," "drafting," and "camera operator" are equally accurate and far less offputting for the female aspirant. The U.S. Census Bureau has recently released a list of non-sexist job titles which should be used by agencies and employers alike.

There is another device that's used to disguise hollow promises. Lower level jobs emphasize the work atmosphere—"plush offices"—or the qualities of the boss—

"groovy vice pres." Don't be duped. Better jobs stress what the actual job has to offer.

An abuse that affects both sexes is the "lure" ad. In a 1971 investigation, the Better Government Association, Chicago's civic watchdog group, found that thirteen employment agencies regularly advertised non-existent glamour jobs—frequently promising women exciting airlines opportunities. When she came to the agency office, the applicant was told that she didn't fit the job and after a lot of fast talk she was "switched" to a lesser position. Unless a legitimate job order from a real company backs up every ad listing, an agency can lose its license. If you're a victim of "switching," don't just go away mad; take your testimony to the Better Business Bureau.

2. *Job orders and referrals.* An employment agency cannot accept any job order specifying sex unless sex is a BFOQ. In a 1973 survey, the National Organization for Women and the American Jewish Congress Women's Division found that 82 per cent of the agencies contacted in New York, Chicago, Philadelphia and Los Angeles "were ready and willing" to accept job orders specifying male applicants for positions as management trainees, systems analysts and retail merchandise managers. In response to the study, New York Attorney General Louis J. Lefkowitz filed charges against 118 employment agencies.

How do agency spokespersons answer these charges? They contend that the survey was inconclusive and irresponsible because no "real" job orders were placed. (The NOW group had telephoned agencies on behalf of an anonymous company that they said would soon need "college men," "fellas," or "guys" for these job categories. NOW claims that only thirteen agencies refused to accept the job order because it was discriminatory.)

3. *Sex-segregated treatment.* Jacqueline Bradford, deputy director for the Northwestern region EEOC, says that her investigators have found Byzantine violations such as: agencies that maintain a male staff for male applicants, counselors who won't refer women for technical jobs, agencies who keep applications filed by sex, agencies that send men out first for the plum positions (on the theory that if a man is hired, he'll get a higher wage and thus the agency will get a higher commission), and even a few agencies with separate waiting rooms and separate entrances for male and female jobhunters.

Edward Valenzuela, EEOC Director for Arizona,

Southern Nevada and part of California, reports that many Chicana women are filing charges of discrimination both on the basis of sex *and* national origin—a fact that parallels historic bias against females who are members of any minority group.

Mistreatment of the most egregious sort is on the decline. However, deeply entrenched sexist attitudes crop up in the form of put-downs or offensive questions during the employment interview. (See Chapter 11.) Try to remember one simple rule: if it's *offensive*, it's probably *illegal* as well. Unless the information requested about you is *job-related*, you may decline to answer on the grounds that it might infuriate you.

4. *General malpractice.* Since an agency's service may cost you a fee, and since their efforts may mean the difference between work and welfare in your life, you should choose an agency with deliberate care. Employment agencies that scour the job market, train their counselors well and treat applicants with respect can be your best friend. But an agency is only as effective as the individual counselor who helps *you*.

That's why so many agencies now carry "Errors and Omissions" insurance to cover liability for their own employees' mistakes. Eileen Lesberg, who specializes in this form of insurance, describes what can go wrong: "Lawsuits occur when counselors fail to check references, when they omit pertinent data about an applicant, or send a person's résumé to their own current employer by accident, or misrepresent the nature of a job to an applicant."

These errors may be infrequent but it can't hurt for you to be aware of potential slip-ups and ask questions to be sure your application is being handled properly.

Image and reality

While women and activist groups are scrutinizing agencies' practices, the industry claims to be policing itself twice as rigorously. They report that their ethics committee surveys ads and even turns wrongdoers over to law enforcement agencies. The local and national associations of employment agencies hold periodic seminars and workshops and circulate booklets on the law of discrimination. Individual agencies require their counselors to sign pledges of fair treatment and statements reaffirming their understanding of the relevant laws.

Until these efforts filter down to every single placement counselor, the best safeguard against discrimination and mistreatment is an informed jobhunter. Know your rights, demand them, and if an agency doesn't deliver on its promises—though they needn't guarantee you a job—make waves. Complain to the National Employment Association, to your state's personnel association, to the state human rights commission, to the EEOC, the Department of Labor or your local Office of Consumer Affairs.

However, if you *do* find an honest, peppy job agency, you'd be smart to team up with them and let them do your pavement-pounding for you.

11

Avoid These Bummers: The Dead-Beat Interview and the Dead-End Job

Sixteen years ago, when I went from agency to agency with my college diploma under one arm and the Help Wanted ads under the other, three of my best friends were making a beeline for the state teachers' examinations.

I thought teaching offered satisfaction and security, but no career surprises. To me the endless frontiers of business were beckoning and I believed publishing was my manifest destiny. While I dreamed of someday editing another *Gone with the Wind,* my three friends were running their own classrooms and pitying me for having to type and file.

"Each to his (her) own taste," goes the French proverb. And it usually works like a charm in the American labor market. As if by divine order, the occupational aspirations of working people vary widely; teachers and telephone operators, lawyers and librarians define success in their own ways. What they have in common though, is a dread of barricades to the free access to that success.

Some say there are no hopeless jobs, only jobs that make some people *feel* hopeless. A housewife taking her first employment plunge at age forty may be overjoyed to work as a receptionist. But an economist is likely to recoil at a receptionist job even if she is assured that it's only an entering wedge into the upper echelons of the company. A high school graduate might jump at the chance to be a legal secretary; but a female attorney who is asked to take notes at a conference or type a colleague's brief will not consider these duties tolerable.

Obviously, one woman's primrose path is another woman's poison. While there are no absolutes about good and bad jobs, there are particular jobs which would be pure torture *for you.* These should either be avoided altogether or else endured only as a stepping stone to your goal. Whether you're working or jobhunting, you'll find these danger signals a useful early warning system to identify the occupational hazard known as the dead-end job:

1. When you present your credentials for an administrative position the first question you're asked is "How fast can you type?"

2. The job is described as a great opportunity "for a woman." Or "for a woman your age."

3. Personnel is more interested in your marital status or your method of birth control than in your expertise or experience.

4. When you inquire about advancement opportunities, they distract you with the company's policy on coffee breaks and Christmas bonuses.

5. You notice that no women in the firm hold jobs above the middle-management level.

6. The emphasis is on your appearance, charm, personality and willingness to "serve" an executive.

7. The company is waterlogged in tradition. Some telltale comments are: "All our girls start out this way." Or, "Women have *always* been researchers." (Both *Newsweek* and *Time* required legal action to break their hallowed tradition of freezing women in low job categories.)

8. Fun and glamour are offered as substitutes for a fair salary and an honest job title. Watch out for the boast: "Some women would pay *us* for such an exciting job!"

9. Your boss is a confirmed misogynist. (He believes that if the good Lord wanted woman to be equal, He would have made her out of more than one rib.)

10. Company politics and departmental back-stabbing is a full-time job in itself. It's not what you do that counts; it's whose side you are on.

11. You're creative, productive, eager, cooperative, loyal and true. But you don't move up because the company never promotes from within.

Many of these offenses take place during the pre-employment rituals. Job interviews, for example, reduce most of us to nervous wrecks; overanxious and trembling to please. Filling out employment applications is a similar ordeal—we feel like school children performing for a passing grade.

There are dozens of books designed to prime you for the jobhunting process and help you get yourself hired. The guides are full of tips like: *do* list your accomplishments; *don't* be a braggard; *do* let the interviewer talk as long as he likes; *don't* lean your elbows on his desk. And so it goes—catechism of what to say, what not to do and how to impress.

But where can you find the dos and don'ts for the man (or woman) on the other side of the desk. How much can they get away with? Which are valid inquiries and which are invasions of privacy? Do you have to answer everything an interviewer asks? Apart from questions and answers, can a personnel man make insulting statements to you with impunity?

There is a code of behavior for employers and personnel agencies, and it's up to you to hold them to its highest standard. For example, you should not be asked what child care arrangements you've made for your two-year-old. That's none of the agency's or employer's business—unless they're offering you a stipend for child care expenses. Similarly, if they think a forty-year-old woman is too old to be a management trainee, that's their problem. Age discrimination is against the law.

It works both ways, too. If your brother wants to switch from driving a cab to becoming a nurse, no interviewer has the right to cast aspersions on his masculinity.

Case histories—or the hiring process can be a bad trip

During one job interview I was asked what method of birth control I use; another time an interviewer asked me how many children I plan to have.

This kind of treatment shoots daggers from the eyes of Dee Alpert, former employment discrimination counselor for the National Organization for Women. "When a woman reports such an experience I tell her to answer that the past, present and future use of her genitalia is none of her employer's damn business." This is Dee's graphic way of restating the fact that an interviewer may not inquire about your sex life or procreative plans since the company can't claim sex has any relevance whatsoever to your competence on the job. Chances are that same employer does not ask a male applicant what kind of contraceptive protection he uses or how large a family he contemplates. And though the question may be asked of both sexes, if the question is not job-related; it's out of order.

Before passage of Title VII of the Civil Rights Act of 1964, employers were free to treat women as a *class* of people, not as individuals. They could make generalizations like "Women will have babies and quit, so they're all a bad risk"—and there was no room for explanation. One Virginia employer went so far as to ask a woman to submit to a sterilization operation as a guarantee of her dependability. But now the law requires that each of us be treated as individuals to be hired or rejected on the merits—not on capricious assumptions of what women do or don't do.

The job application form asked me to state my bust, waist and hip measurements.

If you are a bathing suit model, fill in the information. Otherwise, scrawl across the application: "This is in violation of Title VII." Unless body measurements are a Bona Fide Occupational Qualification necessary for the performance of the job in question, those figures are something only you and your diet chart should know for sure.

The interviewer at an advertising agency turned me down on the spot, even though I had twelve years' experience as an account executive. He said: "You're perfect, but the client won't stand for a woman on his account."

Then the client will have to sit down and listen to a lecture on the facts of life and law. Consideration for a client's or customer's preferences or tastes has been judged an inadequate reason for denying someone a job on account of sex.

Recently, an airline refused to hire a male cabin attendant. The airline claimed that travelers are predominantly men, and men prefer pretty stewardesses. The court ruled that customer preferences are no excuse or justification for a discriminatory policy that excludes one sex from the job. Both men and women can perform the functions of a flight attendant, just as both can administer an advertising account.

When I applied for a front desk receptionist job, the personnel man ignored my resumé altogether and said: "You're hired. With legs like yours, you don't need qualifications."

This man's statement doesn't call for legal action (because you *were* offered the job); but it does warrant feminist action. It illustrates what the phrase "sex object" is all about. Do you really *want* the job if your legs are what got you in the door—and not just literally? Would you feel comfortable working in a place where a woman is merely a brainless ornament? And what are the prospects of promotion for an employee who is nothing more than a pair of legs?

I'd answer the sexist pig: "With legs like mine I'm going to march around in front of this place in the company of twenty other women, carrying placards that inform the public about your antediluvian hiring policies." If you're not up to a picketing demonstration, how about a press conference? With a few more citations of other women's experiences at the hands of that sexist company, you would build quite a story for the local newspapers. Corporate embarrassment is a great consciousness-razor!

A group of us turned up to apply for a specific job opening. I noticed that the men were given written tests and we women were given typing tests.

Sex-segregated tests for the same job wave the red flag to signal a flagrant violation of the law. But when the test *content* is slanted or loaded in a way that favors men, discriminatory intent is harder to prove. (Watch for questions that depend for their answers upon military experience. A tiny percentage of women have served in the armed forces. A question about your "athletic scholarships" is another blatant bummer. What colleges are offering football scholarships to women?)

Black people have wised up about exams that are culturally weighted in favor of those with a white middle-class background. Now we've all learned that questions which have nothing to do with the job, but tend to lower an applicant's score because of his or her unfamiliarity with a far-afield subject, tend to exclude both women and minorities from consideration for better jobs.

They'll try to get you both ways. A Chicago woman found out that she lost a chance at a job because her test scores were considered "too high for a woman." The company was afraid of the trouble a super-smart woman might foment among the men, were she to be hired.

The company man said I was ideal for the computer sales job. But—before he hired me he said he had to check

*with the wives of the men in the department to see if they
object to a woman colleague among their husbands.*

Does the company check with husbands of secretaries to
find out if any of them objects to his wife working for a
male boss or dealing with the men in the mailroom? Ludi-
crous, of course. But some companies try to justify clear-
ing an applicant with staff wives on the basis of "company
morale." *Whose* morale? Nobody really expects us to believe the company is concerned about those wives at
home. What they *are* worried about is the ancient
woman-as-temptress myth. It's the woman's fault if a male
employee is lecherous; it's the woman's fault if this leads
to domestic tension in the man's life; and it's the woman's
fault if this tension decreases the man's productivity.

To its everlasting credit, the United States Navy has dis-
counted the objections of Navy men's wives who protested
the assignment of WAVES aboard ship. An insecure wife
has our sympathy. However, she cannot be permitted to
visit her sexual jealousies upon the unsuspecting woman
who is applying for a job.

*The interview came to a grinding halt when the man
asked me how old my children are. When I told him
they're three and four years old, he said that any responsible parent knows children that young need a full-time
mother.*

It can't be repeated often enough: generalizations and
judgments about women as a class—i.e., "A mother's
place is in the home"—may not be dragged out to deny a
woman a job. Suppose your children are in a day care
group; suppose your husband works nights and stays home
during the day while you're at your job; suppose Dad is a
student or a paraplegic and Mom has to support the
family. Whatever the situation, *this is your life*. And you
don't need a personnel man to tell you how to run it.

*When I applied for a job listed as "Convention
Hostess," the company representative leered: "You'll have
to put up with a certain amount of male lust for the sake
of the firm."*

Let's call a call girl by her rightful name. Disguised
prostitution has no place in legitimate business and the
casual exploitation of your body is not recognized by the
Department of Labor as a "valid condition of employment." One woman filed a sex discrimination complaint
because her employer had insisted that sexual intercourse
was part of her duties as a secretary. She pressed charges

under Title VII on the grounds that having sex with the boss was not required of the *men* on his staff.

Education for survival

They can really put you through the wringer. But you're not as powerless as you think. Take your free-floating rage and focus it on survival tactics, for your sake and on behalf of all the women who'll come after you. For the doer who would rather fight than bitch about injustice, there are ways of making them change.

In the employment interview, grasp the initiative and insist that the discussion center on your experience and references, not on your looks, age or steno speed. Refuse to be typecast as a typist. Renounce the servile role if you're equipped for greater endeavors. Find out if men with comparable credentials are required to assume these roles. If you feel qualified for a promotion, request a trial assignment, an aptitude test, an application for the company's training program.

On the job, organize a women's caucus with your sister workers. Break up into committees and assign yourselves research tasks to investigate the company's pattern and practice of discrimination. Find out whether your company is covered by federal or state laws against sex bias. Talk to the "equal opportunity" or "compliance" officer, or ask the personnel department to show you the company's affirmative action plan, if one exists. Consult a lawyer or ask questions of the various federal agencies that enforce sex discrimination laws.

If you belong to a union, find out how much support they'll provide in your campaign against discriminatory policies. Or turn your guns on the union itself if women are unrepresented victims of a sexist sweetheart deal. Learn how to start a union if there is none in your work unit.

Inquire about maternity benefits when the interviewer asks you about contraception. You can always turn the tables when you know that the law is on your side.

Dead-end jobs may be inevitable but they cannot be permitted to bear the label "For Women Only." Analyze the career ladder and point out where rungs are noticeably missing for women employees. Read the Equal Pay Act (see Chapter 19). Understand that a woman's dead-end job can be more moribund than a man's dead-end job if there is a persistent pay differential. Many brave women who have filed sex discrimination complaints have been rewarded with thousands of dollars in back pay.

By choosing the path of direct confrontation you will inspire and strengthen other women and serve the common cause. Nevertheless, employer retaliation is a very real danger. Though they are illegal, company reprisals against "troublemakers" can result in the ultimate loss of your job. If you honestly can't take that economic risk, there are still pragmatic moves you can make from within.

Many women have chosen a more circuitous route out of their ruts. They hitch their wagon to the rising star of some promising executive who has a healthy attitude toward assertive women. If he or she has no ego hang-ups, that type of boss can run interference when you make the end run.

You'll be better off in a field with well-defined standards of performance where your expertise can be clearly measured and evaluated. It helps to find a new industry like computer science where there are relatively few rigidified notions of what women can or can't do.

You might also explore government jobs which judge applicants on the sex-blind basis of competitive civil service examinations.

I have long believed that, for white collar women and college-educated women, the key question is "how to succeed in business without really *typing*." But secretaries are now in great demand and the overwhelming majority of employers are still touting the advantages of clerical work as an entry-level job *for women*. You may well discover that it's the *only* job you can get. In that case, your skills should be good enough to get you the job but not so good that you become indispensable—unless you want to be. Most bosses still consider a first-rate secretary too valuable to promote to a decision-making spot.

In a sense, of course, a secretary is in the best position to learn her boss's job from the inside out. Read the files until you understand the anatomy of every project. Study the firm's prospectus; analyze its annual report. Ask questions of all your superiors. Never file or type a document that you don't understand. Challenge your boss's decisions and ask him to explain his reasoning. Think of your routine job as a business seminar with pay.

When the work becomes effortless, boring, repetitive or stultifying, that's when it ceases to be on-the-job training and it threatens to become a dead-end job. Here's where the motivated high-achiever turns the corner.

You've done your time on the treadmill and you're ready to assume some of the controls. Time for the showdown. You want a promotion and a raise. Ask for them. Don't undersell yourself now. Remember the career counseling lesson and throw "feminine" modesty to the winds. Carry on a "creative conversation" to articulate who you are, what you want and what you can do for the company in a bigger and better job. You'll probably win without a struggle. Few of us are as expendable as we think.

However, once confident and resolute, if they refuse to promote you, if they give you an argument and you're convinced their motives are unfair (if not legally suspect), you *must* be ready to leave. There's nothing noble about masochism or humble pie. Only someone in dire economic straits should continue to work for a company that refuses to reward her in due time. Incidentally, I've never known a woman to change jobs without improving both her working conditions and her salary!

Once you decide that a dead-end job needn't be your destiny, you're halfway out of it. The only incurable occupational diseases are hopelessness and resignation.

12

The Sexual Dimension:
Even Virgins Get Screwed
by the System

Presumably, by this time we all know what everybody always wanted to know about sex—and more. Still, there's something enduringly fascinating about the subject of sex on the job. Perhaps it's because at any point in our working lives, someone else's sexual experience can suddenly happen to us.

Sex has been used, abused and accused of many things. Some bosses extort sex in return for giving a promotion. Some women still believe they can enhance their job status by making an alliance with a corporate bigwig. And some husbands use the spectre of wild office sex as a scare tactic to discourage their wives from going back to work. (How does the husband know that the working world is so thick with seducers and tawdry scenes—unless he's gotten into the act from his end, I wonder?)

The public in general, with the aid of pulp novels and X-rated movies, has vastly exaggerated the clichés of the swinging career girl and the orgiastic Christmas party.

During thirteen years in business, I never saw an orgy. And I have met more average working women who consider a job a job, than frivolous husband-hunters who consider a job to be a cruise ship mixer. Needless to say, sex is a big part of life. What I object to are the myths and misconceptions that make sex a special problem for the working woman. Take the following common axioms and you'll see what I mean:

When a man and woman work together they can't help having a sexual dimension to their relationship. It's only natural.

The words "only natural" are a reliable cue that someone is trying to keep women down. Notice how the *vive la différence* men, who emphasize and rejoice in our "femaleness" also use it to deprive us of employment. Like the Supreme Court justice who wouldn't hire an attractive female law school honors graduate—because it would "look bad" when they had to work together late at night in his chambers. Or the film distributor who refused sales jobs to two experienced women because they would have to travel around the country with the men on the sales force. The employer was afraid the trips would involve more sex than selling.

As long as a woman is viewed *primarily* as a pretty face and a sexy body—instead of as a person with a brain and particular capabilities—then people will continue to read sex into every male/female encounter. And women's job advancement will continue to suffer as the ever-present "sexual dimension" gets in the way of our fair and equitable treatment.

"The men in my office see me as an object for sexual conquest," says an adjustor in an insurance company. "None of them takes me seriously when I try to talk business. They think I'm there to choose a bed partner, rather than to make a living."

A Detroit blue collar worker is bewildered by a recent experience. "One of my co-workers and I were good friends both in and out of the plant. People couldn't believe that a man and woman can be just friends. Nasty rumors started and I lost my job—but my friend is still there. Why is it always the woman who pays?"

"My boss is always teasing me or making suggestive comments," says a woman in magazine circulation. "I know he'll never promote me. He looks on me as a potential mistress, not as a potential manager."

An administrative assistant asks: "How can a man listen to my project report if he's concentrating on my blouse buttons?"

In a case that epitomizes the sexual bind for women in business, a courageous woman went to the president of the company and reported that she was virtually paralyzed in her work because of the flirtations and advances of her immediate superior. Though most top management is

male, few of the officers of a company will tolerate ineffi-
ciency—even in the name of the precious male libido. In
another case, a company president was found guilty of sex
discrimination when he reacted to news of an affair by
warning the male partner but dismissing the female one.

I don't believe that women are less sexual than men. On
the contrary, we're learning that our sexuality is dense and
full and potentially tireless. What we rightfully resent and
recoil at is the attitude that views us as objects for male
sexual fantasies, as automatic partners in daytime pecadil-
los or as porno diversions at a dull sales conference. This
attitude both dehumanizes women and costs us money.

Admittedly, for every ten men who treat a woman as a
sexual trick around the office, there may be one woman
who exploits her own sexual attractiveness for all its
worth. Because she flirts, teases, dresses provocatively and
seems savagely competitive with other women, we usually
say she's asking for whatever she gets. I suspect there's a
more complex and compassionate interpretation. Such a
woman is usually so lacking in self-esteem that her sexual
allure seems to her to be her only bargaining tool. Call a
woman a "broad" long enough and she'll start to act like
one. Erode her self-confidence, thwart her aspirations, notice her only when she arouses your hormones and she's
apt to believe that sexuality is the only barter she can
trade on. Which brings us to the next popular myth . . .

Women can sleep their way to the top of any business.
The underpinnings of this lie are more pernicious than
the lie itself. What it really suggests is that a woman
couldn't possibly have achieved success by virtue of her
superior ability and hard work. If she's been given a directing job, she must have slept with the producer or the key
investor. If she's promoted to corporate vice president, she
must have had an affair with the president. This assumption that we travel up the hierarchy by lying on our backs
is demeaning at all levels of employment. But it becomes
particularly fierce in the upper strata of big business where
a successful woman is a threat to male dominance of top
salary jobs.

I'm not claiming that no woman has ever tried the bed-
room route to the board room. Only that it's far from
common, it rarely works, and no one has the right to dis-
miss a woman's achievement by chalking it up to sexual
trickery.

We might learn something from the women who *did* buy this myth and tried to make it work for them.

"I was looking for a Henry Higgins who could make me his Fair Lady," admits a public relations woman. "I fell in love with my boss's hero image and I expected all his business knowledge to rub off on me in bed. It didn't happen that way. Close up, his mask crumbled. I saw that he was a scared phony just one step ahead of his own mistakes. It set me back a lot. If that's what people are like at the top, who needs it!"

A media buyer talks about her affair with an account executive: "I wanted an exciting job with lots of responsibility but I knew that women could only go so far at our agency. So I made it with a man who had what I couldn't have myself. Power.

"Behind the scenes I helped him make decisions and solve problems. Living vicariously was pretty frustrating. I began to wonder if he loved me or my secret contributions to his work. Finally I realized that his power was only mine on loan for as long as the affair lasted. You can't sleep with power, or marry power; you have to get it on your own."

"I was living with him at home and spying for him in the office," says a private secretary about her ex-boss. "From the information I got for him on the secretarial grapevine, he was able to maneuver a major promotion for himself. But the deal was when he moved up, he had to keep his predecessor's secretary. So without a word he moved out of the house and left me behind at my desk. I loved him and wasn't with him for what he could do for my career. But I've learned that sex on the job usually hurts your self-respect."

Women who have consciously determined not to play the sexploitation game, offer some cogent comments on their decisions:

"Some men accuse me of being 'masculine' because of my strong commitment to my career," explains an actress. "I found that they wanted to get into bed with me to cut me down to size—to make 'a woman' out of me. That's a pretty sick need."

"I'm thirty, I'm single and I'm no virgin," confesses another businesswoman. "But I don't mix work and sex. Having an affair at the office would diminish me, who I am and what I'm doing on this job."

A copy editor takes the practical approach. "Getting involved with a man sexually would affect my negotiating power. I would feel uptight about asking for a raise if I were sleeping with the guy I have to ask. I know I'd shortchange myself rather than have a confrontation."

"I'm the only unmarried woman in our school," says a young suburban teacher. "The principal intimates that he won't recommend renewal of my contract if I don't warm up to him. The gym teacher hints he'll make trouble for me in the teachers' union if I keep putting him off. It's all so sordid and sneaky. I like to have sex for pleasure and love—not under fear of reprisals."

More and more frequently, we are hearing a new, freer approach to sex. An artist says, "I'm learning to equate sex with pleasure. I may even be the one who initiates it with a customer or someone working in the gallery. I think women should stop seeing themselves as the victim who gets taken—and we should start taking pleasure for pleasure's sake without considering sex a lifelong investment."

If this point of view is still a minority position, there are countless women who simply state that the question of sex has never come up in their work. And thousands more married and single, divorced and in-between, whose moral standards just don't leave room for debate on the issue. For them, sex still belongs after marriage and only with one's husband—and that holds true whether the woman works or not.

Marriage means less in the business world. Married men and women fool around more readily on the job than elsewhere.

This myth should be patently absurd on its face. We each carry our standards with us wherever we go—and it's a cheap shot to blame the surroundings. Marriage either means exclusivity and monogamy or it doesn't.

There are those who make *liaisons dangereuses* in the pantry at a neighborhood dinner party. But when those same people get together behind the water cooler, it's blamed on the corruptive influence of the business world. Nonsense. I'd much prefer to hear straight talk from real women about their feelings, attitudes and experiences. Someone else can depend for their information on the latest *Cosmopolitan* exposé.

A woman lawyer describes a satisfying affair she had before her marriage: "This man and I were equals. Neither of us were playing status games and the sexual intimacy enhanced our working relationship in the law firm. We paid closer attention to one another's sensitive spots as well as to our ideas. I still remember this relationship fondly, even though I'm happily married to someone else.

"Now when I feel sexual vibrations toward a man, I measure the risk. If it's not an *enormous* attraction, I can't see why I should compromise my husband. I suppose if an affair were ever to appear irresistible, I would have to think seriously about whether I should stay married at all."

A waitress admits she's never cheated on her husband but she does use the suggestion of other men's attentions to keep her husband interested. "I don't want another man, but I have the feeling my husband needs to believe that other men want his wife."

"At first I thought my affair would be therapy for a bad marriage and an unsatisfying sex life," says a nurse. "Now I see that I got involved with another man because I needed an excuse to leave my husband altogether."

"I married young and I never had sex with anyone but my husband," reports the owner of an antique shop. "When I went on a buying trip, I met a man who was attending a convention in my hotel. Both of us were far from home and felt like kids let out of school. I had sex with him out of curiosity and I don't regret it. My husband will never find out so the marriage hasn't been affected—but at least I'm not curious anymore."

Some single women consider an affair with a married man to be a safe bet. No commitment, no pressure. Others say married men are bad news because no matter how much they say they love you, they rarely leave their wives. That's an old story. But with the new feminist consciousness, women are also thinking about the innocent third party—the wife we're helping a man betray. Who wants to make another woman miserable?

The "sexual dimension" is not our fault or our cross to bear. Sexuality is one facet of the human condition and it materializes in individual men or women in ways as different as personal metabolism or one-of-a-kind fingerprints. It only becomes a special burden for women in business when men blame us for their own weaknesses or temptation. Exempting us from competing beside men, branding us seductive because we have breasts and hips is a bizarre response that results in a double victimization. It is rather like putting the women behind bars when there's a rapist on the loose.

13

Are You Ready for Women in Power?

A woman who owns an advertising agency enjoys telling about the time one of her copywriters brought in rough copy for a cosmetics ad and asked her to: "Pretend you're a woman and tell me what you think of this."

The point was, of course, that this competent woman boss had become "like a man" in the eyes of her staff.

While the story may amuse some, it is a discouraging reminder of another kind of double-bind endured by working women. Those who occupy positions of power and authority are often held up to special scrutiny. Depending on her style, the woman boss is either accused of "acting like a man" or "acting just like a woman"—and both assessments add up to a put-down.

Since there are only two sexes to which she can be compared, the woman boss may find that according to others, there is no "right way" for her to behave on the job. As Margaret Mead has said, in our society men are desexed by failure, but women are desexed by success. Just as a man who is unemployed tries to explain himself, a woman who is an over-achiever becomes defensive about her "superiority."

The double-bind isn't limited to women who are business proprietors or hot-shot executives. Criticism is directed as readily toward factory foreladies, department supervisors, executive secretaries, head nurses, office managers and any other woman who assumes some form of managerial responsibility over the work of others.

Given the current movement to correct underutilization of women in the labor market, it is more likely than ever that you will either become a woman boss, or have one, sometime during your work life. What can you expect from them and from yourself?

General social prejudice

Most men don't want to work for a woman because they find it hard to believe women can be capable administrators. Some think being subordinate to a female reflects badly on their masculinity. Others resent any woman earning higher wages than a man.

Many women also prefer male to female bosses. The reasons here are more complex and disturbing. As we've noted, men compete comfortably for rewards, while we have concentrated on competing with one another for men. Men vie for worldly approval and status. We vie for husbands. Men strive for excellence, we strive for beauty and youthfulness. Our competitiveness with each other is not an act of selective treachery, but the survival tactic of a second class human being. Bereft of self-esteem, we play the only game in town that seems to offer a pay-off, with the only players we think we can beat—other women.

Lacking normal occupational options and job mobility, women's conditioned competitiveness becomes distorted and magnified when we compete for male approval on the job. We feel threatened or excluded when one of our own sex appears to be getting closer to the male inner circle. Working for rewards, such as money or position, seems indelicate. Because we have not developed a tradition of sex-pride, or sisterhood, one woman's triumphs are seen as an affront to another woman, rather than a cause for celebration or a happy sign that doors may be opening for all women.

Both sexes have trouble living with the idea of women being active rather than passive, decisive rather than compliant, or authoritative rather than subservient. Sadly, we women have externalized our feelings of female inferiority to the point where we doubt that *any* woman can be fit for a leadership role. How could she be worthy of respect when we think so little of ourselves?

Men, on the other hand, have been taught from childhood that they are the rightful occupants of the Boss's

Chair. They are meant to rule, supervise, make decisions, plan, organize and control others simply because of the accident of having been born male. That is why we see mediocre males rising inexorably through the ranks while superior women have to struggle for every boost.

Our society has outlawed concrete forms of prejudice toward the woman boss. But it will take more than legislation to undo the entrenched psychological bias. A first step is to get inside her head and try to understand her problems.

The take-charge woman: thorns in the bed of roses

A woman is often passed over several times before being promoted to the next spot. As a supervisor she is usually given less money or less power than the man who held the job previously. Often, she is the only supervisor in her category who needs a male superior's approval to order equipment or commit company funds.

Common sexist attitudes demean her. She is called by her first name while men in comparable jobs insist on being addressed as "Mr. So-and-so." Men feel at liberty to pinch her cheek, pat her on the head, or call her "Honey" —all of which diminishes her stature. (Imagine calling a male boss "Butch" or "Baby.") If she's assertive or strong-minded about her work, she's called aggressive and tough; if she's the jovial, casual type, then she's labeled "frivolous." If she makes a mistake, rather than attribute it to human error, people blame "her time of the month" or (if she's older) her menopause. Her immediate superior refers to her as "my girl"—though a male supervisor with the same duties would never be called "my boy." Office gossips call her the "womb at the top." I've heard worse, too.

The people who work under her also seem to categorize her instead of viewing her as a person, unique and non-imitative. They may call her "the motherly type" if she is gentle and understanding, or "the castrating bitch" if she is somewhat distant and curt in her directions to her staff. The working mother may be under special surveillance by those who believe that her home responsibilities will inevitably impinge upon her work. They're waiting for a phone call from school or home to topple the boss from her supervisory perch and send her back to "woman's place."

The defensive reaction

With her every move under critical scrutiny, the woman boss reacts defensively. She has become the repository for other people's stereotyped expectations of women's behavior under pressure. Unless her position is absolutely secure (as may be the case with an owner or a woman in a family business), she recognizes that her authority is tenuous and largely dependent on the benevolence of male superiors. Because she's a woman, her success is threatening to people above and below. Underneath it all, she knows she is basically *powerless*.

Rollo May has written that it is not power that corrupts human behavior, but powerlessness. This is particularly applicable to the woman boss. For some, asserting and reasserting her authority and her rightful claim to it, becomes the primary challenge. And here is where the caricature of the tough "Boss Lady" may take shape and come to life. She grows compulsive about her work and rigidly demanding of her underlings. She thinks that she and her department must be perfect (or at least twice as good as anyone else's). Otherwise, her imperfections will open her to the charge of being "just like a woman" and she will lose whatever clout she had. This defensive reaction builds a hard shell around her. She papers over her feelings and focuses a cold stare on the job to be done. She becomes intensely competitive, watchful of rising young stars or protective of her status as "the only woman who . . ."

If her Queen Bee style arouses cries of "emasculating bitch" or "she acts just like a man," then the woman boss may add a dose of extra "femininity"—perfume, a frilly blouse, a sing-song little voice—to take the edge off.

When a woman boss lives up to this caricature, she can be immensely difficult to work with. Her paranoia directs so much of her energies into self-protective exercises that there is little left over for human relationships. However, one shouldn't forget that there are countless eccentric and demanding male bosses whom we tolerate or deplore without casting brickbats at the entire male sex. Moreover, most women bosses are able, resilient human beings who are miles removed from the stereotype. The great majority have taken the hard knocks in stride and have even been positively humanized by them.

A few testimonials

For the most part, those who have worked for women have found the experience no different from working for a man. Some even find reason to praise the special qualities a woman can bring to the work relationship. Particularly on a woman-to-woman basis. Now that women are beginning to define their identities differently, we see the futility of dueling with our own sex. We understand why, when we attack one another we both become victims, and the spoils go elsewhere. Many women have begun the long process of disengaging our foils and giving our sisters all the honors they're due.

An editor has this to say about the female publisher she works for: "She has no ego invested in her role as my superior. She's honest and straight-forward and it's delightful to work for someone I don't have to flatter or flirt with."

Many women remark on the relaxed atmosphere in a woman-to-woman work relationship that is unsullied by overt or covert tensions of the "sexual dimension." More work can be turned out in an all-woman environment, some claim.

"When I said how tedious it was working on figures all day, my boss gave me responsibility for the Petty Cash disbursements so I would have a chance to meet other people in the company who come to cash their vouchers," says a bookkeeper who is responsible to a female comptroller. "She also arranged for me to keep a radio on my desk and I think having music in the background has made my job more pleasant. She always seems to understand our problems and be willing to go to bat for us."

Women don't have a monopoly on thoughtfulness, but many seem more sensitive to the nuances of office atmosphere and worker dissatisfaction.

"She taught me everything she knew. I feel as if our work was collaboration," says an associate producer about her boss. "Her confidence in me gave me the courage to get involved in more complicated projects on our TV show. When the station fired her, they offered me her job. Instead I left with her. First of all, I couldn't be disloyal to her. Secondly, since she had let me in on every aspect of her job, I had seen how they dumped on her. Why should I follow her to the slaughter?"

Men who work for women managers don't necessarily

grin and bear it. Some feel, as does this assistant to a female stockbroker, that it's a definite advantage. "If I work late, she'll say 'Go out to dinner and send me the bill,' or 'Take a cab home on the company.' She has more compassion than any man I've ever worked for—and more insight."

Other men discover, despite initial misgivings, that they forget about the gender label altogether. "You can't be a male supremacist in my situation," says a man who teaches under the jurisdiction of a woman high school principal. "She's simply the smartest, most professional *person* of either sex that I've ever met in the educational field."

At the same time as women are asking the culture to take female bosses for granted, many take-charge women have become more analytical about their own demeanor. They don't want to be treated as token symbols of a company's progressiveness, nor as freaks, nor as "imitation men." They want to carry out their duties in their own way—which often means making procedural changes and challenging "man-made" hierarchical systems.

"I'm a committed feminist, so I try to practice both brotherhood and sisterhood," says an office manager. "We have periodic rap sessions to give people a chance to express their hostilities and clear the air. Job classifications aren't rigid which means people can ask for assignments that interest them. We try to spread around the drudgework so it doesn't all fall on a few workers at the bottom of the heap. Eventually, we hope to eliminate hierarchical titles altogether. They only make people uptight."

An actress turned stage director recalls: "At first I was scared, so I came on mean. I made a lot of enemies and terrified a lot of young actors but I didn't get the performances I wanted from anyone. When I began to share my worries with the cast and to treat every actor as a professional, the play jelled. Knowing I was scared inspired them to work *for* me, not against me."

The publisher of a business newsletter says: "I believe in the product, not the process. In this world too much attention has been paid to who's doing what and not enough to how it gets done. I never remind anyone that I own the place. It's irrelevant. What matters is that we all want to get out a good paper."

In the final analysis, perhaps our problem is that power

is a sex-typed entity. We admire men who seek it and wield it effectively. We must learn to be equally supportive of women who want to make decisions, influence policy and direct the activities of others. While we ourselves may hope to assume positions of authority without trauma and indignity, we must also heed those who are questioning the whole concept of power. It may be on its way out altogether.

Liz Carpenter, former press secretary to Lady Bird Johnson and now vice president of a public relations firm, has an uncanny ability to defense attacks on her competence. Humor is her sharpest weapon.

Once, after Liz's book *Ruffles and Flourishes* was published, she was approached by one of the grand old men in Congress. "I loved your book, Liz," he said. "Who wrote it for you?"

Without skipping a beat, Liz answered with a smile, "Thanks for the compliment, Congressman. Who read it to you?"

14

Procrustes Revisited:
Making the Job Fit the Person

One of the more visionary innovations of recent years is the concept of flexible work schedules.

Take your choice. You can work from 9:30 to 3:30 five days a week; from 8:00 to 6:00 four days a week; eight hours a day beginning at whatever minute you arrive between 6:30 A.M. and 8:30 A.M.; three mornings one week and two afternoons the next; any twenty-five hours during each week—and other arrangements too numerous to mention.

Right now, all over the country, millions of working people are enjoying such schedule options. Many factors account for the growing change in America's employment habits. The Work Ethic is colliding with the pursuit of leisure. High unemployment levels suggest that jobs must be split so there is enough work to go around. Behaviorists and efficiency experts find that job satisfaction is a prerequisite for worker productivity, and many workers feel dissatisfied with the five day forty hour week. Finally, women who are entering the job market in unprecedented numbers cannot accommodate home responsibilities, and men cannot share them, under the standard workday schedule.

Responding to these developments, several foresighted employers have instituted alternate work schedules of one kind or another. If you're lucky (or if you crusade for it) you may be able to find an enlightened firm that offers one of the following new arrangements.

Part-time work

In 1972, about 10.5 million people voluntarily worked less than thirty-five hours weekly—about two-thirds of them were female workers. For decades, women with families have answered ads to sell greeting cards or magazine subscriptions in our "spare time." But now that half of all mothers work and one-third of these choose to work less than forty hours a week, the p/t job has come of age. It has matured to mean *permanent* jobs in the mainstream of the work force (and not just in cottage industries or the low-paying job categories). And more importantly, it heralds an end to arbitrary fiats about work. Most jobs *can* be tailored to be more responsive to the worker's need for time, without penalizing the employer's need for productivity.

By way of illustration, a dietician describes the tandem part-time system that she and another woman had in a Minneapolis hospital: "Our employer made up our work assignment as if we were one person. Then we split the hours to suit ourselves. We worked out a schedule that had me on duty two days one week, three days the next and then five days off. With five consecutive days free, each of us had plenty of time for personal appointments. Our employer benefited because he had one full-time dietician's job filled by two experienced employees. We were paid by the hour and our vacation and fringe benefits were computed for part-time accordingly."

In a well-publicized experiment, Catalyst (the non-profit research organization) persuaded the Massachusetts Department of Welfare to hire fifty case workers on a part-time basis. A later study showed that while paying half-time wages, the Department was getting 89 per cent of full-time workers' productivity. Furthermore, these half-timers had a lower rate of absenteeism and only one-third the turnover rate of full-timers.

Another Catalyst project paired two teachers in one elementary school class. They shared one full-time salary. One woman worked mornings and the other afternoons, with an hour overlap at lunchtime. The teachers were less tired, more enthusiastic and grateful to have a partner with whom to discuss students' progress. The school had an automatic backup substitute to fill in when the "other-half" was ill. Not only was this a great success for the people involved; it suggests a constructive national alternative to increasing teacher unemployment. If more teachers can work half-time, fewer teachers will be faced with not working at all.

Theodore Karger, president of Nowland Organization, a consumer research firm in Connecticut, calls his flexible work plan "customized schedules." About half his staff are p/t women who do in-depth interviews, code data and analyze consumer habits. They average twenty hours per week, choose their own hours, take work home during kids' school vacations, and have every convenience except fringe benefits.

United Publishing Corporation used fifty-four p/t women writers and researchers among the staff of two hundred who prepared its New American Encyclopedia.

Peter Lewis, president of Progressive Insurance Company in Cleveland, told the *Wall Street Journal* that his successful experience with p/t clerks has persuaded him to hire women as p/t claims adjusters, underwriters and managers.

Professionals too, are joining the part-time trend. Two women lawyers share one full-time position at the Smithsonian. At Downstate Medical Center in New York, Dr. Barbara Delano has organized a program extending doctors' internships to either eighteen months or two years to allow time for family life. Other hospitals offer extended programs to women who are residents in a medical specialty.

Carol Greenwald, Assistant Vice President and Economist with the Federal Reserve Bank of Boston, works from 9 A.M. to 1 P.M. and spends afternoons with her pre-school daughter. She depends on skilled cooperation of her staff and a "team management" system worked out between herself and another supervisor.

"I do exactly the same job I used to do, but for less pay," she explains. "I rarely take a coffee break, don't eat lunch on bank time, and of course I take mountains of work home."

As an economist, Ms. Greenwald has become an expert in part-time employment. She emphasizes that shorter work schedules must be matched by equitable pro-rated fringe benefits.

"Employers can pay half salary for full vacation periods or simply give half the vacation time," she explains. "They can cut insurance benefits in half or let the employee pay half the premium. And unless the job pays more than $12,000, employers need not pay any more in Social Security. Blue Cross and Blue Shield are more complicated, but economists can help employers find a fair formula."

Another problem is beyond the control of either employer or employee. As mentioned in a previous chapter, the new tax law allows deduction of child care expense only if you are employed during three-quarters of the cutomary work week or more. The absurdity of this limitation is clear. Mothers—the very people who want part-time work—are the workers most likely to need babysitters *and* thus to need the deduction for that expense. Without this right under the tax law, it is difficult to have much left over from a p/t salary after a child care person is paid.

Part-time work should not be viewed as a solution for women only. Men who have the option of shorter work schedules can become more involved fathers and greater participants in the home.

And finally, the benefits to the employer can be enormous. Newtime, the New York employment agency pioneering in flexible shift jobs, puts it strikingly in their ad: "If Madame Curie were alive, but could only work from 9:30 to 3:15, would you hire her?"

Employers who can say yes to that question will attract high quality workers from the pool of educated and motivated family women. They'll get more output and lower unit costs because part-timers have shown themselves less prone to absenteeism, lateness and turnover. They'll enjoy greater productivity from workers who can maintain a faster pace in a concentrated period. (Western Electric found that production line workers performed at peak efficiency during the first four hours of work and declined to fifty per cent efficiency toward the end of an eight-hour shift.) And, if they open full-time jobs to paired part-timers, employers can satisfy federal affirmative action plans by employing more women workers in more good jobs.

Four days/40 hours or three days/36 hours

About a thousand companies operate on a three or four day work week which affords workers a full salary with extra days at liberty. Those who support the short work week cite the boon of a three or four day weekend with more time for travel, hobbies, chores and family activities. They note that the ten or twelve hour day puts them on the roads when there is minimum commuter traffic.

Objections to these truncated work weeks seem to center on the fatigue factor. Unions assail the inroad into the hard-won eight-hour standard and the concept of overtime. Perhaps this is why some firms are becoming even more liberal.

Employees of Group Health, Inc. of New York, work a four-day week, eight and three-quarter hours a day. In the summer, Bonne Bell, Inc. in Cleveland pays employees for forty hours even though they work four days of eight and a half hours each.

Workers polled on their preferences seem to choose 4/40 or 3/36 over the standard five-day week because of the extra free days and the twenty per cent reduction in commuter fares, child care expense and restaurant meals. Nevertheless, there are some conflicting opinions about some of the benefits.

"On the Fridays when my husband and I are both off work, I have the 'freedom' to clean, cook, market and do the wash," says a Los Angeles factory worker. "He uses his extra day to play golf."

Opposing this view, another woman raves about her three day/thirty-six hour schedule: "When I worked an eight-hour day I hardly had time with the kids by the time I got home, anyway. Now I barely see the children at all three days a week, but for the other four, we have uninterrupted time together. Whether we travel or stay home, every four-day weekend is a holiday."

Gliding hours or flexi-time

If you're a 9 A.M. person working in a firm where everything starts at 8; if you hate morning stress, rush-hour traffic and rigid routine, then flexi-time is for you.

Hewlett-Packard Company with 14,000 employees throughout the country, is entirely pleased with their system. They let manufacturing workers arrive anytime between 6:30 and 8:30 (office workers come in between 7 and 9). Everyone works eight hours from the moment of arrival and there are no time clocks, only an honor system.

John Flaherty, personnel manager at the Medical Electronics Division in Waltham, Mass., reports that 65 per cent of the employees "choose to get in early and get out early to enjoy the extra hours of daylight in summer. It lets them beat the traffic all year long and avoid driving in the dark during winter snow storms."

While employees are free to vary their schedules from one day to the next, Mr. Flaherty reports that most people tend to evolve a convenient pattern and keep to it.

"Even the production line works more smoothly," he says. "People are capable of filling in at various stages on the line. There is always someone who'll work overtime or someone else who has chosen the later part of the flexi-time cycle." After one year, Hewlett-Packard noted no change in productivity, a decrease in absences, an increase in job commitment and worker enthusiasm and, of course, an end to tardiness altogether.

John F. Auderer Laboratories in New Orleans has had its dental technicians and office staff on flexi-time for twelve years—with a time clock. "Our people are free to arrive whenever they want between 7 and 9 A.M.," says Mr. Auderer. "They're usually waiting at the gate at a quarter to 7 and they're eager to work overtime to get time and a half. But I also have women who choose to work twenty hours a week, and I have office workers who split one full-time job between them any way they want."

Mr. Auderer also gives employees the option of choosing eight Mondays or Fridays instead of one five-day vacation week.

The Nestlé Company in White Plains, New York, works it this way: 8 to 9:30 A.M.—flexible arrival; 9:30 to 12—fixed work time; 12 to 1:30 P.M.—flexible lunchtime; 1:30 to 4 P.M.—fixed work time; 4 to 6 P.M.—flexible departure. If she or he has completed the full thirty-five-hour work week by 3 P.M. on Friday, an employee can start the weekend at 3 P.M. on Friday. Workers plan each week's schedule with the approval of their supervisor one week in advance.

Stephen Korsen, manager of public relations for Nestle, says that 650 people are covered by flexi-time on the honor system, and a questionnaire survey indicates that they strongly favor it. "Only our data processing department is excluded," he explains. "With such expensive machinery, we have to have round-the-clock definite shifts."

Union reaction to alternate work schedules

A small sampling of opinion indicates favorable reaction to flexi-time (although none of the above-named companies is unionized), an "iffy" reaction to part-time, and a negative response to 4/40 or 3/36.

Leon Stein of the International Ladies' Garment Workers Union says flatly: "Organized labor fought hard for the eight-hour day. I think four days and forty hours is no bargain. Talk about a thirty hour week for the same pay and then you've got something. In the garment industry it's all piece work and in some parts of the season our people work a short week and earn less money whether they want to or not."

Jim Gary of the International Union of Electrical Workers (where up to fifty per cent of the membership are women) says the big move is toward making all national holidays fall on Mondays. He likes the sound of flexi-time but it's not yet an issue in his contracts. "As for the 4/40 week, we maintain that an eight-hour day is enough for most people doing physical labor—especially over age fifty-five," Mr. Gary says. "Otherwise, they deserve time and a half even on a four-day schedule."

Emanuel Vitale of the Civil Service Employees Association, which pro-rates its union dues for members working twenty hours a week or less, has this to say about part-time work: "Hospitals and schools depend on part-time employment. School districts are lucky to get bus drivers willing to work four hours a day with dead time in between, or school cafeteria employees available from two to six hours a day for a steady job. We've won for them pro-rated benefits and the recognition that they are *full-time* workers on the part-time schedule that the county sets for them."

From all indications, work options of many kinds are increasing. Among them, flexi-time may well be the work revolution of our generation, and part-time work may become the alternate norm. From the workers' viewpoint, it's hard to imagine anyone in this depersonalized society who could object to a new system based on recognition of individual efficiency cycles and respect for the demands of one's private life.

15

Out of Work but Still in the Running

"You're fired"

"I quit!"

There's a world of difference between these two statements. But if you can't find another job immediately, it boils down to the same thing: you're unemployed.

The U.S. Department of Labor considers you an unemployment statistic if you are out of work but available and actively looking for a job. By this definition, in September 1974 nearly two million women were unemployed (and while the overall jobless rate was 5.2 per cent, married men experienced less than half that average rate). Joblessness is hardest on women, singles, minorities and young people.

Be prepared before unemployment strikes. Run through the following checklist and learn rights and obligations before you quit or get fired.

- Must you give advance notice of your resignation? How much notice is required? Must notice be given in writing?
- Will you get your unused vacation and sick pay if you quit? What happens if you're fired?
- What are your chances of getting a good reference?
- Can you continue group insurance coverage after you leave?
- Does your company have a voluntary or manda-

tory retirement policy? What are your pension and profit-sharing entitlements? Are pension benefits portable to your next job?

• Do you know what job security measures protect you from dismissal? Have you read your employment contract, union contract, tenure provisions, company policy statements on justifiable reasons for termination?

• In case you are fired, can the company force you to leave on the spot? How much notice must they give you?

• Is there an appeals procedure or a grievance review?

• What severance pay can you expect if fired or laid off? How is severance correlated with duration of employment?

• What happens to your accumulated vacation time from previous years?

• What termination reasons would disqualify you for unemployment insurance in your state?

• Does your company have a layoff plan detailing who will be let go first if cutbacks become necessary? Is this based on seniority or departmental priorities?

• Is your employer a participant in the unemployment insurance program? Are you covered? Do you know where and how to file your claim?

The government recognizes four types of unemployed persons: "job losers" (those who are fired or laid off); "job leavers" (people who quit); "new entrants" (people who have never before held a full-time job); and "re-entrants" (those who have been out of the labor force and want to return).

A fifth group has also been identified and labeled. "Discouraged workers" are potential workers who aren't presently looking for jobs because they think nothing is available for them.

Should you find yourself in one of these five categories, it can't hurt to have a larger perspective on your situation.

Job losers

A TV news anchorwoman is fired because "we don't feel you come across on camera." A hospital worker because of lateness after repeated warnings. A sewing machine operator is laid off due to seasonal cut-backs. A secretary loses her job when the boss hires his niece instead. An editor gets the ax because management objects to her politics.

Unemployment statistics suggest casualties like these. But the fact is that only 43 per cent of the unemployed were fired or laid off—and proportionately much fewer women than men are job losers.

Whatever the workers' sex, the more education they have the less likely they are to lose their jobs. Job losers also tend to experience longer periods of unemployment than job leavers or first-time job seekers. In 1972 for example, six out of ten women who were out of work for twenty-seven weeks or more, had been fired or laid off. (The average duration for women's unemployment is ten weeks.)

Certain industries and localities are more unemployment-prone than others. Blue collar women are laid off because of decreased workload, seasonal manufacturing cycles, shifts in production or business failure. Obviously, a national downturn puts many jobs in peril. During the 1970–71 slump it was engineers and space workers; in the 1974 energy crisis it was airline, automotive and leisure industry personnel. Some observers say that nearly half a million people lost their jobs in the first three months of 1974 due to energy-related belt-tightening.

Thirty-three cities seem to take the brunt of high unemployment, but small areas are not immune. (In 1974 in Anderson, Indiana, unemployment doubled in just six months.)

Job leavers

During the early Sixties, I quit three different jobs in less than two years before finding a good position with bright possibilities. It seemed to me that moving around was the fastest way to move up. Each time I changed companies my salary increased and I gained more experience.

Some women quit for reasons of illness or excessive home responsibilities. Others move on when promotion seems impossible in their present job. Still others quit in order to change fields entirely. Within the last year I've watched a social worker go into teaching; a teacher switch to public relations; and a magazine editor decide her future was in urban planning.

Ideally, one shouldn't leave a paying job until another position is lined up. But it doesn't always work according to plan—and that's why about 19 per cent of unemployed adult women are job leavers who are still searching for work.

In times of job scarcity people are reluctant to leave their jobs voluntarily, no matter how discontent they may be. Therefore you should watch the general economic picture and stay put during a job squeeze. When economic conditions improve, the traffic from job to job increases and you'll have more openings to choose from.

Most job leaving occurs in the years when people are still exploring career options—between ages twenty and twenty-four. Also, since there are still few tempting opportunities for most women workers, and since few husbands are now willing to share the domestic load, many women leave the labor force to raise their young children. As the motherhood mystique fades, and more employers hold out the carrot of career advancement to women, we are bound to see women remaining at work after their children are born.

New entrants

If you've never worked before and you can't find a job now that you want one, chances are you're under twenty years of age. Each year when the June graduates descend, young people suffer a peak period of unemployment and fierce competition for entry-level jobs. A few Junes ago, for instance, 1.9 million graduates were looking for jobs, of whom 1.1 million were unsuccessful!

Relatively few adult women are new workers; most have held jobs at some point in their lives and thus are considered—

Re-entrants

This is the most familiar scenario. You once held a job but you've been absent from the labor force for years because of personal reasons. Now, after five to fifteen years of full-time home work, you're ready for another career. Or you're divorced and you need the income. Or you're turned on by the idea of a specific career that had never appealed to you before.

As soon as you start looking for work—and until you land a job—you count among the 34 per cent of unemployed women who are in the re-entrant category. And you probably feel the most vulnerable because interviewers want to know: "What in the world were you doing all those years?"

Discouraged workers

Because discouraged people aren't actively seeking work, the Bureau of Labor Statistics doesn't have much data on them. Rough estimates put this unfortunate tribe at 680,000—the majority of them, women—who feel their job-hunting efforts would be in vain. They are the "hidden unemployed."

Writing about this unknown labor force reserve, Jacob Mincer, professor of economics at Columbia University, differentiates between "inhibited entries," who feel it would be futile to even try to find work; and "discouraged drop-outs," who have given up hope after a fruitless search. No wonder women dominate both these discouraged groups. Negative conditioning about our expendable work role (impressed on us by school, family, husbands and the media) has made us "inhibited entries." Employer resistance and job market discrimination has made us "discouraged drop-outs."

In 1972 only 8 per cent of jobhunting males were unsuccessful while 20 per cent of jobhunting women had to give up without ever finding a job.

Jobhunting methods

How do the unemployed look for work? According to a study done by economist Thomas F. Bradshaw, 70 per cent of all job-seekers apply directly to the prospective employer. Newspaper classified ads, public or private employment agencies and contacts through friends and relatives account for other job search methods. Although there is duplication—most individuals try two or three methods simultaneously—certain patterns have emerged.

Men use more methods than women; more whites than blacks use private employment agencies; women rely heavily on newspaper ads; young people go directly to employers more often than any other group; people who are job losers tend to look for work through agencies or ads rather than by direct employer contact.

Whereas men seem to find out about openings through their unions, professional registers and word-of-mouth referrals, women have traditionally been excluded from the information network. Why not make a special effort to plug in? You needn't be satisfied with the clerical offerings in your local paper. Exhaust every method: agencies, company personnel offices, blind letter inquiries enclosing your resumé, referrals through working friends, clubs, ex-employers, husband's colleagues or the neighborhood grapevine. Best method? Apply in person at the employer's door.

It costs money to look for work—transportation, time, printed resumés—and you lose money every day that you could be earning it. Being out of work is an expensive proposition, unless you qualify for—

Unemployment insurance

Of the 85 million people in the work force, roughly 70 million are covered by unemployment insurance and about three million jobless people are receiving benefits at any given time. (Most domestics, farm workers and state employees are exempt.) State eligibility rules vary widely but in general, assume you may collect benefits if you have: lost your job through no fault of your own (not fired for misconduct); been willing, able and available to work immediately; worked a minimum number of weeks during the past year; been making good faith efforts to find "suitable" work; been let go by an employer who is a participant in the unemployment insurance program.

Twenty-six states still disqualify pregnant women altogether—even where the woman has medical approval to work and satisfies all other state eligibility rules. But the writing is on the wall and several states have changed their laws to conform to Title VII guidelines and to honor recent court decisions granting due process and the right to work to all pregnant citizens.

Fifteen states still deny insurance to those who leave work for unavoidable marital or domestic reasons—such as quitting in order to accompany one's spouse to a new job location. There are many other provisos that may give you trouble in your state. Check with your nearest unemployment insurance office for full details.

If you're eligible for benefits how much can you collect? Again there are enormous variations. At this writing, maximum weekly unemployment benefits range from $47 in Mississippi to $87 in Colorado to $97 in Illinois to $117 in Washington, D.C. to a high of $138 in Connecticut. The White House has proposed a standardized formula of minimum benefits amounting to two-thirds of the State average weekly wage. At present, only four states have achieved this goal.

In most states, the maximum period during which you can collect benefits is twenty-six weeks.

Unemployment is everyone's occupational hazard. With expanded benefits, more job security and greater part-time work opportunities, perhaps joblessness—when it happens to you—will not be the life-shattering crisis that often it is today.

There's nothing shameful about losing your job. And there's nothing honorable about staying in a job that is suffocating you. Being *between jobs* puts you in the fine company of actors, writers, consultants, ministers and millions of other splendid folks. You'll make some marvelous friends while waiting in line at the unemployment office.

16

Job Satisfaction:
The Last Litmus Test

After all you've gone through to get a job—and to work and play well with others in your office or plant—suppose it just doesn't add up. Something is wrong. The job is repetitive, exhausting, unchallenging. You feel trapped. Underpaid. Taken for granted. You're excluded from decision-making, mistreated by your boss or discrimination against because of your age, race or sex.

These aren't idle complaints—and you're far from alone in your malaise. Discontent with working conditions has serious consequences, such as excessive lateness, absenteeism and turnover. Unhappy workers slack off, do poor work on purpose, vandalize, steal and even sabotage the production process. They are prone to depression, apathy and an escape into drugs.

Recent polls conducted by Gallup and Louis Harris indicate that Americans feel a growing dissatisfaction with their jobs. It's so serious that the Senate has examined the problem and the Ford Foundation has commissioned research on it. An American Assembly conference on "The Changing World of Work" spent four days studying blue collar blues and white collar woes and their cure. To put it simply though, the government's massive "Work in America" study tells us that only a tiny minority of people would choose the same kind of work if they had it to do over again.

While your job complaints may not have been translated into sabotage or drug use, you've probably felt at least the urge to act out your frustration in one way or another. And things will get worse before they get better unless employers, government, labor specialists and non-profit institutions learn to solve problems such as these:

Boredom

According to the Harvard University Institute for Policy Studies, the ten most boring jobs in the world are assembly line worker, elevator operator, pool typist, bank guard, copying machine operator, keypuncher, highway toll collector, car watcher in a tunnel, and housewife.

That doesn't necessarily mean that if you have one of those jobs, you hate it. Nor does it mean that you're thrilled with your job if it isn't on that list. In a survey of 2,800 executives, the American Management Association discovered that the big wheels feel just as bored and demeaned as the rest of us little cogs. And there's no sex difference in job dissatisfaction either. According to a University of Michigan study, both men *and* women consider unchallenging work to be disagreeable—although women are much more likely to have such jobs.

And don't we know it! A dental hygienist complains that she cleans peoples' teeth all day, when she could be varying her job by giving injections or taking X-rays. A file clerk wonders why some typing, research or even mailroom work can't be interspersed into her job. An assembly line worker wishes she could rotate positions on the line to keep her mind from going dead at one repetitious task.

People are sick of serving the gods of efficiency and specialization. They respond best to diversification and job enrichment—as long as it's not a work speed-up trick to get more output for no more pay.

An AT&T experiment begun in 1965, is a good example of constructive job redesign. The company saw that its clerical workers took no pride in their work ("a job not worth doing is not worth doing well") and that their productivity was down. So, instead of having one person do all the order forms, another all the bill verification and another only typing, AT&T assigned each person a work "module" composed of several functions. Telephone book assemblers processed and verified whole sections of a given phone book. Billing clerks handled all the duties and follow-up on *their* specific accounts. Workers could see a beginning, middle and end to each project; they could feel some pride of authorship. With the enlargement of these jobs, morale rose and absenteeism fell markedly.

Similarly, Bankers Trust, General Foods and Xerox have reported success with their job redesign experiments. The program at Donnelly Mirrors Inc. in Michigan is especially noteworthy. It proves that even a boring or unpleasant task can become acceptable if the workers have the power to decide where, when and how fast the job will be done. At Donnelly workers are divided into task-oriented teams that set their own production goals, control the assignment of jobs within the unit and set the pace of product assembly. The team members also decide their own pay rates collectively, and pay themselves salaries rather than hourly wages. This set-up is no pie-in-the-sky experiment; it's ten years old and going strong.

One key antidote to boredom is human contact. A woman who left a $95 a week job as an order checker to take a $95 a week job as an insurance claims adjuster, says she feels much more needed and useful helping clients with their problems. A bookkeeper became a saleswoman because she found that "people-work beats paperwork by far."

Workers want autonomy, affect and diversity in their jobs. But critics of the job enrichment concept claim that certain tedious tasks are necessary to a technological society. They say it's naïve to think these jobs can be improved, so we'll just have to pay enough to get people to work at them, hateful though they may be. That argument, it seems to me, ignores the cost to the human spirit. How long will people sell their dignity and self-respect for a price? A more hopeful sign is that those jobs hardest to humanize seem more likely to be the ones phased out by automation. Until that time, if the job can't be redesigned, we shouldn't ask one person to tolerate it for too long. More rotation of tasks and faster promotion would help. If boring jobs became the lower rungs of a career ladder, workers could get on and get off before their minds and spirits have a chance to atrophy.

Work climate and employer attitudes

Admittedly, some workers are just too worried about economic security to notice whether their jobs are "meaningful" or "satisfying." But those whose basic needs are met often find themselves examining the sources of their psychological and emotional discontent—and then demanding changes.

Many teachers, for example, consider themselves professionals and feel compromised by "babysitting" assignments such as cafeteria patrol or study hall duty. One school superintendent, Dr. Norman Haweeli of Herricks, Long Island, devised a creative solution that has resulted in greater utilization of teachers' expertise *and* necessary supervision of students. During free periods, students choose resource labs in math, science or language, where teachers make their special knowledge available on an informal basis. The new program resembles a college seminar. It requires no special preparation by the teacher but rather depends on general knowledge already accumulated, and lets the teacher respond to students' individual needs.

Exclusion of employees from decisions that affect them is another common gripe. Secretaries feel they could improve a company's filing system. Lineworkers are more familiar with production difficulties than are remote administrators. In a soft drink plant where workers' participation is sought and appreciated, it was a lineworker who solved a problem that had stumped the industrial engineers. Some unfilled cans of soda were getting through the line undetected. Why not devise a magnetic arm that can lift and reject short-weighted cans but cannot lift the properly filled cans. Why not? Management heeded the suggestion; the "inventor" got a bonus.

Other complaints arising from the work climate require only management awareness and sensitivity to make change. Employers who solicit information from their employees (either through questionnaires or group discussion sessions) often learn more than those who hire expensive labor consultants. Here are some typical demands of workers whose goal is job satisfaction.

- "Recognize our skills and reward them. Don't ask a biochemist to make coffee for the men. Don't take credit for a subordinate's idea."
- "Give us more direct access to management. We feel like those frustrated White House staffers who could never get in to see Nixon."
- "Too much competition leads to backbiting. We'd

rather compete against other companies' sales records or against the people in another branch office—not against the friends we work with every day. Give us team incentive plans instead."

• "The company is too impersonal. Morale would rise if we had company sports teams, theater parties or family picnics."

• "Get rid of all the status symbols, like the executive washroom. It only makes us resentful. Put everyone on a first-name basis. None of this 'Take a letter, Mary.' 'Certainly, Mr. Jones.'"

• "Let us in on financial difficulties. Otherwise, we pick up bad vibes and don't know if it's our fault or not."

• "If we have serious problems at home—if the kids are in trouble or a relative is dying—we should be able to tell the supervisor that we're under big pressure. Then the supervisor can decide if the company can afford a slowdown in our slot, or whether it makes more sense to tell us to take the day off."

Sex discrimination

Complaints about age and race bias haven't increased during the last five years, but *sex* discrimination is becoming a more frequent job dissatisfaction item. Unequal pay, unfair promotion and hiring practices, sex-separate seniority lists and men-only training programs are some of the obvious grievances. But subtle sexism is even more disturbing to many women because it is less tangible and therefore harder to combat.

This quote from a company "manpower" manual epitomizes the prejudice women find prevalent in employers' attitudes:

"Because most women actually like routine, they are easier to train. Because of what psychologists call their 'dependent nature' women are easier to supervise, thus they take and follow instructions better. And, when handled properly, they are more responsive to criticism."

If female human beings are perceived in this "train-your-pet" image, it's no surprise that women feel they're treated like dogs too! To raise the consciousness of male management, let them substitute the word "blacks" for the word "women" in that quote. Would they publish and promote such racist hogwash? Why should any woman find satisfaction in a sexist firm where she is perceived as a ninny before she is even hired?

Bread and butter issues

Believe it or not, inadequate wages are not among the top five dissatisfaction items in the "Work in America" report, but inadequate fringe benefits are ranked third. Whatever coverage workers have, we seem to want more. One-third of the labor force lacks one or more of the common benefits, like paid sick leave or paid vacations. (Workers with more sophisticated demands won't be entirely content until dental care is included in their benefit package.)

According to the report, nearly three-quarters of the women surveyed in 1973 were entitled to maternity leave with the right to be re-employed. Now women want pregnancy-related medical expenses to be accorded the same disability coverage as any other disabling condition.

Working hours

Those who are dissatisfied with their hours beef not about *how much* they work, but *when* they must work. They resent inconvenient hours and consider compulsory overtime akin to forced labor (regardless of time-and-a-half or double-time wages).

Unions have taken up this battle for the blue collar worker. But no one goes on strike when the corporation president calls a 6 P.M. meeting and the junior executive has to miss her (or his) evening law class.

Oddly enough, the 1973 Labor Department survey found far more men than women reporting dissatisfaction with working hours. Despite the general impression that women complain most about juggling home and work responsibilities, if there are children in the household, men seem to resent unreasonable work hours as much as do women.

They say you can't please all of the people all of the time. However, our jobs are a large part of our complex and demanding lives and if we are pleased with our work, we are likely to do it better. In this respect, it pays to please all of the people as far as is humanly possible. But job dissatisfaction can only be alleviated when each worker is heard. A society that gives as much attention to the people-motive as to the profit-motive would have a winning combination.

SECTION III

Fine Print
and Large Protections:
Working Women and the Law

The letter of the law is clear; but the spirit is lagging. If we are to demand our rights we must know what they are. If we want the laws to be real, we must be brave enough to test them.

17

Title VII: The Working Woman's Basic Tool

In 1966, Lorena Weeks of Wadley, Georgia, was earning $78 a week working the night shift for Southern Bell Telephone Company. As an outside plant clerk she was responsible for making minor repairs on equipment. After eighteen years with the company, she applied for the job of switchman—also repair work, but carrying a salary of $135. At that time, Georgia state law prohibited women from working at jobs requiring them to lift anything weighing more than thirty pounds. Southern Bell refused to promote Ms. Weeks on the ground that the switchman job called for "strenuous activity" and the occasional lifting of thirty-one pound equipment. The company gave the switchman job to a man who had far less seniority than Lorena Weeks.

If this happened to you would you watch your extra $57 a week land in another worker's pay envelope just because he's a man and you're a woman? Would you be cowed by that state law and give up in defeat? Or would you demand your right to work at whatever job you felt able to perform, and drag powerful Southern Bell through the courts as long as it took to win?

Lorena Weeks chose to fight—and thousands, perhaps millions of women workers will eventually profit from her courage and determination. After four years of hearings and litigation, the Fifth Circuit Court of Appeals ruled that Southern Bell was in violation of Title VII of the 1964 Civil Rights Act which prohibits discrimination in employment on account of sex. It took two more years and a court order before Ms. Weeks finally was given the switchman's job. Southern Bell was ordered to pay her $31,000 in back pay (representing the higher wages she would have received had she been given the switchman's job from the date she first filed her complaint), plus the overtime pay earned by the man who did get her job, plus premium pay, travel pay and all legal expenses.

Sex discrimination is no laughing matter

The law upon which Ms. Weeks case was based was originally intended to combat job discrimination because of religion and race. The word "sex" was added by a Southern congressman who hoped it would take the heat off employers with race bias policies. The idea of sex discrimination in employment was initially regarded as comic relief from more profound areas of job bias. As it turns out, sex discrimination is a deadly serious fact of American life. And dozens of companies like Southern Bell have discovered that the legal remedies available to women under Title VII often hit the corporate treasury, rather than its funny bone.

Title VII is this nation's contract with the American working woman and its guarantees are as binding as your right to vote. Very simply, it prohibits employment discrimination on the basis of color, race, sex, religion or national origin. The Equal Employment Opportunity Commission is the federal agency that administers Title VII. According to their latest figures, discrimination against women accounts for as many complaints filed against employers as do complaints filed by all the other minority groups combined. Obviously, the Southern congressman's strategy was a complete bust!

How the Act works

Under Title VII you may file a complaint against an employer with fifteen employees or more, or against a labor union or employment agency whom you believe discriminates against women in any of the following areas: hiring, firing, layoff, recall, recruitment, promotional opportunities, seniority systems, wages and conditions of employment, pension and retirement plans, work assignments, sick leave, vacations, overtime, insurance and health benefits, advertising employment preferences based on sex, training programs or other conditions and privileges of employment.

Read that list again. Post it on your bulletin board. Understand how very thorough and far-reaching these protections are. Bear in mind that they cover blue collar women and executives, teachers and state or city employees. Be prepared to quote your legal rights to any employer who attempts to discriminate against you because you are female.

If you have a Title VII complaint, you must file charges in writing with the EEOC within 180 days after the discriminatory act. Charges may be filed by the aggrieved party (you), or by the EEOC itself. The EEOC must notify your company within ten days after the charge is filed. Beyond that, your complaint is kept confidential.

(If your state or city has a fair employment practice law that is similar to Title VII, then your charges are automatically passed along to the state or local agency which must act upon them within sixty days.)

The EEOC has 120 days to investigate your charges and attempt to secure a conciliation agreement or to bring a civil action in federal court against the employer, labor union or employment agency that did you wrong.

Federal courts may issue temporary restraining orders to relieve the problem situation. Or the court can order "affirmative action"—a programmed commitment to correct the employer's wrongdoing—or it can order "other equitable relief" such as reinstatement or back pay.

Included in the EEOC's most recent revised regulations are the following guidelines that tell you exactly where you stand. As you read them, notice how many bells ring in your mind.

Sex as a bona fide occupational qualification (BFOQ)

It is illegal to indicate a preference for one sex or the other unless sex is a *job-related* occupational qualification.

An actor or an actress, a men's locker room attendant, a model or a masseuse are among the very few jobs that authentically require a person of one sex or the other.

The feminist lawyer, Florynce Kennedy, suggests that the BFOQ test be applied on its narrowest terms: "Okay. They can ask for a man when they need a sperm donor, or a woman when they need a wet nurse. But that's about it!"

The EEOC is somewhat less stringent. However, the agency does outline several instances when a sex preference cannot be used to deny employment:

• An employer cannot refuse to hire a woman because of assumptions about the employment characteristics of "women in general" (i.e., that the turnover rate is higher for women than for men; or that women are less capable of aggressive salesmanship).

• An employer cannot refuse to hire an individual because of the preferences of co-workers, clients or customers. This protection works for both sexes. Remember the case where an airline was not permitted to refuse a man employment as a flight attendant simply because "most passengers prefer a pretty stewardess."

Title VII supersedes state laws

The so-called "protective" labor legislation in various states was undoubtedly enacted with the best of motives. Such laws, where they still exist, require rest periods for women, restrict the kinds of jobs we can hold, the number of hours we can work and the amount of weight we can lift.

Why, pray tell, aren't state legislators protecting us from lifting a basket of wet wash or two sacks of canned goods or a child that weights thirty-five pounds? The inconsistency suggests that, in truth, protective labor laws discriminate rather than protect—by preventing women from earning higher wages in those jobs arbitrarily dubbed "man's work." These laws also give employers reasons *not* to hire women, who would require special treatment.

• The EEOC has found that such laws and regulations do not take into account the capacities, preferences and abilities of individual females. The alternative to these restrictions is not forced labor at jobs that may seem dirty or unpleasant to *most* women, but freedom of choice for *all* women. Do not let any state law intimidate you out of a job. Remember that Title VII preempts state laws.

• The EEOC has also decreed that state laws which restrict the employment of minors, cannot restrict minors of one sex and not the other.

Separate lines of progression and seniority

It is against the law to classify a job as "male" or "female" or to maintain separate promotion or seniority systems based on sex.

• The EEOC recognizes that disguised forms of classification—such as "light" and "heavy" jobs—are also illegal if such labels prevent advancement by members of one sex.

Discrimination against married women

Any rule that forbids or restricts the employment of married women, without similarly restricting the employment of married men is in violation of Title VII.

Job opportunities advertising: Help Wanted—Person

Title VII has been an effective lance to slay another dragon—the sex-segregated want ad. The EEOC prohibits any job advertising that indicates a preference or limitation based on sex, unless sex is a BFOQ (see above).

• The placement of an ad in newspaper columns headed "male" or "female" is likewise considered evidence of discrimination.

What's so bad about Male and Female help wanted columns? ask the newspapers. Under the law, women can *still* apply for any job listed in either column.

Even though the Male columns list a greater variety of jobs with higher pay and more prestige, would you feel comfortable turning to the Male columns of your newspaper to look for work? It's like asking whether you would go into the Men's Room if the Ladies' Room had no paper towels. Most of us have been taught to read signs and follow directions—and Male/Female ads provide subtle discriminatory signposts that inhibit us.

No, the sex-titled columns are just a "convenience," said one newspaper, "because jobs generally appeal more to persons of one sex than the other."

If that were so, then women should gravitate toward so-called "women's interest" jobs no matter where they're listed. But a study performed at Carnegie-Mellon University proved quite the reverse: when all job openings appeared in an integrated listing with no reference to sex, 81 per cent of the women tested preferred the "male interest" jobs!

Employment agencies

Private employment agencies may not deal exclusively with one sex—unless they are servicing jobs for which sex is a BFOQ. (Such as all male or all female models.)

• As much as we might want agencies to recruit women specifically for top-echelon jobs, only *employers* may seek workers of one sex to satisfy their affirmative action requirements. An agency advertising for "Women in Management—$20,000+" is in violation of Title VII.

• Employment agencies that accept a discriminatory job order will share responsibility with the employer who places the job order, and will be equally culpable under the law.

Pre-employment inquiries

A job application or employment interview may not solicit information regarding the applicant's sex or marital status, unless the inquiry "is made in good faith for a non-discriminatory purpose."

• An employer can ask if you're married in connection with your health insurance coverage, but not as a clue to whether you might have children or not.

Fringe Benefits

• Employers may not discriminate between men and women in medical, hospital, accident, life insurance and retirement benefits; profit sharing and bonus plans; sick leaves and vacations.

• Benefits may not be restricted to the "head of household" or "principal wage earner" in the family unit, because this tends to favor male employees.

• If a benefit is available to the wives of male employees (for example, medical coverage for maternity), it must also be available to female employees.

• Benefits that are made available to wives and families of male employees must also be available to husbands and families of female employees.

• The employer cannot provide fewer benefits to female employees, even if the cost of benefits is greater where women are covered.

• Pension or retirement plans may not contain different benefits or different optional or compulsory retirement ages based on sex.

Employment policies on pregnancy and childbirth

An employer may not refuse to hire an applicant because she is pregnant! Even nine months pregnant!

• Pregnancy-related disabilities, such as abortion, miscarriage, childbirth or its complications, must be treated like any other temporary disability—and should be covered under any disability insurance or sick leave plan maintained by the employer.

• Any policy that regulates when a pregnant woman must begin her maternity leave, or how long she must remain away from work; what happens to her accrued seniority and other benefits; or the circumstances of her reinstatement—all such policies must apply equally to people with other temporary disabilities.

To those who argue that counting pregnancy as a disability favors females, who are the only sex that become pregnant, you might reply that men who undergo prostate operations enjoy disability benefits—although only males have prostate glands! In a recent case the U.S. Supreme Court ruled against the EEOC interpretation but new challenges are in the wings.

Landmark cases

There are two kinds of discrimination: the pernicious kind that consciously and systematically denies rights or excludes benefits to one group; and the subtle, almost unconscious kind that results when vast generalizations are made about one class of people. Women have been victims of both forms of bias—but the subtle prejudices are the most frustrating and embittering. Assumptions about our strengths and weaknesses, about our interests and responsibilities, or about what work we can and cannot do, are subjected to searching analysis when a claim is made in a court of law. It is here that Title VII is given life and breadth.

The first Title VII case to be decided by the United States Supreme Court involved Ida Phillips who was denied a job as an assembly line trainee just because she had young children. The company, Martin-Marietta, made what has become known as the "sex-plus" defense. "We are not discriminating against Ms. Phillips because she is a woman," they said, "but only because she is a woman *plus* the mother of small children."

In a unanimous opinion, the Court held that Title VII forbids employers to have "one hiring policy for women and another for men." In other words, the company could not refuse to hire women with young children *unless* fathers of young children are also refused jobs.

In another early case, the Court of Appeals in Chicago ruled that a woman can't be forced to retire three years earlier than a man, even if compulsory retirement ages are negotiated in a union contract. When union and employer bargain away one group's right to work on the supposedly humane grounds that older women are frail, one can only smile and remind our male protectors that we have a habit of outliving them by nearly seven years.

Title VII cases have brought windfall settlements to thousands of mistreated working women. A few years ago, Anaconda Aluminum in Louisville, Kentucky, had a system of classifying women in "light" work and men in "heavy" work categories. When rehiring employees who had been laid off, the company took back the men first, saying they needed heavy workers—despite the greater seniority of many women workers. The Court held that Anaconda had not given senior women the chance to compete for the available jobs, which may not have been too "heavy" for any of them. Anaconda was ordered to pay 276 women a total of $190,000 in back wages—money they would have earned had they been hired according to their seniority rights.

The guardian angel has feet of clay

With all its best intentions and admirable regulations, the Equal Employment Opportunity Commission doesn't seem able to control the rabid epidemic of sex discrimination. (In fact, in-house discrimination complaints suggest that the EEOC can't even keep its own shop in order.)

In July 1973, the EEOC Chairperson admitted that *not one* of the five hundred largest U.S. corporations was in compliance with anti-discrimination laws. As if acting out of nagging guilt, two months later the agency filed job discrimination charges against four giants of American industry: Ford, General Motors, Sears and General Electric.

Even David had only *one* Goliath. The EEOC now faces a showdown with four giants as well as a backlog of 65,000 cases against smaller adversaries. However, the agency has recently expanded its staff considerably and every month more and more women are getting satisfaction under the solemn covenant promised by Title VII.

Don't be discouraged if the EEOC is slow to act. And don't let *your* perpetrator off the hook. Once your case squeezes past the EEOC bottleneck, you may make labor history for all of us.

18

A Little Bit Pregnant;
A Lot of Aggravation

Remember the old joke about the woman who has just had a medical examination.

"I have good news for you, Mrs. Brown," announces the doctor.

"It's *Miss* Brown, Doctor," corrects the woman.

"In that case, Miss Brown, I have bad news for you."

Whether the pregnancy is welcome or not, if Ms. Brown holds a job and wants to continue working, her impending motherhood may be bad news for her employment status.

Childbearing is still an honored activity in our culture—*except* in the labor market. Here it's a problem and as such it requires "a maternity policy."

Before the 1972 Title VII guidelines were published, and before the Cohen-LaFleur case was decided by the United States Supreme Court, employers were free to set arbitrary rules regarding pregnant workers. It didn't matter if your doctor said you could leap buildings in a single bound; it didn't matter if you desperately wanted to keep your job and needed the income. A company could tell you when you had to leave and how long you were required to stay away from work—and whether you would be allowed back at all. Individual cases were largely ignored and medical evidence carried no weight. The pregnant worker was regarded as an encumbrance in the business world. She had to be dismissed for her own good.

An employer who couldn't care less about your sinuses

or sciatica felt justified to adopt an attitude of romantic paternalism toward your pregnancy. Even today, despite Title VII, the equal protection clause of the Fourteenth Amendment and the Supreme Court ruling, a survey of one thousand companies shows that some employers are still trying to get away with these "protective" maternity policies:

* You may be forced to leave your job months before your due date.
* You may lose all benefits and seniority during this involuntary leave.
* There are often no guarantees of reinstatement to the same job or one paying a comparable salary.
* You may be forbidden to return to work for a specific period of time after childbirth; or required to return earlier than your condition permits—or else forfeit benefits.
* You rarely receive cash payments to compensate for the involuntary loss of income during your disability leave.
* If the company health plan includes childbirth coverage you may discover you didn't work there long enough to qualify for it; or else the insurance only pays a tiny part of your medical costs.
* Or, you may be fired. Period.

While maternity policies still are far from uniform, business seems to be liberalizing the rules in three areas.

Disability leave with provisions for job security

The most discouraging changes have been happening in the area of forced leaves—since that was the issue decided by the Supreme Court in Cohen-LaFleur, a case involving teachers.

Very simply, the law now requires that a pregnant woman be granted a leave of absence on the same terms as any other leave for disability—when the patient and doctor require it. The employer may not force a pregnant worker to leave her job nor forbid her to return for a specific period of time, unless the same restrictions are binding on a male worker (before and after his hernias and heart attacks). Whatever time limitations apply in company policy on other disability leaves should apply to maternity leaves. Therefore, if an ulcer patient gets his job back after twelve weeks disability leave, and if he is carried on the rolls for benefits and seniority during his absence, then the new mother is entitled to the same job security.

Disability pay or sick pay to compensate for loss of wages

Here, the Supreme Court let us down. In its ruling on a California case, the court voted that employers were not discriminating under the Fourteenth Amendment by excluding from a disability program medical costs of a normal pregnancy. Without judicial encouragement employers are home free so far as the Fourteenth Amendment to the constitution is concerned. But Title VII was not mentioned by the court and EEOC guidelines still require employers to treat all pregnancies the same as any other paid disability. As of April 1974, the EEOC had filed suit against eleven employers, including duPont and General Mills. Few companies are as enlightened as Seattle Trust Bank which allows pregnant women to use accrued sick pay (up to twelve days a year) and on top of that pays a woman two-thirds of her salary for the duration of a two-month maternity leave.

Just as a woman has the basic right to take a disability leave on the same terms as anyone else who is incapacitated, she also has as much right to receive disability pay during that leave. Most companies carry Temporary Disability Insurance which protects the employee against loss of income resulting from sickness, ailment or bodily injury. The policy is funded by the employer or by contributions from both the company and the worker. Some states even have *legal* requirements for minimum disability coverage.

Once again, pregnant workers should enjoy the same confidence and financial security during their period of unemployment as any other afflicted employee. Whether through the vehicle of disability insurance or by using accumulated sick leave pay, a working woman who is temporarily off salary for a legitimate reason, must have a stop-gap income.

Allowances for medical care and services

The great majority of union-management health plans include medical allowances of some kind, whether flat payments for maternity expenses or specific fee schedules for surgery, hospitalization and pre-natal care. Most employers agree with the wisdom of including maternity in health plans. The dispute centers around how much coverage is enough. If your bills come to over $1,000, a flat $350 reimbursement doesn't help much. Where a corporate insurance program provides up to eighty per cent coverage of hospital bills it makes no sense to single out maternity expenses for a flat fee. What women want is a realistic scale of medical allowances—and no waiting period for eligibility under medical insurance programs.

Allowances for medical care and services

The great majority of union-management health plans include medical allowances of some kind, whether flat payments for maternity expenses or specific fee schedules for surgery, hospitalization and pre-natal care. Most employers agree with the wisdom of including maternity in health plans. The dispute centers around how much coverage is enough. If your bills come to over $1,000, a flat $350 reimbursement doesn't help much. Where a corporate insurance program provides up to eighty per cent coverage of hospital bills it makes no sense to single out maternity expenses for a flat fee. What women want is a realistic scale of medical allowances—and no waiting period for eligibility under medical insurance programs.

How to argue for your maternity rights

All three maternity provisions are eminently reasonable and buttressed by EEOC guidelines. If you have to debate your employer on the merits of the law, here are some arguments that are as rational as they are just:

Employer: "Special benefits for pregnancy and childbirth would give women workers privileges not afforded to men."

You: Agreed. In righting a wrong, we don't want to tip the scales in our direction any more than men's. We recognize that exceptional treatment for pregnant women would be resented by our co-workers. Moreover, if the special benefit costs the company money, it could be used as yet another excuse not to hire women in the first place.

But we're not asking for *special* benefits. We only ask that childbirth be treated the same as any other temporary disability and that complications of pregnancy be considered an illness like any other. We demand no more and no less than the company already provides to any worker who is temporarily unable to do her or his job.

Prostate problems are unique to men. Childbirth is unique to women. Yet both "ailments" require medical care, hospitalization, possibly surgery, a recuperative period and temporary leave from the job. Why then is this male condition just cause for sympathetic treatment, while the female condition is cause for discriminatory policies?

A Federal judge in Virginia says it shouldn't be: "Because pregnancy, though unique to women, is like other medical conditions, the failure to treat it as such amounts to discrimination."

Employer: "But maternity is not like other disabilities. It's not an illness, it's a normal physiological condition."

You: We have to separate the three phases of maternity. There's the pregnancy, the childbirth itself, and the post-delivery-early-motherhood phase.

We can agree that in the first phase, a healthy, uneventful *pregnancy* is normal. So normal that I want the right to work through as much of the nine months as I and my doctor feel I can. But if that "normal" pregnancy period is fraught with complications like toxemia or hemorrhaging, it is no longer normal. Only then does it satisfy the definition of a temporary disability.

The second phase, *childbirth,* may be "normal" in the sense that it is universal. However, every woman knows that labor and delivery is no picnic. Again, it requires a physician's care, hospitalization and recuperation. Parenthetically, there is always the possibility of death. For these reasons, the childbirth phase of the maternity period qualifies as much as any other disability.

The third phase, early *motherhood,* is the period when women may ask no special favors and employers may make no special prohibitions. We expect a reasonable recuperative period to be included in our disability leave. Beyond that we do not expect an open-ended leave of absence for childrearing.

The Citizen's Advisory Council on the Status of Women has issued this definitive statement: *Childbirth* and *complications of pregnancy* are, for all job-related purposes, the only valid temporary disabilities of maternity. It should be clear that the obligations are mutual—the employer may not be punitive and the employee may not be privileged.

Employer: "Pregnancy is voluntary and therefore different from all other ailments that count as disabilities."

You: Rubbish! For millions of women whose religion prohibits the use of contraceptives, pregnancy can hardly be called voluntary. In a sense, however, the right to be pregnant is as meaningful as the right to avoid pregnancy. Reproductive freedom, like any other freedom, must insure choice. Asking me to choose between my job or my child is not choice but punishment.

If the word "voluntary" carries such weight, what about the man who voluntarily smokes his way to lung cancer? And what about the man who volunteers for the armed services? Why is he granted a leave of absence and reinstatement? Why are you willing to recognize an obligation to the man who bears arms for his country, but not to the woman who bears children for the survival of the race?

Employer: "Women are fragile and vulnerable during pregnancy and after birth."

You: That's a matter for me and my doctor to determine. Most obstetricians approve and even encourage continued work. Besides, there are no data indicating a higher accident rate for pregnant women, so don't worry about us, thanks. In wartime, women have endured incredible hardships and still delivered healthy babies. Women athletes have won Olympic medals while they were pregnant. In other cultures, women till the fields, give birth and return to the plow hours later. And right now, pregnant women are skiing, working on assembly lines and doing arduous housework with no ill effects.

When choreographer Ethel Martin was eight months pregnant she was dancing in *Pal Joey*. Billie Jean King played tennis while pregnant and jockey Mary Bacon rode winning horses in her sixth month. A pregnant nurse went from her last shift right into the delivery room at the Pittsburgh hospital where she worked. Like these women, I believe my body is my business, not businessmen's.

Employer: "Pregnant women can't expect to be taken seriously in the business world."

You: Perhaps if we were more commonplace, we would become less noticeable. But even now, women themselves report that they feel better and happier when pregnant and therefore they are more effective. An expanding uterus doesn't cramp the brain.

Employer: "Women don't come back to work after

childbirth so why should I waste benefits on them?"

You: Eleanor Holmes Norton, Commissioner of Human Rights for the City of New York took that job when she was seven months pregnant. She worked until the day her daughter was born and returned to her office four weeks later. The fact is that well-paid women with good jobs go back to work and poorly paid women in dead-end jobs (the great majority) do not. It is not a matter of sex and motherhood, but of income and status. If you limit my aspirations and rewards, it's your own fault if I choose not to return.

Employer: "Women will be absent and late during pregnancy."

You: Not so, says the Public Health Service. Time lost from work because of childbearing is only a fraction of the time lost because of other conditions. Then too, a man's accidents and illnesses come without warning and who knows how often. Conversely, you have several months' advance notice when I become pregnant. Temporary help can be arranged for my absence. And as an average woman, I am not likely to have more than two pregnancies during my entire working lifetime.

Employer: "It costs too much to maintain maternity benefits in health plans and disability insurance policies."

You: In 1972, the Aetna Insurance Company showed that the additional cost of including this coverage is *very small*. In a typical policy, about sixty cents extra per month per employee would assure a sixty dollar a week benefit during a new mother's six week disability leave. Insurance carriers are willing to write maternity disability into their policies and discuss terms. Just ask them.

So much for arguments and rejoinders. The dialogue has begun in the courts, at the bargaining table, in state legislatures and federal agencies. The progress is encouraging, but far from satisfactory.

In almost any country in Europe, Asia or Africa, this chapter would not have had to be written at all. Other countries have national social insurance systems that would entitle you to free medical care at your employer's expense (Guinea); or two months leave with full salary (Finland); or a legal guarantee of reinstatement to the same job (France). Where rights of the pregnant worker are concerned it's time that the United States caught up with the rest of the world.

19

The Equal Pay Act:
Desexregating Paychecks

Are you being paid less money than the man at the next desk? Did the company pay higher wages to the man who held your job before you? Was your starting salary lower than that paid to the fellows in your training program?

If you can answer "yes" to any of these questions, why in blazes haven't you filed a complaint under the Equal Pay Act?

The University of Michigan Research Center found that nearly 95 per cent of women surveyed were underpaid; yet less than eight per cent of them believed they were victims of discrimination. And none of them were seeking redress under the law.

"There are interesting reasons for women's failure to demand their rights under the Act," explains Francis W. McGowan, Director, Division of Equal Pay and Employment Standards of the United States Department of Labor. "Some women assume the procedures are too complicated or they fear employer reprisals. Other women don't recognize pay discrimination because they've lived with it for so long. Those who do see the inequity will simply excuse it with statements like: 'That's the way it is' or 'At least it's a good job for a woman.'"

McGowan deplores this attitude of hopeless resignation. He feels that the Equal Pay Act is a sweeping protection for working women and he wants more women to use it to seek their just rewards. His department has over 350 offices throughout the country with more than one thousand compliance officers standing by to make equal pay for equal work a reality for every woman. Why not give them some business?

Other workers' windfalls

• In the Brookhaven Hospital case the court ruled that nurses' aides (women) and hospital orderlies (men) did substantially equal work. The aides got back pay and a thirty cents per hour raise.

• Three female lab technicians won $44,000 back pay, plus $20,000 legal costs, from the Miller Brewing Company.

• A large university made a $300,000 adjustment in unequal salaries; one woman professor got a $3,000 raise.

• In an Arkansas case involving press operators, women's wages were raised to equal men's even though the work was not precisely equal. The ruling established that a woman's great *mental* stress working on high speed equipment was equatable with a man's great *physical* stress working with heavy equipment.

• A bank was directed to pay male and female tellers the same wage, even though officials claimed the male tellers were being groomed to become bank officers. (An employer cannot grant one sex a privilege and then penalize the other sex for not having that privilege!)

• In a whopping windfall, two thousand women at Wheaton Glass Company received back pay of $900,000 plus 6 per cent interest to compensate them for six years of underpayment.

• J. M. Fields, a retail chain, was found guilty of paying women department supervisors less than men doing *substantially* equal work. The women had supervised "soft-line" goods (like apparel) while the men had supervised "hardline" goods (like appliances). The court found no difference in the effort or function of these supervisory jobs and ordered the retailer to pay *eight* years of back pay to women supervisors in sixty-six branch stores.

• In June 1974, the Supreme Court ruled that Corning Glass could not offer lower-paid, formerly all-female *day* shifts to men, or higher-paid, all-male *night* shifts to women in an attempt to cure the equal pay violation. Regardless of whether both sexes perform a job, and whatever the hours of the shift, if the jobs are equal the pay must not be unequal. About 950 women *and* men at Corning have been awarded $600,000 back pay.

• Several newspapers have discovered that the Equal Pay Act doesn't condone paying Women's Page Editors less than editors of other sections of the paper.

• At General Electric's Fort Wayne, Indiana, plant, 350 women were awarded $300,000 back wages, $250,000 in increased salaries and the right to bid with men for the same jobs.

• When men and women at AT&T were promoted into computer jobs, they each received a 10 per cent raise. But, due to previously sex-typed job policies, the men came to computer work from craft jobs and the women came from clerical jobs—where they had earned $40 to $70 less per week than the male craft workers. Even with the across-the-board 10 per cent increase, men and women were performing the same computer jobs while the women were still being paid $40 to $70 less. In a bonanza settlement, AT&T consented to pay $7.2 million to correct this differential. (One discouraging aside: the consent decree provided that every AT&T job would be open to both sexes. Ironically, men have harvested most of the benefits. More than four thousand men have taken jobs as operators but only 1,400 women have moved into traditionally male jobs with their far superior salaries.)

What the law provides

Whereas Title VII covers a wide scope of discriminatory practices (including wage bias), the Equal Pay Act of 1963, which was amended to the Fair Labor Standards Act, is a laser beam focused only on money problems. The Act which applies to men and women alike, prohibits "discrimination on account of sex in the payment of wages by employers." Because women have been the traditional targets of discriminatory pay scales, the Act is our great ally. Its intent is plain: women and men in the same establishment who perform substantially equal work on jobs requiring comparable skill, effort and responsibility must be paid the same wages for their labor. (It does not require that jobs be *identical*.)

The law also considers fringe benefits, such as pension and insurance plans, to be subject to equal pay treatment. It does not allow an employer to either raise a man's wage or lower a woman's wages in order to offset the higher cost of pension benefits for women. Nor does it permit an employer to penalize a woman for the extra cost of her pregnancy benefits.

In attempting to get salaries into alignment, the employer may not adjust a man's salary *downward* to equal a woman's. And unions are specifically prohibited from causing an employer to discriminate in pay during the collective bargaining process.

The only pay differentials considered legitimate under the Act are those based on bona fide seniority, merit systems, piecework rates or any system in which sex is not a factor.

When a violation is established, the employees who have been affected are entitled to a raise to equalize their wages with those of the opposite sex. In addition they are entitled to two years of back pay (three years if the violation was willful, repeated or deceptive). Willful violators are also subject to criminal fines and imprisonment.

The Equal Pay Act also includes a specific prohibition against employer reprisals—and the government has been tough on employers who have retaliated by discharging or harassing a suspected "troublemaker."

Who is covered by the Act?

About sixty million wage and salary workers engaged in interstate commerce are under the Act's jurisdiction; virtually every industry, from agriculture to advertising, is accountable. Blue collar women have been covered from the start, but in 1972 the Act was extended to executives, administrative, professional and outside sales people. You may be protected by the Act even if you are not subject to the minimum wage and overtime provisions of the Fair Labor Standards Act, of which Equal Pay is an amendment.

Exempt from coverage are household workers, employees in a retail establishment that grosses less than $250,000 annually and employees of state and local governments (other than school and hospital workers).

(Those who *are* covered under the Act should rethink the old commitment to salary secrecy. It's supposed to prevent jealousy and friction among co-workers. But what salary secrecy really does is keep employees ignorant of discrepancies based on sex, race and other irrelevant factors.)

Getting in on the Act

You can do it with a phone call, a short letter or a visit to your local compliance officer. (They're listed in the phone book under "United States Government—Labor Dept. of—Wage & Hour Div.") Just state your complaint simply. There are no official forms or affidavits. Confidentiality is assured. The compliance officers I've interviewed seemed uniformly personable and took their jobs seriously.

How is the Act administered

The Wage and Hour Division (WHD) of the Department of Labor intervenes in a company's pay policies in two ways: First, on its own initiative WHD makes routine checks to determine whether a company is in general compliance with all sections of the Fair Labor Standards Act, including minimum wage, overtime and equal pay. A second method by which WHD can investigate a company is in response to a complaint—by someone like you.

Under the law, WHD officers can examine payroll and other records. They can see right through "job titles" (bookkeeping vs. junior accountant) and "job descriptions" which the company may use to mask the similarity of two jobs. With a sharp eye on pay differentials, the officer will investigate the company's practice of sex-typing jobs, or the sex discrimination built into a union agreement, or the pattern of non-compliance in an industry. But they need you for personal input and job-content specifics.

The beauty of the Act is manifold. All complaints are held in strictest confidence so the company need never know whether WHD is poking around in response to your complaint or as part of a regularly scheduled investigation.

Action is immediate. Investigations begin about two weeks after a complaint is registered.

WHD's enforcement powers are strong. They achieve satisfaction in 95 per cent of their cases without litigation. And your complaint can result in raises and back pay for all other women in your job category. When Equal Pay cases do go to court, the aggrieved working woman is represented by the Secretary of Labor—and the record of victories in these cases is impressive. Of 242 cases decided by July 1973, the Labor Department had won 205 on behalf of complainants. The payoff is similarly impressive.

During fiscal 1974, 17,000 workers, most of them women, were awarded nearly $7 million in back wages.

If you file a private suit under the Act (rather than a suit brought by the Secretary of Labor), you may be awarded back pay plus legal fees, court costs and extra damages for your trouble.

Any way you look at it you have everything to gain from a justifiable Equal Pay Act complaint. And nothing to lose but your anger. But don't make the mistake of assuming that equal pay for work is the final solution. It's only the tip of the iceberg.

If you and twenty other women work in a dead-end, low-paid clerical department, the Equal Pay Act is a meaningless tool. Without male co-workers against which to compare your salary, you have no claim under the Act. Since the poorest-paid jobs are held by women in those occupations that employ mostly women, many of us must seek other means of upgrading our wages. Equal pay for equal work is a fine concept but it only applies when women and men are employed in roughly equal numbers in the same kinds of jobs.

Until we women have *equal access* to equal work, we don't have real equality at all.

20

More Help for the Working Woman: Courtesy of the Executive Branch

You can skip this chapter only if you're sure that your employer has no financial dealings with the federal government.

But federal contractors—companies or institutions that do business with the federal government—are subject to a special executive order signed by President Lyndon Johnson. Executive Order EO 11246 amended by EO 11375 prohibits discrimination on the basis of sex and requires the holder of federal contracts to take "affirmative action" to hire, train and promote women into jobs where women have been underrepresented or underutilized. The protections specified by EO 11375 parallel those of Title VII, though its application differs in some respects.

To determine whether you are covered by EO 11375 find out if your employer holds a federal contract of $10,000 or more. Do you work for a college or university that does research for the government, or a manufacturer that supplies defense materials, or a construction company that bids for federal building projects? These are but a few examples of federal contractors who fall within the purview of EO 11375.

Suppose your company sells staplers to the State Department but you work for the branch of the company that makes paperclips—your job status is still protected by EO 11375.

An institution or company receiving more than $10,000

but less than $50,000 in federal contracts must fulfill the non-discrimination provisions of the Executive Order but need not have a written plan. However, an institution or company that employs fifty or more people and receives $50,000 or more in federal monies must have on file a *written* affirmative action plan—detailing goals and timetables to correct the underutilization of female employees. They must submit this plan to the contracting agency—the Department of Defense or Health, Education, and Welfare, etc.—on request. The contracting agency is supposed to check on an employer's compliance with non-discrimination guidelines, before the government can award a contract of $1 million or more.

If an investigator discovers that women are underrepresented in the employers' work force at all levels; if there are obstacles to female advancement; if recruitment or promotion policies favor men; if job advertisements indicate a sex preference; or if other unfair practices are found, hearings are scheduled and the employer stands to lose a big, fat, juicy federal contract.

Ask to see your employer's affirmative action plan. It's usually in the personnel department's files. You should be able to check out the company's expressed intentions against the reality of your job experience and the situation you know exists in the company.

In April 1972, the Department of Labor published Revised Order No. 4, a list of criteria for affirmative action that is expected of employers who are subject to EO 11375. It decrees that particular attention be paid to those job classifications where women are scarce, such as officials and managers, professionals and technicians, outside sales workers and skilled crafts. (In the educational field, this order carries special urgency for those who want to increase the number of women principals, department heads, supervisors and administrators.)

The Labor Department requires that employers set target goals that it will reach within a specific period of time, or else face cancellation of federal business. To implement goals for fuller employment of women the employer must ascertain:

• the degree of female unemployment in the immediate labor market area.

• the proportion of women in the total work force in

the area and how this compares to the proportion of women in the company.

• how many promotable or transferable female workers are already employed by the company.

• methods of improving recruitment and training procedures to attract and upgrade women.

Under EO 11375 your sex discrimination complaint can lead to back pay awards (to you and to all other women similarly affected), cash settlements, or reinstatement where it is determined that you were fired on account of sex.

New guidelines published in December 1973 further expand EO 11375 to bring it in line with Title VII. Included in these new guidelines are non-discriminatory guarantees for pregnant women and women with young children, as well as prohibitions against sex-stereotyped job titles (foreman, cameraman, etc.), distinctions based on marital status, or sex-specific retirement and pension policies. At this writing, the Department of Labor was still undecided about whether to insist employers provide equal fringe benefits for both sexes or let employers make equal financial contributions to fringe benefit programs. The second alternative would give female workers less benefits, since it usually costs more to cover women in insurance, pension, and welfare programs.

About 250,000 companies and institutions come under the jurisdiction of EO 11375. If you have a complaint against one of these companies, you have 180 days from the discriminatory act to write to the Office of Federal Contract Compliance, Department of Labor, Washington, D.C. 20210. Though the wheels of justice grind exceedingly slow, the threat of losing millions of dollars of Uncle Sam's business has made many an employer shape up.

• One federal judge even ruled that the "last hired, first fired" policy can't be used to lay off women and minorities whose low seniority were due to past discrimination. Women hired by order of the OFCC shouldn't be considered the most expendable workers in the event of cutbacks.

• In the spring of 1974, nine major steel companies negotiated with the EEOC and the OFCC (the two agencies are trying to coordinate better) a series of "goals and timetables" that will affect over ten thousand women. Within one year, the steel companies are bound to hire females to fill 20 per cent of production and maintenance job vacancies and 25 per cent of supervisory and management training jobs. Fifty per cent of the openings in trade and craft jobs will be filled by women and minorities. In addition 5,600 women will share (with 34,500 minority males) a back pay settlement amounting to nearly 31 million dollars. Despite several controversial "Catch-22" provisions in the consent decree, if EO 11375 can help squeeze millions out of such giants as U.S. Steel and Bethlehem Steel, imagine what it might help you accomplish to reform *your* company.

• The Hesse Envelope Company of Dallas has been declared ineligible to receive government money because of deficiencies in its affirmative action program.

• Martha Griffiths, the Michigan congresswoman, found that the OFCC too rarely exercises its power to deny federal contracts. But Labor Secretary Peter J. Brennan declared that the agency has reorganized and in 1975 it plans to review the equal opportunity records of nearly fifty thousand government contractors.

21

Oldies but Goodies

Abigail McCarthy once made a moving, almost poetic declaration:

> I am the way I am.
> I look the way I look.
> I am my age.

In this culture, few women have been comfortable enough about aging to make such statements. Frenetic worship of the youth cult has afflicted many of us with a kind of loathing for the inexorable passage of time. Women, more than men, have been victims of the new "ism"—ageism—which puts a premium on "young skin" and "bikini bodies."

Everyone has a different definition of "the mature woman." The plateau ages of twenty-one, thirty, thirty-five, forty and fifty all seem to bring on profound attacks of reassessment, if not existential shock. One forty-five-year-old considers herself a washed up old lady, while another woman won't answer to the words old lady, while another woman won't answer to the words "old," "mature" or "senior citizen," though she's sixty-two.

Wouldn't it be nice to dispense with such labels altogether so that a woman may be described by her unique qualities and potential, rather than by the gray in her hair or the date on her birth certificate.

Women's groups such as OWL (Older Women's Liberation) and The Gray Panthers, and the monthly newsletter, *Prime Time*, have been working hard to restore dignity and value to the mature woman. They offer consciousness-raising groups, job seminars, loans and scholarships, medical programs and lobbying assistance to women who are refusing to be discarded in the rubble of America's youthquake. Because aging is inevitable and ineluctable, every one of us, whatever her present age, should wish that such groups multiply and prosper.

Wishing aside, special problems do accrue to specific age groups. In connection with the problems relevant to the working woman, it becomes important to admit and accept one's true age.

To begin with, for purposes of statistics, the U.S. Department of Labor considers the "mature woman" to be between the ages of forty-five and sixty-four. Half of all American women in this age group have paying jobs. Of them, seven out of ten work at full-time, year-round jobs. The great majority of these women are married. Also, as is the case for women of all ages, most of these mature women work because they need the money.

According to the National Organization of Women's "Over-45 Committee," more than half the women workers in that age bracket hold clerical or service jobs. Less than seven per cent are in management positions, and fourteen per cent are professionals or technicians. The Women's Bureau furnishes even more depressing information: in 1971, among year-round, full-time workers, the median income for men ages forty-five to fifty-four was $10,700; for women it was $5,800!

What keeps upper-age women in lower-wage jobs?

Cultural attitudes and employer discrimination. An old maxim holds that a man of forty is in his prime, but a woman of forty is over the hill. Such flippant myths tend to replace the truth, simply by being repeated often enough.

According to a Labor Department study made by Ohio State University, employers have even elaborated on the basic myth. They think the woman *over thirty* is hard to train, more likely to be absent, and more likely to quit. Yet objective data show that both turnover and absenteeism is lower among older workers. The 1971 White House Conference on Aging cited research indicating that mature workers are *more* trainable than younger workers. While mathematical ability may decline slightly with age, conceptual thinking actually improves as we get older, and our I.Q. score is higher at fifty than it was in college.

Add to this support for the viability of the older worker, the following information about the superlative older *woman.* It is women who live nearly seven years longer than men—witness the fact that there are four million more mature women than men alive today. Women are spared men's high incidence of heart disease and ulcers. With a healthy psychological attitude toward menopause (and hormone treatment, if necessary), women can function in the working world with new energy and new freedom. (Meaningful employment is one of the best antidotes to the "empty nest" depression that women often experience when their children leave home.)

Men, on the other hand, have been found to suffer a sort of "emotional menopause" from which it is difficult to bounce back—and which cannot be alleviated by hormones. Because of the great pressure to achieve success and power, the American man who has not reached the top of his field in his forties often feels despondent and beaten. His occupational status seems to reflect on his virility, his masculinity and his role as provider. He is expected to have "arrived" by the age of forty while his wife at forty is either expected to have "settled in" (resigned herself to the dead-end job she's had for twenty years) or to "re-enter" (start from scratch after raising the kids).

Here is yet another example of the vastly different standards that apply to women in this sexist society. If a woman has always worked at a paid job, her career was supposed to have taken second place to success in her personal life. If she accepts this assignment of priorities, she is in effect admitting that she lacks career commitment and job dependability. This implicit admission gives the employer an easy rationale for keeping her in a second-rate job despite her years of seniority.

Meanwhile, the woman who devotes her years exclusively to home and children discovers that when she goes job hunting, she gets no credit for life experience. So she too must settle for a job with low-status, low responsibility and low pay. All this begins to explain why women earn little more than half as much as men in the prime life decade of ages forty-five to fifty-four.

Women's most common experiences with age discrimination

• Employers say they prefer to invest time and money in training a young worker so that the company can get long-term service in return.

While a woman of forty has a life-expectancy of between thirty-five and forty additional years, the employer is telling her she has no future.

• Employers are reluctant to hire women over forty for fear they will resent working for a younger executive.

Some of us find it hard to work for people who have loud voices or long hair. Still, we do it—and more important, we are not denied a job on the *possibility* that we might not get along with our loud-mouthed, long-haired boss.

• Employers claim that older women are *overqualified* for various jobs because of their long previous work experience.

It is up to you to decide whether you are suited to a job or vice versa. If an unemployed physicist is *willing* to work as an elevator operator in order to feed her family, she must be given her turn at the controls. "Overqualified" is frequently an employer's way of saying that you've worked too long to be hired for a low-level job, but you're too old and too female to be hired for the job you deserve.

• Employers pay a pittance starting salary to mature women who enter the labor force without work experience. ("You have a lot of catching up to do," they tell you.)

Then five years later, after a few five dollar raises, when you are quite expert at your job, you are still earning far less than your male or younger colleagues—and far less than the job is worth. For many older women there seems to be no such thing as catching up.

• Employers worry that older workers will be a drain on the company's retirement and medical programs.

In addition to the legal answer (see section below), there is a logical reply to this contention: by excluding the over-40s from the work force, we force them onto the welfare rolls. Either way, whether through company pension plans or public welfare, a humane society must take ultimate responsibility for its older citizens. It is therefore a highly political act when an employer rejects a mature woman who may consider work as essential to her dignity as to her economic survival.

How are you legally protected against age discrimination?

As we've shown, Title VII of the Civil Rights Act of 1964 prohibits employment discrimination based on sex. Since acts of injustice committed against an older woman can overlap both issues of her age and her sex, it is important that you first check out Title VII coverage.

For example, an employer may have expressed the preference to hire a forty-five-year-old unemployed man as opposed to a more qualified forty-five-year-old woman, in a generally depressed job market. The common generalization about males being heads of households and therefore having a greater economic need for work (or the unspoken ego support men give to each other) is no justification for passing over a more worthy woman.

Remember that Title VII Guidelines state that it is unlawful for an employer to use sex as an excuse for maintaining a pension or retirement plan with different retirement ages or different benefits for women and men. Some plans have paid women lower monthly retirement benefits based on the rationale that women live longer and therefore will collect more benefits in the end—a rationale which means nothing to those women who don't live as long as the actuarial tables promised.

A second Title VII guideline specifies that an employer can't use the fact that it costs more to provide the same retirement benefits to a woman, as an excuse for not hiring a woman or not paying a woman equal monthly benefits.

Beyond Title VII, your most formidable ally is the *Age Discrimination in Employment Act* (ADEA) which applies to private firms that employ twenty-five or more people. This federal law prohibits job bias on the basis of age for women and men between ages forty and sixty-five in such matters as hiring, discharge, leave, compensation, promotions and other areas of employment. A few examples will suggest the scope of ADEA protection:

1. A company cannot force you to retire earlier than age sixty-five unless it maintains a legitimate retirement

benefits program that requires an earlier retirement age *and* you are included in the coverage of that program.

2. Let's assume you're fifty-eight and you're looking for work. Don't let anyone refuse to hire you simply because the company has a compulsory retirement age of sixty-two. Even though you may only work a maximum of four years and your coverage might raise the company's retirement costs, you cannot be denied employment on this basis.

3. Unless there is a bona fide occupational qualification (BFOQ), classified ads or recruiters seeking younger persons for a job are in violation of ADEA. The Act recognizes as a BFOQ the need for a young person to model clothes for teen-agers but the company's desire for a nubile young convention hostess wouldn't hold up in court if a middle-aged woman had been qualified for the job.

4. Private employment agencies are also subject to ADEA. In fiscal 1973, three hundred agencies were found to have violated the Act through use of illegal advertising phrases such as "young go-getter wanted" or "script *girl*" or "student to train."

5. No labor union can exclude you from membership, or classify you, or refuse to refer you to a job opening because of your age.

6. You cannot be refused a promotion or job assignment because the employer believes "this job needs a younger person." Preference is no defense to injustice.

7. Discrimination *within* the forty to sixty-five age bracket itself is also forbidden. Thus, a forty-three-year-old woman cannot be favored over a fifty-three-year-old if the grounds for the preference is the decade difference in age.

The Age Discrimination in Employment Act is administered by the Wage and Hour Division of the U.S. Department of Labor, Washington, D.C. 20210. When you file your complaint every attempt at conciliation is exhausted before the Secretary of Labor seeks court action. (You can also bring your own civil suit under the Act.) If your complaint is upheld, you may win equitable relief in the form of employment, reinstatement, promotion or back pay. In 1974, $2.5 million was found owed to six hundred people who had been victims of age discrimination in employment. The 1975 figures will reflect the largest ADEA settlement to date. Standard Oil was ordered to pay $2 million to 160 former employees who were fired on the basis of age.

If maturity implies wisdom, it is not too much to ask that mature women be informed about their rights and wise enough to insist upon them. At age forty, you have scores of productive and rewarding years ahead of you. Use them, fill them, and don't let anyone cheat you of them.

To paraphrase Ralph Waldo Emerson, your years should not be counted until you have nothing else to count.

22

The Equal Rights Amendment:
Everywoman's Emancipation
Proclamation

What do the National Welfare Rights Organization, Gerald Ford, the YWCA, the United Auto Workers and the United Church of Christ have in common?

These disparate groups are unanimous on one of the key issues of our generation: support of the Equal Rights Amendment to the Constitution of the United States. But the ERA is not solely the concern of big shots or lobbying groups. It is a resolution that will affect the everyday lives of all Americans—most particularly, the working woman.

The wording of the ERA is almost eloquent in its simplicity: "EQUALITY OF RIGHTS UNDER THE LAW SHALL NOT BE DENIED OR ABRIDGED BY THE UNITED STATES OR BY ANY STATE ON ACCOUNT OF SEX."

This short, declaratory sentence will invalidate all federal, state and local laws that require or allow women and men to be treated differently. Where present law *confers* a benefit or privilege to one sex only, that benefit or privilege will be extended to the other sex as well. Where current law *denies* a benefit or restricts a privilege, that law will be rendered unconstitutional by the ERA.

Here are some aspects of your life which may be affected when the amendment goes into effect:

State protective labor laws

These are the local laws covering the number of hours a woman may work, the number of pounds she may lift on a job and the kinds of work she may perform. As we've stated, these laws don't protect, they *eject* women from occupations which offer more money or advancement, and they give employers a reason to refuse work to a woman. (It's easier to hire a man and not have to worry about complying with special rest periods, weightlifting or nightwork restrictions applicable to female employees.)

Protective labor laws have always varied from state to state. Most of them have already been struck down by challenges filed under Title VII. But it has taken years of expensive court actions to chip away at discriminatory statutes one by one. Those who say that the ERA is not necessary because Title VII provides adequate remedy, are simply naïve about the slow and capricious judicial process.

The Equal Rights Amendment would make *unconstitutional* all limitations and generalizations about women's working capabilities. It would allow a strong, healthy young woman to compete with any man for a job requiring some physical effort. It would open all off-limits occupations from bartending to bowling pinsetters. It would leave the question of job competence up to each individual and the judgment her employer makes of her abilities. It would relieve us of the common denominator labels of "weak," "passive," "fragile," and "delicate." It would not *force* the frail woman to operate a crane, but neither would it *prohibit* robust women from becoming crane operators if they are interested and able.

Those who fear that the ERA will lead to sex integration of rest rooms can relax. The well-established "right of privacy" will keep the men out of our powder room.

Educational equality and free access

"Sure, I'd hire a woman if I could find one who's qualified." This common employer's disclaimer sounds fair, but it ignores the vicious cycle syndrome: Policies which discriminate against women at the level of educational opportunity come home to roost when those women go jobhunting. And if tax-supported schools or government sponsored training programs are perpetuating sexism, then we women are underwriting our own oppressions with our tax dollars.

The Equal Rights Amendment would make it unconstitutional for schools to deny girls technical training provided to boys—such as woodworking, mechanics or metal working. It would prohibit colleges from requiring higher IQ and grade point averages when admitting female students. It would eliminate male favoritism in grants and scholarships; open specialized boys' high schools of science and technology to girls; do away with all sex quotas in colleges, medical schools and state training programs; and assure equal pay to women faculty and staff in all public and state schools and colleges.

(Title IX of the Educational Amendments Act of 1972 is supposed to accomplish the aforementioned miracles, but it too requires countless court tests before it can be a watchdog with teeth.)

The ERA would establish a *national commitment* to fulfill the potential of America's girls and women by training them to become that magic adjective: *qualified*.

Social Security

Both sexes have legitimate beefs in this area. You pay into the Social Security fund all during your work years but when you die your husband receives nothing from your account—unless he has been dependent on you for more than half of the family's income. Meanwhile, any wife, no matter how wealthy, is entitled to collect her husband's accumulated benefits.

At present, only widows can collect a reduced benefit when they are sixty. The ERA would allow widowers to do the same.

Today, a married woman who retires can draw Social Security either as a worker (her own input) or as a wife (her benefits under her husband's earnings contribution). Most often she chooses the wife's rate because men tend to earn 40 per cent more than women and therefore a man's wife's benefits are higher. Male workers do not have the option to draw Social Security as "husbands" in cases where the wife's overall earnings have been greater. The ERA would correct this.

Government employees

Though the amendment would not affect private industry, it would guarantee equality in pay, pension and retirement to workers employed by federal, state and municipal governments.

Married women's rights

Right now, there are states that restrict the property rights of married women (she can't sell property without the consent of her husband) and states where a married woman is not permitted to engage in business as freely as men (she may need court approval to buy a store or business).

Right now, it is considered "desertion" and therefore grounds for divorce if a married woman refuses to follow her husband wherever he chooses to move. If she does not take her husband's domicile (place of residence), she may be denied the right to vote, run for office or take advantage of lower tuitions at state schools.

The ERA would nullify these laws of domicile and would give a married woman the same right to independent domicile as married men. (To understand the importance of this right, refer back to Chapter 7 on the Dual Career Family.)

Men too will benefit from the ERA's sweeping equalization. Husbands will not automatically have to shoulder the burden of support. In this sense, the ERA will bring law up to date with reality. In millions of homes, family income is brought in by both spouses. Though our faint-hearted sisters fear that their husbands will instantly desert them, the fact is that a man who wants to split the home scene can (and does) do so now—without an ERA.

Under the amendment, alimony and child support payments will be determined according to need and ability to pay. The man will not necessarily be billed for the wife's legal fees. The wife will not automatically be granted child custody; instead the welfare of the child will be the primary determinant of who the caretaker parent will be.

Is this really such a radical notion? Can't you think of a few couples in which the father is the best parent of the two?

And on the subject of alimony, the well-provided-for

ex-wife is a cliché and a myth. As things stand now, only 2 per cent of all divorce settlements provide permanent alimony to the wife. More to the point, one year after the divorce decree, only 38 per cent of fathers are still in full compliance with alimony and child care payments! Records show that men are not held criminally liable for fault in payments unless their ex-wives are destitute.

The ERA will not deny maternity benefits to working mothers, nor will it change the criminal offense of rape. Though these two issues affect only women, they are the results of the *reproductive* differences of the two sexes and neither rape nor childbirth can be experienced by the opposite sex in the same way as they are experienced by women. Therefore, here the ERA is irrelevant.

The military question

This is where tempers flare and reason falters. During the Congressional debate on the ERA we heard incredible testimony about how women are incapable of throwing grenades, how women will be bombed and napalmed, how women will give up the home for the barracks, if the ERA forces them into the infantry.

While it's true that with our rights women must assume our responsibilities, scare tactics shouldn't be permitted to muddle the facts.

Remember that we now have an all-volunteer army. In the past, women were also allowed to volunteer and thousands have sought a service career. The ERA would continue this practice while eliminating restrictions on women's role in the armed forces. Even if the draft were restored, women who cannot throw grenades would not be assigned front-line duty—just as weak-armed men are kept in the orderly room. (At the height of the Vietnam war, only 14 per cent of the *men* saw ground combat.) Since Section 456 of the Selective Service Act already allows exemptions and deferments in special circumstances, women would be exempted under those existing classifications when they are not physically suited to an assignment.

A repugnant prejudice is revealed by those who attempt to make an emotional case against the ERA by brandishing visions of bombed and napalmed women. Are these people claiming that dead and wounded young *men* have been any less tragic than dead and wounded young women would be? If we deplore killing and carnage, we should not send *anyone* to war.

Assuming we continue our habit of killing for peace, we must recognize that modern wars depend on technological rather than brute strength. In a sophisticated nuclear war, a muscular man is no better able to defend himself or others than is a petite woman.

Finally, if a woman prefers the barracks to the back yard, she must have the right to make that choice. Minority groups have long valued the armed services for job opportunities, veteran's benefits, inservice training, housing loans, medical care and travel. Under the ERA, women could avail themselves of these same options.

Jury service

It can be a big drag to sit in a courtroom for a week or two. Nevertheless, jury duty has been recognized as one of the crucial obligations of citizenship. Women are citizens and yet they are excused from juries in some states and exempted altogether in other states. For the defendant's sake, a jury of peers should include female peers. The ERA would standardize the requisites for jury selection, without regard to sex.

The significance of the Amendment

Advocates proclaim that the ERA will be as far-reaching in its impact on women as the Fourteenth amendment has been for black men. (Let's not forget that black *women* endure a double stigma. While their status as a race may have been improved, their status as a sex has excluded them from many of the privileges of citizenship now enjoyed by their husbands and brothers. Where civil rights are concerned chivalry vanishes and "ladies last" is the rule.)

Opponents of the ERA claim that women are already covered under the Fifth and Fourteenth amendments by the phrase that says "no state shall deprive any person of life, liberty or property without due process of law; nor deny any person within its jurisdiction, the equal protection of the law."

The word "person" should, of course, include the female, but it has not been construed as such by the Supreme Court—the final authority on questions of constitutional interpretation. The Court has rarely considered sex discrimination cases and its rulings have been so narrowly confined to the facts of the particular cases that the classification of people on the basis of sex has never been declared unconstitutional.

In fact, in 1962, the Court refused to hear a case in which women were refused admission to a Texas state college. So although the Fourteenth amendment does exist, it has not yet included female persons in its definition of those who are guaranteed "life, liberty or property" and "due process of law."

If, as a woman, you've ever felt excluded by the phrase "all men are created equal" then the Equal Rights Amendment is your emancipation proclamation. It will close all the loopholes. It will be an emblem of America's commitment to a non-racist *and* non-sexist rule of law. It will be an act of national conscience and an end to second-class citizenship for any woman or man.

After forty-nine years of trying, proponents of the ERA celebrated its passage by the Senate on March 22, 1972. (The House had approved the measure five months before.) But before the ERA becomes the Twenty-seventh amendment to our constitution, it must be ratified by three-quarters (38) of the state legislatures. At this writing, thirty-three states have approved the amendment—and not without vituperative battles. Five more states must ratify by 1979 in order for the amendment to go into effect. We are watching the remaining state legislatures with passion and with hope.

Perhaps, by the time you read these words, American women will have won their freedom.

SECTION
IV

Getting Yours Your Own Way

Taking control of your life may be a life-long occupation. Changing yourself and institutions is an organic, never-ending process. It would be foolhardy for anyone to promise you truth or transcendence.

23

Re-entry: The Change
of Life *You* Can Control
(without hormones or hot flashes)

You're a widow beginning a new life at an age when many women feel life is over. Or else, you're a married woman—a mother who is trying her own wings before her children leave her with an empty nest. Or perhaps you're separated or divorced and you couldn't be a dependent wife if you wanted to. In any of these cases—whether by choice, chance or necessity—you are forging a new independence for yourself in the world outside the home.

There are thousands of women just like you who are re-entering the work force after five, ten or twenty years of full-time family life. Re-entry women can't easily be compared with young graduates or life-long careerists because they experience a whole range of extra problems, pressures and challenges.

That's why talking with re-entry women about resumés or job interviews is only skimming the surface. Beyond the details of the job hunt is a psychological purgatory that lies between the Hell of indecision and inertia and the Heaven of commitment and personal progress. At its most painful, this purgatory can be literally paralyzing.

I'm thinking of the friend who started trembling, stammering and suffering dizzy spells when she tried to set up interviews with employment agencies. She had been a wife, mother and community volunteer for about twelve years. Now her three children were eleven, eight and seven years of age and she knew there was nothing preventing her from going back to work. Her husband was supportive and encouraging. She had many good leads—

people who offered to refer her to promising job openings. She had created an impressive resumé that emphasized her skills and translated her volunteer efforts into marketable business experience. She was ready to move.

Then, without warning or discernible cause, anxiety took possession of her body with the force of a demon. Her symptoms could neither be ignored nor overcome. She became an insomniac. She couldn't eat; couldn't even prepare a cup of coffee. Her hands shook so violently that she was unable to hold anything. A doctor finally prescribed tranquilizers and escalated her dosage to twelve pills a day. She knew she was afraid and she knew it was a fear totally associated with returning to work, but she wasn't able to locate its source and exorcise it.

When I last spoke with her, my friend had stopped taking the pills because she believed they contributed to her anxiety. But she also stopped thinking about getting a job. Her determination was simply that she wasn't ready; that she had too many family and household details on her mind. She decided to put off her re-entry for maybe a year. Like Scarlett O'Hara in *Gone with the Wind,* she would think about the problem tomorrow.

Without psychological analysis it would be impossible to reliably trace the roots of this woman's paralysis. To me, it seemed she was afraid to give up the easy challenges of cooking a tasty meal, or making all the phone calls on a charity list, or taking estimates from housepainters. The potentially greater challenges that might lie "out there" were just too threatening. She was, in my view, fearful of spoiling her image as the all-capable housewife and mother by becoming a possibly fallible, vulnerable wage earner who would be evaluated by more objective observers than a husband and children. She seemed too terrified of failure to even give work a try.

I am not equipped to probe into other people's dense psychic jungles. But I *have* discovered that there is much to be learned from women's *own* assessment of their re-entry experience. What is fascinating is their hindsight on the years they spent at home. Or why they suddenly went back to work. Or what feelings accompanied this drastic change in their lives. The women who pulled it off without paralysis may save others an unnecessary anxiety attack.

*

Mary Y., one of sixteen children, had to quit college after one year to earn money for family expenses. In 1953, she married and took a clerk-typist job, but when her husband got out of the service he announced that he wanted her to stop working and stay home. "I never questioned; I just quit my job," Mary remembers. "I was deeply in love and I wanted only to please him." She was twenty-two-years old.

For the next eighteen years, she devoted herself to her home, her two children and her husband. She followed wherever his job opportunities led, finally settling in California. In April 1973, the couple celebrated their twentieth wedding anniversary and Mary thought they were exceptionally happy and remarkably fortunate people.

Then in August of 1973, the bombshell dropped. Mary's husband came home one night and told her he was leaving her.

"I thought: 'He's forty. He's going through changes; he needs to be alone.' But we were so close, I was sure he couldn't mean it."

He meant it. In October he moved out of the house. Mary fell into a profound depression. One of the children took the break-up very hard and required psychological help. There was no money.

"At first it seemed nobody was interested in someone who's forty and hasn't worked in more than eighteen years. Then I took the clerk-typist test at Lockheed and got a job for $4.30 an hour. I was beginning to feel I might make a go of it when I got laid off. I just don't know how the kids and I got through Thanksgiving and Christmas. By January, I was desperate. I simply couldn't find work. Finally, I had to apply for welfare."

With the assistance of the Urban League, Mary eventually got into a training program at Tenneco Company where she is now employed as an accounting clerk—with excellent ratings. She plans to return to college to earn a bachelor's degree in sociology.

"For twenty years I thought only about pleasing my husband; in return he handled everything for me. Now I have to do everything for myself *and* the children and I find I can make decisions and pay the rent on time. Next I must create a Mary; I had a husband and kids but I never had a Mary in all those years."

*

Barbara S. was a working child. From age eight to eighteen, she was a professional child model and actress. But show business was her mother's passion; Barbara wanted to become a teacher ... and a wife.

She married in 1953, graduated from college in '55 and proceded to have two children in three years. From 1956 to 1965 her entire job was homemaking. "It's amazing that someone with my strong work orientation could accept the social pressure to stay home," she comments. "I expect to live a long life. I don't mind having given nine years of it to childrearing, but there was never quite enough to do. I was isolated in an arid suburb—reading, cleaning and counting the hours. If my husband was one train late I went buggy."

In 1965 a friend accused Barbara of being "an underachiever." This spurred her to look in the newspaper and blindly take the first teaching job that advertised morning work hours. For the next eight years she held various part-time teaching positions while working toward a Masters in Education. Her one requirement for any job was that she must be home when her children came home for lunch.

"Even though I had free time, I was so conditioned to be a super-mother and super-housekeeper that I never realized I could have worked on a master's *and* doctorate without hurting anyone."

When the children were seventeen and fourteen Barbara accepted her first full-time assignment. Since July 1973 she has been an Educational Consultant and Director of a curriculum project.

Pat S., 59, remembers the Depression well. In 1933 she married a machinist whom she describes as "an incredibly demanding man who insisted that no wife of his would go to work." Despite the family's tight finances, Pat could only persuade her husband to "let" her work (as a babysitter, cashier and Avon representative) for a few scattered periods during the first fifteen years of their thirty-five-year marriage. But from 1948 to 1968, her husband insisted that she stay home caring for their two children, getting his meals on time and tending to the collection of 250 parakeets he kept in their basement.

"I gave in because I thought of myself as uneducated, inferior and worthless," Pat explains. "I resented feeding and cleaning cages for his damned birds and I regret all those crazy lost years, but I never had the guts to leave him. Instead, I took up tennis and volleyball. Sports were my outlet."

After her husband's death in 1968, Pat took a sales job, sold the parakeets, cleaned the basement and converted it into a picture frame shop. Discovering that she had a real talent for framing, she followed a friend's recommendation and got an interview at one of New York's most prestigious framing companies. She was hired in 1970.

"Except for my children, the years of my marriage are a complete blur," Pat admits. "I feel and look better now than I did in 1945. I've got confidence, new friends, new men, a great job that pays me $10,000 and an apartment overlooking the river. In the past year I took a vacation trip down the Colorado rapids and a cross-country business trip. I'm living at last."

Mary Lou W., 36, got married in 1961, a year after her college graduation. At first she kept her full-time job in a publishing firm. When her children were born she quit the job and only took on free-lance editorial assignments calling for about two hours' work each week.

"It was my way of staying awake without having to really prove myself," she says. Like many homemakers, she found volunteer work challenging, particularly when she published a newspaper to publicize local school problems—and learned everything about journalistic writing, printing, advertising and layouts.

The rest of the story can only be told in Mary Lou's own words: "One day I discovered after a doctor's visit that my son was slowly deteriorating from muscular dystrophy. For four years I was the ultimate mother-martyr. I used to have a recurrent dream that I staggered and fell down like my son did. I was getting lost in my child. I was atrophying too, to show how much I loved him. From that dream I realized I was in peril. My husband and I saw how precious and important life is, not only for our son, but for all of us."

Mary Lou joined the staff of a Connecticut regional newspaper and for two years she has earned both money and praise for her writing—a direct result of experience gained in her volunteer newspaper project. She has also begun to contribute articles to national magazines. Most of her $125 weekly wage goes to pay a young man who helps cook, clean and care for the child in a wheel chair, but Mary Lou has no complaint. She and her husband believe their family is healthier now that each of them is focused not on disease but on living productively.

Susan G. is another re-entry woman whose volunteer work carried weight in the job market. She was married in 1959 and divorced in 1974. She has two daughters, ages eleven and seven. During ten years of her married life, though she didn't hold a paying job, Susan was very involved in community work, serving as editor of a local magazine in Seattle, board member of the League of Women Voters, and chairperson of the Seattle Head Start Volunteers.

In 1968 she returned to college with the intention of becoming a librarian because "it's a flexible career for a wife and mother." When the marriage broke up Susan realized that she had chosen a profession for others, not for herself. Her real love was, and had always been, shipping. She was a boat freak, a devotee of dockside activity, and she had never dared follow that passion because it was an "unseemly" vocation for a wife and mother.

By a fluke, she was at a party where she heard of *the* perfect job opening. She had spoken openly of her love of shipping and she had thereby attracted opportunity like a magnet. Susan G. is now Director of Community Affairs for a large city port authority—and she couldn't be happier.

"I've noticed two big changes in my life since I went from volunteer work into this paid job. People respect my opinions as they never did before; and I worry less about money now, even though I have less of it than when my husband doled it out. The point is that I'm a responsible, worthwhile adult for the first time."

Jean C., a high school graduate, worked as a secretary, married in 1955 and a year later quit her job to have her first child. For eleven years she thoroughly enjoyed homemaking and caring for her three sons.

In 1967 when her mother-in-law came for a long visit, it occurred to Jean to get a sales job at a department store just to earn some Christmas money. With Grandma as a babysitter, Jean could relax and concentrate on three days of sales training. But after eleven years as "just a house-wife," she was extremely nervous about her first day on the selling floor. "I thought I'd never get the hang of that huge register, yet in a few days it became automatic to me."

After the holidays Jean tendered her quitting notice. But management was so impressed with her work that they asked her to remain on the job on her own terms. She arranged a part-time schedule that was successful for six years, until a new store manager came in and objected to it.

Jean left the department store and was promptly hired by a small dress shop that was happy to have her on part-time terms. She now has a devoted clientele who especially seek her sales help and fashion advice. A Christmas job has thus become a profession. "I started working for the money," Jean says. "But I'd have to admit that if we won a $100,000 lottery, I'd still work. It makes me feel like I'm a Mommy, a wife and a person too."

Amy S., 52, believed that her children were to be her only product. She had four of them in neat girl-boy sequence after her marriage in 1949. She remembers: "If my kids ever looked unhappy I was ready to hit them because it meant I had failed."

Amy's interest in enriching her children's lives led her to become active in a local arts center. "From 1953 to '61 I was on this seesaw: gracious housewife and great mother on one side; cultural leader in the community on the other. Fine. Except I had to spend years with a psychiatrist to find out why I wasn't content."

She decided to do graduate work in history. At school one day in 1961, she attended a campus meeting protesting fall-out shelters. "One consistent commitment of mine has been an abhorrence of war," she remarks. "So at this meeting I found myself speaking out, and when the meeting was followed up by a demonstration at the United Nations I ended up being interviewed on the TV news. I became a founder of Women Strike for Peace (we had 150 women at the first meeting and 5,000 at the second); I went to Geneva to plead for disarmament; I called press conferences; got Congresspeople to take a stand on the issue; got the press to ask President Kennedy questions about nuclear testing at his press conferences. Through the sixties I went on peace missions to Hanoi, to Paris, to Cuba.

"This certainly marked the end of my feelings of powerlessness. But I was schizoid. I came home from Paris or Vietnam and I did all the shopping and cooking and never let my husband lift a finger. I used my family as an excuse to stay domesticated and stop myself from professionalizing. As a volunteer, I never had to put myself on the line."

In 1970, Amy became deeply involved in the Women's Movement. Two years later she enrolled in a master's program and the following fall she became associate director of the Women's Studies Program at her college as well as serving as a lecturer. Not surprisingly the course she teaches is "How to Organize Movements for Social Reform." Her salary is $11,000. In this dovetailing of the interests, skills and ideological commitments of twenty years, Amy is still in the business of social change—but the biggest change has been in herself.

"The re-entry crisis" is a demonstrable phenomenon among many American women in their middle years. But it needn't be the negative, traumatic ordeal that some women fear. Webster's Dictionary has an accurate and heartening definition of the word "crisis:"

"The decisive moment; the turning point . . ."

You have every right to seize *your* decisive moment and make re-entry into the turning point that changes your life for the better.

24

Answering for Your Values

We've traveled from the demise of the Queen Bee and the passive drudge, to the birth of a new kind of woman. She doesn't embody a single ideal or espouse a single solution. She is extrapolating from her specific pain; she knows that her problems are not the cause of society's afflictions, but the symptoms. She is experimenting with life in the laboratory of the self.

You are that new kind of woman. As you survey the terrain of your personal and your work lives, you are deciding which areas you will sow and cultivate and which you will let lie fallow. You are learning how to grow yourself in any climate and in all seasons.

After the household is reorganized, the job counselling courses are over, the promotion is won, the work schedule is revised, the law suits are filed—after all this is underway and you are flourishing, there is still the question of values. For you are what you care about, not what you do.

So, where are you now and where are your values taking you? Are you working for something greater than a paycheck? Do you want to be a success; or is success an outdated ideal? Can women change the meaning of success by the ways they seek and use it?

I've often felt that success is just a dream from which we awaken in order to continue living and working in the real world. Unable to confront my own vague and somewhat troubled feelings about success, I started asking questions of a great variety of women. From them I discovered that success is neither a fact of life nor a state of mind—it is a combination of the two, or else it doesn't exist at all.

For many women the whole concept of success is off-base. They challenge the finality of it; they prefer to talk about growth.

Some call success a "male invention"—a product of the "must-win" mentality that men are taught from boyhood.

Others say that in a sexist society, women can only achieve second-rate success. ("It's a terrific victory, for a woman.")

I found a number of women who want to succeed at *something*—an assignment, a personal relationship, a difficult job. But no matter how famous, prosperous or accomplished the women might appear to an observer, surprisingly few call themselves "a success."

What does success mean to you?

Bounce your own values off the springboard of these remarkably incisive comments taken from my interviews:

"Success is whatever you don't have. It's the brilliant article I haven't yet written."—*Freelance writer*

"It's accomplishing something according to my own standards. When I perform to someone else's expectation, I'm not a success, I'm just a grown-up teacher's pet."—*Administrator*

"I feel successful in my commercial art when I'm paid well. But as a painter, money can't convince me I'm good if my own eyes tell me different."—*Artist*

"Ambitious people can never feel successful; we're always focused on the next hurdle. I can't even retain the memory of my past successes. Maybe I don't believe them."—*Lawyer*

"Anticipating success is more fun than getting it. I really looked forward to my promotion, but now that I have it, I don't feel it."—*Postal worker*

"Success is different things at different ages. It's getting A's in school, getting into the 'right' college; getting married to the best guy around. Only lately has success changed from 'getting' something to 'being' somebody yourself."—*Journalist*

"When I feel in charge of my own life—while still being able to ask for help—then I'll be a success."—*Actress*

"You can't be a success unless you know you've earned it. You can fake your way to the top. But you can never fool yourself that you belong there if you don't."—*Confidential secretary*

"It depends on how you define failure. When I'm not frightened of failure, then I'm successful."—*Film-maker*

"There's no such thing as success. There are only breakthroughs that lead to other breakthroughs. If you're lucky, it never stops happening."—*Sound technician*

"To be a decision-making person in a meaningful job; to be surrounded by people I can learn from; to take risks and grow from them; to feel myself changing for the better."—*Editor*

As measures of success, how do you rate fame, status and money?

It comes as no surprise that being rich, famous and powerful is no guarantee that you'll feel successful. Women who want or already have these trappings are quick to establish the conditions under which they can be enjoyed. Those who devalue wealth and celebrity do so philosophically or out of bitter experience.

Tony Award-winning actress Rae Allen says: "Fame is like an addictive drug—the craving for it distorts and overshadows all other goals. I'd rather have power behind the scenes and do what I believe in."

Liz Carpenter, public relations executive and former press secretary to Lady Bird Johnson, believes those in the spotlight should cast their light on important issues. "Fame is a precious gift," she says. "Because fate once cast me into the White House I now have a name that draws crowds and allows me to reach people on matters I care about, like the Equal Rights Amendment.

"But most of the successful women I know aren't famous. They're just exuberant people who are stretching themselves to the limit."

Meteoric success hasn't changed the self-image of Marcia Seligson, author of the bestseller, "The Eternal Bliss Machine." But Ms. Seligson admits that when her paperback rights were sold for $350,000, she found herself being secretive about her money: "I saw my financial success as a threat to the men in my life. I ignore my money; it's unreal."

Folksinger Mary Travers compares her present success as a solo performer, to her ten years as part of the singing group Peter, Paul and Mary.

"My partners' male chauvinism created terrible friction. I was their equal in the group, yet they expected me to be the 'dependent wife' off-stage. When we split the group, it was a marriage break-up. After all those years of thinking 'we' I had to develop the concept of 'I.' Now I've grown up and I think I'm as much in charge of my own life as any woman with four children can ever be."

Speaking of the effect of her success on her husband (Gerald Taylor, publisher of the magazine National Lampoon), Ms. Travers says: "He loves me, loves my talent and thinks I'm beautiful. But it wasn't always roses. The money part was tough. When we married in 1969, he was making $30,000 and I did $250,000. He had to face the fact that he might never top my income. Big deal.

"But that wasn't as hard for him as tolerating being called Mr. Travers. For the first two years he winced. Now he laughs it off as one of the givens when you have a famous wife."

Congresswoman Bella S. Abzug feels she was always successful—as a student, lawyer and political activist. However, since entering the Congress she finds her recent fame useful to popularize such vital issues as peace, women's rights and expanded democracy. "Success is when you're personally satisfied with what you've accomplished," says the Congresswoman. "Fame is when others see you as successful for reasons that may or may not meet your standards. It becomes a problem when people see you only as a *celebrity*."

Muriel Siebert, the first woman ever elected to the New York Stock Exchange, bought her seat in 1967 for $445,-000. "My sudden fame and visibility brought with it great obligations," says Ms. Siebert. "Not only did I have to prove to my colleagues that I had bought the seat for business reasons, I also had to be a fitting model to all those young women who said, 'You're my ideal; you've inspired me.'"

Eleanor Guggenheimer, Commissioner of Consumer Affairs for New York City, introduces the element of chronology into her view of success. "When you're sixty-two you don't take your triumphs for granted; you work much harder for everything you get. A lot of my friends complain about getting older but I'm just hitting my stride."

Dorothy Haener of the United Auto Workers' Women's Caucus, started out working in a bomber plant during World War II. Now, after twenty years with the UAW she became a candidate for vice president of the union. "That election was the zenith for me," she says. "Blue collar women like myself have limited opportunities for success on the job. Our only chance to excel is in the union movement or at home."

Eleanor Perry, screenwriter (*David and Lisa; Diary of a Mad Housewife*) isn't recognized on the street, though her name cuts through red tape at airports and restaurants. "It makes life easier, but that's not what success is about," she says. "When I've written a movie, I can hear my words on the screen and watch the audience. They're laughing, they're crying—I have evidence that I've moved them. That's the real love trip."

Gloria Steinem, the well-known feminist writer and activist, says: "When you're famous, people react to you without content. They want your autograph because you're just a name, not a person. On the positive side, if fame gives you visibility, credibility and access to the press, then you can use your clout for good causes. But this public power comes with personal impotence: people can hurt you and you can't fight back. You're closely watched because you're expected to stand for something.

"Fame loses friends, too. Both women and men can be hostile for no reason, or overly friendly for the wrong reason. The nice people stay at a distance. They're worried about imposing on your time, or else they don't want the burden of sharing a famous person's scrutinized life. Often you find yourself left with the opportunists.

"As for money, it's important to have enough so that you don't have to think about it. Then you're free to pursue satisfaction."

Despite her fame, effectiveness and income, Ms. Steinem perceives herself as incomplete: "When people call me a success, I feel falsely accused. I might feel successful if I could write one book that mattered."

In their own smaller spheres, women without national prominence also contend with the effects of fame and money. Professional jealousy can sour intimacy among colleagues. And fame, in small towns especially, carries added responsibilities. It is the town celebrity who is badgered to endorse political candidates, host fund-raising events, make large donations (everyone assumes that famous people are also rich); speak at luncheons, counsel young people. Many highly motivated women report that fame can actually sap your energy and make further success impossible.

Or it can make women feel guilty.

"To my old school friends I'm the glamorous superachiever," says a much-honored newspaperwoman. "Their awe for my accomplishments becomes an excuse for them to diminish themselves by comparison. They get masochistic; then I get defensive and go into my false humility act to assure them that I'm no better than they. It makes it hard to savor whatever success I have."

Celebrity is not at issue for a merchandise manager. "Accepting prosperity is my problem," she says. "I was raised to think poor equals virtuous, yet in business, recognition equals money. I have yet to feel worthy of what I'm being paid."

Few of us have to struggle with either too much money or too much fame. But every woman travels an orbit that carries her from the personal to the professional sphere every day of her life. It isn't necessarily a smooth trip.

Can you feel successful with an unhappy private life?

It seems the consensus is a qualified "no." Woman after woman told me that blissful success is the total integration of professional *and* personal satisfaction—and I would agree.

While several women claimed they can forget their troubles in their diverting careers, most argued that a disturbed homelife or love relationship blights career achievement.

A theatrical director remembers, "My show got rave reviews but opening night was a disaster for me because a long love affair had ended that afternoon."

"My personal life is my secret career," says an investment analyst. "I don't get a raise when my marriage is going well but without excellence in that area, I can't experience excellence professionally."

"I felt fantastically successful when I was nine months pregnant and I presented my research paper to the academy," admits a biochemist. "That day the best of me was rolled into one."

A staff writer quit her magazine job and got divorced in the same year. "I felt scared to be without the institutional identity for my work. And without my identity as a wife, I felt like a complete loser. Recent success with freelance writing has relieved the first anxiety, but not the second."

"I've made it in business. People listen to my opinions. I have a staff of twelve, a $28,000 salary and a great reputation in my field," says a public relations woman. "I wouldn't give up *any* of it for a man. But I also won't feel like a success until I find someone to whom I can say 'I love you'—and mean it."

Is success different for women than men?

This time the answer is an unqualified "yes." Ulcers, heart attacks and mid-life depression, as we've seen, are the more familiar components of the success syndrome for men. (Feminism, with its plea for equal distribution of roles, might liberate men from their present destiny of dying years ahead of women.)

Then too, men seem to separate career from private life much more than do women. A mediocre businessman doesn't call himself a success just because he's a great husband and father. By the same token, neither broken marriage, expectant fatherhood nor a scandalous affair puts the curse on the career of an up-and-coming male dynamo.

Since men are expected to be striving, ambitious creatures, they rarely have to explain themselves if their marriages fail, while the divorced professional woman is thought to have sacrificed her husband and children to her "unnatural" craving for success.

Thanks to studies done by Dr. Matina Horner (now president of Radcliffe College), we can understand the conflicts women have felt about their own achievement. Because our culture says that competition, independence, competence and success are male goals, "inconsistent with femininity," Dr. Horner found that women develop a "motive to avoid success."

Women fear "social rejection and/or feelings of being unfeminine as a result of succeeding." Rather than be thought "aggressive," many disguise their abilities and drop out of the race. Depending upon the age groups studied, Dr. Horner found that from 47 to 88 per cent of girls and women actually *fear* success.

One hopes that this fear is fading. For those who still fall victim to femininity tremors, I offer a piece of advice that has worked for several in my women's group: spend more time with other strong, confident women. As the support from women increases, the need for male approval decreases. Rather than take refuge in familiar "feminine" wiles (to gain popularity with men at the expense of your self-worth), you may find yourself pressing on with the work you love. Even if it leads to great success.

Will success spoil a love relationship? If it does, the man probably didn't deserve you in the first place. A vibrant, accomplished woman is a complement to a man, not a threat.

If you have unconsciously "promised" not to be successful, it may have less to do with your self-doubts or your expressed disinterest in worldly reward, and more to do with your having adopted someone else's values instead of your own.

Sociologist Cynthia Fuchs Epstein writes that women are assigned "supporting roles in the human drama. They are almost never heroes ... [but] women who *have* had any success find that in fact, it is more pleasant than failing."

Wherever you are, whatever your job, however you define success for yourself—perhaps you can agree that we must together create the first generation of women heroes.

With the help of other women I have finally come to understand my own definition of success: Love. Work. Knowledge. And not having to choose between them.

Author's Note

As often happens in a letter to a friend, we save the short, punchy details of life for the post script—a place for afterthoughts, reminders, up-to-the-minute news.

The following pages constitute the P.S. to this book, or rather a triple P.S.

First, there is a brief sampling of diverse career situations. Second, a "Where to Get Help" section. And, finally, one man's view of life with a working wife.

Dip into the P.S. wherever you find it interesting, relevant or helpful. For those who need no more encouragement, I'll sign off here. Warmest wishes for your own kind of personal success and best of luck getting yours. You deserve!

Sincerely, in sisterhood

Letty Cottin Pogrebin

Letty Cottin Pogrebin

SECTION
V

Post Script
Career Sampler:
"Oh, but my situation is special."
"That's what *you* think."

Each one of us is different, and special. As working women, we have problems that are different, and special. Yet the more we learn about one another, the more awesome becomes our commonality. Before we are anything else in this world, first we are all women.

Union Women Unite!
You have nothing to lose but your powerlessness

Today, labor is big business. Nearly nineteen million union members (20 per cent women) pay dues and rally behind elected leaders who bargain on their behalf for pay raises, better health and life insurance, pensions and fair treatment on the job.

How well do unions represent today's Union Maid?

Most women who are union members acknowledge the great advantages of collective action. But many women have found that a double standard exists in the labor movement itself. Too often, when the brothers fear competition from the sisters, the union family doesn't count for beans—on the job or in the union hierarchy.

Wages

According to a Bureau of Census study, union women earn a median of $1,540 more per year than their non-union sisters, but the earnings of union men are still disproportionately higher than those of women.

The National Labor Relations Act decrees that unions must bargain for and fairly represent *all* workers covered by the union agreement, whether or not those workers are union members, black or white, male or female. In addition, Title VII of the Civil Rights Act prohibits sex discrimination by unions as well as by employers. Nevertheless, there are times when a union may seem more an enemy than an advocate—particularly toward women.

In 1971, a U.S. District Court judge found that Local 604 of the Amalgamated Clothing Workers "blatantly bargained away the salary rights" of twenty-one women employees at Sagner, Inc., a men's clothing plant in Maryland. Five years before, the union had accused the company of violating the Equal Pay Act by underpaying its female workers. When Sagner agreed to pay the women nearly $30,000 in back wages, the union suddenly stopped representing its women members and started sucking up to its men. The Union instructed Sagner to pay the women only $7,500 and to distribute the rest of the money among the hundred male workers as an *ego payoff* "in order to keep peace within the union."

As a result of sabotage like that, women have learned to keep a sharp eye on their own unions whenever wages are at issue.

Seniority

Basic to job security is seniority rights, or credit for time worked. The Equal Employment Opportunity Commission (EEOC) has found that a union is in violation of Title VII if it is party to a collective bargaining agreement that contains a discriminatory seniority system. That means you may not be placed on a segregated women-only seniority list. It also means you must not be laid off ahead of a male with less experience and such a male may not be recalled to work before you.

Seniority is money in the bank. Don't let your employer or your union steal it from you.

Job classification

With rare exceptions, the EEOC has found that the concept of "male" jobs and "female" jobs violates Title VII and tends to discriminate against women. Watch for job descriptions using the phrases "light" and "heavy" work—common euphemisms for "women's" or "men's" jobs. Companies have tried to establish these separate classifications in order to pay women lightly for "light" work. Labor unions are violating Title VII if they fail to *challenge* any company that practices such restriction of women to one class of jobs.

Women in the union hierarchy

According to 1972 statistics, not one major union had a woman president. Though women comprise twenty per cent of all unions, only 4.6 per cent of all union officer-holders were women. There were no women on the executive council of the AFL-CIO or of the Teamsters Union. The United Auto Workers have one vice-presidency slot that is reserved for a woman—out of a twenty-six member executive board—though the UAW has 200,000 women members. Of those unions with large female contingents, the American Federation of Teachers had six women v.p.'s out of twenty; the ILGWU had only one woman vice president and the Communications Workers of America and the Bakery Workers had no female officers whatsoever. At the local level, the situation is somewhat better, though women rarely exceed ten per cent of the local leadership.

Women's issues

If the union leadership weren't predominantly male, unions might better represent the interests of women workers. Men do not easily support, empathize or strike in sympathy with issues like child care or maternity benefits. If we are to win these important gains, more women must take an active role in union politics and stop electing men to do their bargaining for them. Check your union's stand on three crucial areas which should be top priorities.

1. *Child care.* Did your union lobby for the child care bill that Richard Nixon vetoed? Are they trying to get this legislation out of committee for a Congressional vote in this session? Do they have the facilities to provide a child care center at union headquarters? Could they cooperate with your company to start a center? Are they bargaining for employer contribution to child care expenses?

2. *Maternity policies.* Does your contract include paid disability for delivery? Reinstatement to the same or similar work after childbirth? Good health insurance coverage for delivery and possible complications? A few unions are trail-blazers.

The Newspaper Guild favors unlimited benefit payments in maternity health plans and demands paternity leave so that fathers can share in the birth and care of the baby.

The teachers' unions have led the fight against forced maternity leaves, an issue that was finally resolved in favor of women by the United States Supreme Court. The ILGWU insures that their members qualify for full pension if they've worked twenty years out of the past twenty-five—a provision that allows women some leeway for childrearing absences, without penalizing their security upon retirement.

3. *The Equal Rights Amendment.* After some resistance and much debate, most unions are now committed to the addition of this amendment to the United States Constitution.

When full ratification is achieved, the ERA would nullify those state protective labor laws which Title VII has not entirely cleared off the books.

What's happening now

Trade union women have organized to fight for equal job opportunities, greater leadership roles for women unionists, fair maternity policies, ratification of the ERA and quality child care. Union W.A.G.E. in California and the Coalition of Labor Union Women (CLUW) are most notable activists. (See Reference Section.)

White collar organizing is a major union growth area. By far the most active in this field is the Office and Professional Employees Union (OPEU). In 1972 OPEU began a vigorous campaign to unionize one million bank employees, most of them women. Perhaps your office should be next. For step-by-step details on becoming unionized, contact Arthur P. Lewandowski, Director of Organization, OPEU, 265 West 14 Street, New York, N.Y. 10011. Mr. Lewandowski warns it is prohibitively expensive for a union to send a representative to organize a one or two-woman office. However, if you're part of a group of fifteen or more, and if about 80 per cent of your group clearly favors union representation, and if your group comprises an "appropriate bargaining unit" (which means that none of you are supervisors or management personnel and none of the secretaries are responsible to executives handling labor negotiations for the company), then the union will send someone to get you moving.

A representative from the nearest local or a business agent or international representative will come to inform your group of the laws and procedures, and later to provide experienced help when you bargain your first contract.

If your group is too small to justify the organizing efforts of an existing union, you may still form a bargaining unit and constitute yourselves a union. For information about how to achieve union certification, contact the nearest office of the National Labor Relations Board.

A few years ago, legal workers including secretaries, receptionists and clerks who work in law firms in New York City contacted District 65 to represent them in bargaining a contract with their lawyer bosses. Their final contract gave the workers sixteen paid holidays, up to five weeks' vacation, "adequate" maternity leave and a grievance procedure to handle "sexist slurs" suffered on the job. The union's newsletter, which covers problems shared by white collar workers in various industries, may be ordered from Legal Workers Guild, District 65, 13 Astor Place, New York, N.Y.

A union that is devoted to upgrading women deserves to have you as a member. But any union whose overall good intentions can be sacrificed to the self-interest of its male leadership, is not giving you your money's worth, no matter what you pay in union dues.

Carry On, Nurse!
(Women in White: Part I)

The nursing shortage is acute. In 1970 there were 700,000 Registered Nurses in this country. *Occupational Outlook Quarterly* projects a need for at least a million nurses by 1980.

While graduates can decide to work in public health, doctors' offices, schools, industry, nursing education or private homes, two-thirds of all R.N.'s go into hospital nursing.

The profession offers great choice and flexibility: a

two-year (associate degree), three-year (diploma) or four-year (baccalaureate) course will make a woman a nurse for the rest of her life. She can be a clinician, consultant, educator or administrator—and she can practice anywhere in the world.

Many nurses see bedside nursing as a true specialty. They're disturbed that the housekeeping, record-keeping and other scutwork keeps them from their primary role as the patient's friend, confidante and helpmate.

Nurses are hamstrung by a professional ethic that forbids them to divulge to the patient any serious medical facts about her or his case. According to the code, the nurse must tell the patient to discuss all such questions with the doctor. At the same time, the nurse is aware that most doctors avoid emotional confrontations with their patients at all costs. Cool medical detachment is their protective mask.

So the patient has nowhere to turn. And the nurse—particularly if she has a patient with a terminal illness or incurable crippling—is forced to evade questions and falsify her relationship with the patient. Compulsory pretense on the part of the nurse cheats the patient of honest communication at a critical time. And it cheats the nurse of another one of her *nursing* functions. As a coronary care nurse puts it: "The patients should be able to trust us and to know that we understand their cases and care about them."

Fright and pain are frequent components of hospitalization. Less recognized is the fact that human beings feel terribly vulnerable when confined to a sickbed. Wearing a hospital smock, submitting to sponge baths or intravenous feeding make adult patients feel defenseless and childlike.

A staff nurse has a sensible intepretation of the petty sexual attacks she endures from some male patients: "I suppose I could feel like a sex object, but I try to understand what sick-bed flirting represents. The guy is usually terrified that he won't be sexually healthy because of his illness. He's trying to prove his manhood by talking sexy or grabbing for me. I can handle it."

A nurse in the women's wing shows warm insight when she says: "I take a lot of abuse from my patients because I know they have to act bossy to make up for how helpless they feel."

Mothering is the key word used by all the dedicated professional women I interviewed. But the system doesn't program mothering into the medical process. There's no time for it, and not enough nurses to go around.

Crazy schedules covering nights, days and weekends in arduous eight-hour shifts take their toll. Unless nurses work a part-time schedule, their family lives or social lives take a back seat to the demands of their work. When they do get home, they're often too tired to enjoy a private life. The hospital census is so high in most places that four nurses may have to care for forty-five sick children!

For such labors, a major city hospital pays about $10,000 to a staff nurse and up to $16,000 to an administrative supervisor. Though nurses' salaries have nearly doubled in fifteen years, it seems clear that for their training, hard work and heavy responsibilities, they are still vastly underpaid. Moreover, the R.N.'s don't feel they are getting to use their training in a way that justifies the years invested in it.

Dr. Judith Lorber, Professor of Sociology at New York's Fordham University, suggests that the movement to professionalize nurses is partly to blame. "College graduated nurses acquire skills, like pharmacology or psychiatry, which prepare them to be more than mothers to patients," she explains. "They're ready to be Assistant Doctors."

This trend has its positive aspects, of course. It has resulted in such innovations as the development of Pediatric Nurse Associates, who are trained to examine and care for "well babies" in a program jointly endorsed by the American Medical Association and the American Nurses Association. Professionalization has also allowed nurses to become anesthetists, coronary care specialists or Nurse-Midwives. (Delivering babies was women's province until recent times. Now, doctors have begun to return the specialty to women and have given the AMA stamp of approval to midwifery.)

Professionalization has established a career ladder with specialized status levels beyond the usual progression to head nurse, supervisor and director. These are excellent options for the motivated nurse-scientist, but an implicit put-down of the nurse who wants to stay on the ward. As women rise in the professional ranks, the bedside becomes more remote and the classical nursing functions suffer.

It's not farfetched to say that sexist attitudes have made bedside duty low in prestige. After all, care of the sick is what mothers and wives have always done. It's women's work and we all know the value put on *that*.

Sexism may also be at the root of the common assumption that nurses are just frustrated doctors. Though it is true that women's quotas in medical schools and discouragement from counselors may have diverted some women from a medical career, the assumption that nursing *must* have been a second choice for the bright and gifted woman reveals a deeper value judgment. Are we holding that medicine, because mostly men do it, is first rate; and that nursing, because women predominate, is second rate?

If nursing could somehow be valued as *different* from but *equal* to doctoring . . . if caring could be as important as curing . . . if the nurse's mother-surrogate role were as revered as the doctor's role as healer . . . if both could be seen as life-giving functions of comparable importance— then perhaps the nurse would achieve her rightful status and the profession would grow to fill our pressing health needs.

Women Lawyers Plead Their Case

Did you ever want to be a lawyer?

When I was small, I didn't dream about becoming an actress or a ballerina. I saw myself defending innocent people in dignified courtrooms. I practiced making eloquent speeches before the Supreme Court. And in wild flights of fancy, I imagined my wise and impartial face peering down from the judge's bench.

I have discovered that I was not alone. Thousands of women once wanted to be lawyers and many little girls secretly play-acted in black judicial robes rather than a white nurse's uniform. But gradually most of us were deflected from that goal. The discouragement of parents and guidance counselors, the general joking attitude toward "lady lawyers," discrimination in law school admissions and the expense and time taken up in training, persuaded most of us to give up the impossible dream and watch Perry Mason instead.

That's why less than three per cent of the nation's 325,-000 lawyers are women. Of all the sex-typed occupations, the law is perhaps the most rock-ribbed male preserve. (Even medicine, which requires longer study, can boast that seven per cent of all doctors are female.) But women's role in society and conditions in the legal profession are changing so radically that we frustrated would-be attorneys owe it to ourselves to reconsider this career no matter what our age or educational background.

Let me offer in evidence some findings which may help you reach a new verdict about becoming a lawyer.

Just the facts, Ma'am

Results of several recent studies indicate that two-thirds of the practicing female lawyers surveyed were married and about 70 per cent of them had children; in 1970 male lawyers could command a starting salary between $11,500 and $15,000, while their female counterparts averaged $1,-500 less. Despite these two facts, women attorneys put in as much time as men in a given work week, and change jobs far less frequently than men.

In order to practice law in the courts of any state, you must be admitted to the bar. To take the Bar Exam you must have completed up to four years of college study and also be a graduate of an approved law school. A few states will recognize apprenticeship in a law office as a partial or full substitute for law school attendance. In some places, you must complete a period of clerkship before being admitted to the bar.

Your college record plus your performance on the Law School Admissions Test (LSAT), added to subtle personality and character judgments made about you during the admissions procedure, will determine whether or not you are accepted to law school. If you attend full-time, it's a three-year program, but a quarter of all law students take the four-year night school curriculum, which may be better suited to your life too.

Admissions

Women are applying to law schools (and getting accepted) in record numbers, but sex bias is not licked yet.

While some schools have up to 50 per cent women in their entering classes, Harvard (which only began accepting women in 1950) has moved from eight per cent in the Class of '73 to only fourteen per cent in the Class of '75.

One activist law school woman explains why equity is impossible under the traditional admissions procedure: "After they accept the few top-rated applicants and reject the few bottom-rated ones, the faculty admissions committee reviews the middle group of students on the basis of something called 'sparkle' which translates to impressive extra-curricular activities in college. However, it is mostly male college students who can qualify for Rhodes Scholarships or varsity football teams; and it is mostly males who get to be editor of the college paper or work in a State Senator's office during the summer. On that basis, no wonder even the most glittering female applicant has no 'sparkle.' "

Ironically, despite the propaganda about the important job women do at home, we get no tangible law school admission credit for performing the demanding tasks of child-rearing, household organizing, entertainment and diplomacy, budgeting or putting a husband through school. So even with good college grades and top percentile LSAT scores, you'll just have to convince admissions officers that all *your* extra experience adds up to "sparkle."

Law schools cannot justify a preference for applicants by sex. But it is no solution to accept the top ten per cent of women and the top ten per cent of men, either. Were they simply to choose the top fifty students, regardless of sex, law schools might find that thirty-five of the top fifty applicants happen to be women. If this turns out to be the case, we should start taking credit for women's high academic achievement, rather than let it get lost in the shuffle called "separate but equal."

Recruitment

It's unlikely that someone will tap you on the shoulder in the supermarket to ask if you'd like to apply to their law school. Your husband, on the other hand, might stumble upon a law school recruiter at his alumni association or athletic club. Recruiters tend to go where men gather. Law schools have too few contacts on the campuses of women's colleges. While women's groups can make some effort to attract their sisters into the law, it is the proper responsibility of the law schools themselves to seek candidates of *both* sexes.

In class and on campus

A 1969 study shows that of 2,500 law teaching positions, only fifty-three were held by women. Recent activist efforts coupled with the threat of governmental action has increased the female ratio somewhat—but it hasn't been easy.

In both admissions tests and law school performance, women by and large have done splendidly, despite the myth that "feminine" qualities are ill-suited to the tough demands of the legal discipline. In 1971, fifty per cent of Radcliffe's graduating class were accepted and went to law school. In 1972, the top-ranked student at Hofstra Law School was a mother of three. In 1973, three women students were on the prestigious Columbia Law Review.

On the average, women outscore men by seven points on the LSAT. One study found that at fifty-six schools, the cumulative grade average of women law students exceeded the overall student average! Perhaps women are "naturally" suited to the law after all—once we're given a chance to prove it.

Hiring

At last law firms are being held accountable for their law school recruitment practices as well as for their in-house record of discrimination against women attorneys. Firms have been banned from using the job placement facilities at a few schools. Interviewers have been taken to task for making statements to women such as: "If you don't use birth control measures, we can't hire you." Or, "We've already hired our woman this year."

On the job

The sex-typing of specialties within the law is another hallowed tradition. Women are routed into trusts and estates, domestic relations, research, poverty and tax law. Litigation, criminal, labor relations and corporate law are considered "masculine" specialties.

But today's woman attorney is not limiting her practice,

and she is pressing for equality in the bar associations as well. She is fighting the generalization that women will marry, bear children and automatically cut down on their professional endeavors. She is taking *pro bono* (no fee) cases to help women suffering job discrimination. And always, she is coping with sexism in her own way.

Carol Libow, a member of an all-woman law firm, remembers that the first day she was admitted to the bar, she asked a family court judge for a conference in his chambers. "I never had a chance to discuss my case. I became a woman alone with him in a room—not an 'esteemed counselor.' The judge chased me around his desk until I finally backed out the door."

New York's Shirah Neiman was the first woman in the criminal division of the U.S. Attorney's office in more than twenty years. As a prosecutor she is on the receiving end of defense lawyers' attempts to charm or discredit her. "It's a double bind," she explains. "Either I'm supposed to have an advantage with a jury because I'm a woman; or I'm supposed to have trouble getting a jury to believe me because I'm a woman."

Under the American system of justice, equality for women under the law should be a national priority. But equality of women *within* the law will only be possible when more of us enter the profession to plead the case for woman attorneys as well as we represent our clients.

A Secretary Is Not a Toy

If you have a college degree and you want a career in management, don't skip this chapter. In the current employment market, you may discover that the most available entry level positions with the best starting salaries are secretarial jobs.

Computer science, commercial art, show business and

retailing are among the very few exceptions where a woman can begin her career as an apprentice or in a training program. Otherwise, the corporate mentality continues to classify female beginners as little minnows who must wade through the typing pool before becoming big fish. One out of five women with four years of college or more, becomes a secretary or clerical worker. Some consider it a training course in business administration. They don't mind passing through on their way up. Others decide to make a career of it—despite having majored in Greek literature—because it's comfortable and secure. If you have a high school or business school degree, you'll be more apt to consider secretarial work an end in itself.

As for me, I've always felt about a good secretary the way my children feel about a purple cow: I'd rather *see* than *be* one.

This prejudice is the result of having toiled in the secretarial vineyards for seven bosses before tasting some executive sweets myself. Secretarial work was fine for openers. I learned a great deal about high-level business procedures and decision making. Observing management's brilliance (and bungling) at close range was a valuable preview of executivehood.

Yet I resented that, because I was a woman, I *had* to start as a secretary, regardless of qualifications. I was angry that my male fellow graduates were in IBM's executive training while I sat at the IBM executive typewriter. I was often bored by the routine. Many times I felt like an exploited servant (watering plants, mixing drinks, picking up theatre tickets), a scapegoat for my boss's errors (as he hid behind, "*She* must have made a typo"), and a general all-purpose professional possession (like my boss's credit cards).

While thousands of women share my view, it's fortunate for the health of the economy that thousands more feel differently. If secretaries were not so exploited, I might feel differently, too.

"Secretarial works is a profession in and of itself—just as nursing is a profession and *not* a stepping stone to becoming a doctor," says Shirley Englund, editor of *The Secretary* and spokeswoman for the National Secretaries Association, International. "It's a background role but one that has special gratifications and privileges. A secretary doesn't take home the highest paycheck, but she doesn't take home management's night work or worries, either."

Add to my view and Ms. Englund's, a third school of thought: that secretarial work is the ideal interim occupation. It is practical for the wife who has no choice but to follow her husband's job transfers from city to city, or for the woman who prefers only part-time or temporary assignments.

Let's assume your skills have rusted during the years you've been home with the children. Getting back in shape to go jobhunting won't be a major production. If everything's hazy, you can get some typing and steno textbooks from the library and start from scratch. Otherwise, consider registering as an office temporary and start in a low level clerical position. Then brush up your skills while on the job and move into better secretarial slots with each new temporary assignment until you're ready to vie for a well-paid permanent position. Your local high school or YMCA may have a vocational refresher course. To revitalize your shorthand at home, take dictation from radio news broadcasts. Make your target speed 80 words per minute. Rent a typewriter if you don't own one. Then copy the stock market pages from the newspaper to give yourself practice on letters *and* numerals. Try for at least 50 w.p.m. without errors. Ask a friend to give you a few spelling tests.

Secretarial schools

In my opinion, secretarial schools are invaluable for career secretaries, but may be counter-productive for women with a different future in mind.

The Katharine Gibbs School should be typical of the highest caliber institutions available in most larger cities. A two-year Gibbs' course, combining some Liberal Arts classes with secretarial skills, economics, accounting and basic business organization might cost you $1,600 per year. An abbreviated one-year version of that course or an adult training program will cost considerbly less. Gibbs has something called the "Entree" course for under $600 which is an eight-week blitz to teach basic secretarial skills to college graduates. An important Gibbs bonus is their lifetime placement service. Other schools guarantee periodic refresher courses when you need them.

Betty Owen, who runs Secretarial Systems, Inc., has figured out an average timetable for the average beginner who wants to qualify for the average job that requires average skills: Plan to attend forty two-hour classes to achieve that 50 w.p.m. typing speed and about fifty two-hour classes to reach 80 w.p.m. in the Gregg stenography method. Ms. Owen says that you should insist on individualized instruction, moving along at your own pace rather than sticking it out in a padded long-term course. Some whiz kids learn it all in half the time allotted.

What a secretary does all day

In House Springs, Missouri, a secretary for a small manufacturer handles dictaphone work and types all correspondence for three executives, types stencils, financial statements and statistical reports; handles four active telephone lines; processes invoices and purchase orders; take charge of all incoming and outgoing mail; does weight checks on the company's product; files, keeps record books; and serves as a part-time receptionist.

In contrast, a Chicago secretary is responsible to one boss, the producer of a TV talk show. She interviews guests for the show; attends previews and reads current books so that she can recommend actors or authors as guests; she keeps clipping files on celebrities and knows their whereabouts; checks newspapers and magazines for program ideas; takes notes at rehearsals and planning meetings, and types about a dozen letters a week.

Those two women's jobs prove how different one secretary's work can be from another's. "*Secretary* is the most loosely defined word in the job market," says Ms. Englund.

One solution to the muddle is the NSA's Certified Professional Secretaries program, which establishes job performance standards based on skills, efficiency, judgment, organization and problem-solving. But thus far, the NSA has certified only a few thousand secretaries—hardly enough to set standards for three million.

In the civil service, uniform classifications can be maintained by way of competitive exams that rate typing and steno speeds, vocabulary, spelling and knowledge of office procedures. But since the labor market at large does not have a set definition of a secretary, the description of the job is more important than the title; it can camouflage a junior management position, which would command a higher salary if it weren't dubbed "secretarial."

Beware, too, of the "Assistant to the ..." ploy. Here you're expected to be an all-round workhorse in return for a somewhat upgraded title. Check your salary against that of other staff people. While it's nice to have a title, honor without profit should be your choice, not your employer's deception.

During National Secretaries' Week 1974, a group of 150 secretaries gathered to talk about their jobs. The consensus was that a secretary does what her boss requests— including sewing on his buttons or doing his kid's homework—*if he enjoy it*. And if she doesn't enjoy it? The secretaries agreed she shouldn't complain; she should just quit.

What a secretary earns

Not surprisingly, jobs in urban centers pay best. Secretaries in manufacturing concerns often earn more than those in other businesses. The more important the executive you work for, the higher your salary. At this writing, secretaries seem to be a national treasure. In most places there are many more jobs than people to fill them—and you can be choosy.

If companies *are* hiring where you live, you should find that salary levels range from a low of $100–$120 for a beginner with a high school diploma, to a high of $200–$225 for a crackerjack secretary experienced in the fields of real estate, law or import-export. Providence, Rhode Island, might be on the low side of the averages while Los Angeles would compare with New York City's high.

If you want to work in a glamour field (publishing, fashion, advertising) or in a classy part of town (as opposed to the warehouse district) be prepared to earn a little less in return for atmospheric amenities.

For the great freedom, mobility and diversity, consider being an office temporary. Here you are paid an hourly rate depending on your skills and the local ranges. One friend of mine earned $6.50 an hour doing secretarial work on a Saturday—although $3.50 to $5.00 is more usual. A temporary assignment can last anywhere from a few hours to a few years. Do bear in mind, however, that temporaries get no fringe benefits or paid vacations.

White collar unionization is supposed to boom in the Seventies. In the meantime, most secretaries' salaries, promotions and fringes are decided at the employer's discretion. Uniform pay scales and automatic increments may apply in one office while the firm next door hassles and negotiates with each secretary on an individual basis.

In the federal civil service, competitive tests determine your rating and your rating determines your pay. Announcements of job vacancies and information about secretarial exams are available at the Civil Service Commission's sixty-five area offices.

If you obtained your job through the services of an employment agency and the agency's fee was paid by the employer, you should be aware of certain unwritten ethical rules which require you to spend a minimum of one year on the job. You can ignore this guideline if you really loathe your job, and if you're sure that you never signed a guarantee of a minimum term of employment.

With so many options and such a high demand market, one might ask why more men don't become secretaries. In the days of spittoons and roll-top desks, ninety per cent of secretaries *were* men. In many firms a secretary or clerk was considered an apprentice. As industry and business prospered, men carved out a different promotion route for themselves, and it didn't include doing time at the typewriter. The second sex became available for the menial tasks.

As women began to leave farmhouse and tenement, they were absorbed at the bottom ranks of the white collar army—where they were expected to remain. Thus, clerical positions became sex-typed as women's work and for women there was no longer a concept of secretary-as-apprentice.

How infuriating it is to discover that the deck is stacked in favor of men at both ends. Labor Department figures indicate that when a man *does* become a secretary, he earns twenty per cent more than a woman doing the same job.

Nevertheless, if we're to be consistent in our plea for equality, we should welcome men into the secretarial ghetto. Indeed, I like to fantasize about a time when all jobs are sex-blind and lots of women are sitting in those plush private offices, and lots of men are touch-typing outside the office doors. Instead, I have the distinct impression that things aren't evening out. It seems that when *we* make inroads into *their* domain, it costs us something because we're paid less. And when *they* move into our domain, it still costs us something, because *they're* paid more.

Should male secretaries become next year's corporate status symbol, applaud *his* "equal opportunity"—but demand *your* "equal pay."

Teachers: An Endangered Species

While recognizing the benefits and rewards of being a schoolmarm, it's time we debunked the myth that teaching below college level is everywoman's employment paradise.

Of the nation's more than two million public school teachers, 68 per cent are women. Here are some compelling reasons why the profession may be so attractive to so many.

Equal pay

In the area of *salary*, sex discrimination has been virtually eliminated. Teachers are paid according to a formula based upon number of years' experience in a given school district plus amount of postgraduate credits accumulated beyond the Bachelor's degree. Yearly increments accumulate automatically. On top of that, in about half the states, the overall salary schedule is periodically improved according to negotiated contracts arrived at through collective bargaining between teachers' unions and school boards. Where collective bargaining is not provided by law, teachers' raises are taken up in informal negotiating sessions.

Pay rates may vary widely between different sections of the country; but they don't vary between the sexes.

Working hours, holidays and vacations

It's an enviable schedule. Thirty to thirty-five hour work week, thirty-six working weeks per year, vacations that co-incide with those of your own children, and summers off. What doesn't become immediately apparent are the mountains of work that fill a teacher's supposed "free" time. There are test papers to correct, compositions to grade, lesson plans to prepare, parent conferences, staff meetings, participation in students' sports and club activities, and independent reading and research that dedicated teachers consider essential. While all this work can be done at home and on a self-determined schedule, it adds up to more than a full-time job.

The working mother who chooses to teach can coordinate her vacation with her family. On a day-to-day basis, she can generally arrive home at the same time as her own children—so her child care costs are restricted to her preschoolers. If she had energy to spare, at the end of the term she can take a summer school job, work as a camp counselor, supplement her income with temporary office work or take advanced courses in summer college programs.

Job security

Depending upon which side of the fence you're on, the word *tenure* can represent either shackles or security. A community that wants to get rid of an ineffective teacher will discover that tenure ties their hands. But to an experienced teacher, having tenure is a guarantee against a capricious lay-off. In New York, for example, after a teacher has worked in a district for five years, she or he can only be fired for "just cause" (after a full hearing of the facts), or because of an overall reduction of staff in the district. The only requirement is a satisfactory rating and, within those five years, the earning of a Master's degree.

In the past, there was such a serious shortage of teachers that women were assured they could take their pick of jobs in this safest of all professions. Since the beginning of this decade there has been an astonishing change. The National Education Association reports that in 1970, 77,000 beginner teachers did not find jobs; in 1971, 104,000 were turned away. Eventually, the profession couldn't absorb new teachers *nor* sustain those who were employed. Lay-offs increased in every state. If the trend continues, NEA experts predict that in 1975, more than 700,000 teachers will be unemployed. Under these circumstances, job se-curity becomes a tenuous proposition.

Benefits

In most communities, teachers contribute a percentage of the cost of their health and life insurance and pension plans. In other places, the taxpayers shoulder the full cost of teachers' benefits. Retirement policies also vary. A big city teacher might get 75 per cent of her final salary while a rural district teacher might retire with little more than her Social Security. District X pays pensions after thirty years' service or at age sixty-five, while District Y retires its teachers at age fifty-five after twenty-five years in the classroom. Despite these variations, teachers' fringe bene-fits are considered excellent, compared with other trades and professions.

Job satisfaction and social usefulness

The enthusiastic, inspiring teacher is a practitioner of the highest humanitarian arts. She can open children's minds to the world's wonders; she can chart the path for lifelong pursuit of beauty and knowledge. Her potential for satisfaction and social usefulness is absolutely limitless.

So, with all this—convenience, benefits, satisfaction—why are so many teachers miserable? It's not a question of getting stuck with a tough class for one or two semesters; the profession is blighted by some critical flaws.

Advancement, promotion, job mobility

One might suspect that there's an unwritten rule proclaiming that women may be teachers but rarely administrators. The statistics are nearly incredible. Among elementary school teachers, women outnumber men nearly nine to one—but 78 per cent of all elementary school *principals* are men. In the secondary schools, the proportion of men and women teachers is about equal and yet 98 per cent of high school principals are *men!* Out of some 13,000 school superintendents in this country, a mere handful are women. Men wear the pants in the teacher's unions too. Less than one-quarter of the union locals have women presidents.

Should you happen to have leadership qualities, some career ambition, a desire to shape educational policy and a talent for mobilizing others, you might make a superlative department chairwoman, principal or school superintendent. You can earn your M.A. or Ph.D. and attend internship courses in school administration—but don't count on equal treatment when the time comes for appointments to be made in your district. Prepare yourself to campaign hard and to publicize any discriminatory treatment you may receive.

Salaries

Teaching salaries both for men and women are on the low side. It's the familiar vicious cycle: Because pre-college teaching has been considered women's work, it hasn't attracted many men. And where men are not employed in substantial numbers, salaries tend to be low. A few years back, when a teaching job might win a draft exemption, men began entering the profession. Coincidentally, militant union actions, better pay demands and teachers' strikes followed in the wake of the increase in male teachers. Now women teachers, like secretaries, face a knotty dilemma: more men means more pay and more clout for teachers in general. But the influx of men also further reduces women's hopes of beating the preference for male administrators—it just gives the district more men to choose from. And competition for the dwindling number of supervisory and teaching positions is likely to continue as long as the birth rate declines.

Outlook

The status of women in teaching has gotten worse, not better. Forty years ago most school principals were women. In the high schools, where there is greater specialization and more prestige, the proportion of women teachers has dropped from 57 per cent in 1950 to 46 per cent today. In 1972, only one state had a woman as chief school officer. Twenty years before, there were six.

Certainly, some teachers should be men. Men have long been missed in early childhood education where an all-woman learning environment presents the child with a one-sided view of the adult world. However admirable the goal of attracting men, it should not be pursued by sacrificing the resources and loyalties of thousands of qualified

women. Now that Title VII has been extended to cover teachers, anti-female bias in promotions must be challenged wherever it surfaces.

Teachers will never become extinct as long as there is reverence for ideas. But realistically we must accept a new perspective on the profession. Once, women were guided into job categories that were counterparts of their domestic roles. From mother (caretaker of the child at home) to teacher (educator and socializer of the child at school), seemed a logical step. While the brilliant boy in the school orchestra was encouraged to become a composer, the gifted girl was advised to be a music teacher. Today, that advice is not only sexist, but a profound disservice to the young woman who may find that the sign on the schoolhouse door says, "No help wanted."

For those who choose to persist in their goal, one final test will clarify whether teaching represents a commitment or a compromise. If you believe in the old axiom "Those who can, do; those who can't, teach"—then teaching is a compromise. If you agree instead with the paraphrase of Henry Brooks Adams' statement, then teaching is a commitment:

> "A teacher affects eternity; she can never
> tell where her influence stops."

Passing Muster in the Military

By law, women in the military cannot be armed, are not trained to handle weapons and may not serve in combat situations. Nevertheless, because the jobs available to female personnel support the basic fighting function of the services, if you reject war as a solution to anything, your religious or moral beliefs may prevent you from considering this career.

Assuming that you have no qualms, the service does offer certain advantages to working women. In fact, according to George A. Daoust, Jr., Deputy Assistant Secretary of Defense, "The enlisted woman with a high school diploma starts at $307 per month—which is a fine wage when you figure that she gets her food, clothing, and shelter at no cost and tax-free."

Officers do far better. A Second Lieutenant, who is a college graduate, gets about $10,000 a year and can look forward to earning $28,000 annually after twenty-five years in the service.

For both officers and enlisted women, the pot is sweetened by free medical care, an excellent retirement program after twenty years, thirty days' annual paid vacation, subsidized recreation, academic and vocational education and free travel.

In June 1973 there were 45,000 women serving in all branches, and the Defense Department plans to raise female representation to 87,000 by 1977. This would be the greatest number of women since World War II when 100,000 served, although they served in distinctly limited roles. Within just the past two years, dramatic progress has been made in "desexegrating" military occupational specialties (MOS) that were formerly just for men. (The service still requires that women have a high school diploma; this is not the case for men, whose MOS options are greater, nonetheless.) Whereas women had been restricted to clerical, administrative and medical jobs, we are now eligible for 81 per cent of the military specialties. Combat posts are still off limits to female personnel but Army women are in missile repair; Navy women are aboard non-combat ships; and Air Force women are in astronautical engineering. Daoust insists "the military's problem is finding enough trained or motivated women to fill the specialties that are open to them."

Despite expanded occupational opportunities, there has been some sexist tarnish on the military brass. Military regulations on pregnancy and children remain two troublesome issues in every service but the WACs (which removed these restrictions in April 1974). If you are a married woman with children, you must get a special waiver in order to enlist. If your child was born out of wedlock, you must first submit affidavits of good moral conduct and proof that you don't have custody of the child. Women who are already in the service when they become pregnant must apply for a waiver in order to stay in.

The services justify this practice on the grounds that once a woman becomes a mother she is no longer available to work all hours or to travel on short notice.

While it sounds fair, this policy of interfering in a woman's private life is founded on a grossly unjust sexist assumption: that every woman's first service is in the home—and it is up to each individual woman to prove that such is not the case.

The opposite assumption is made for the serviceman who becomes a father. He is still free to pursue his career because the Army, Navy and Air Force rest easy in the belief that he has a wife at home who will do the parenting for both of them. With half of all American wives working outside the home, the stay-home military wife may be a fiction. Forcing the pregnant servicewoman to justify her disinterest in full-time motherhood, and to open her child care arrangements to scrutiny, is a true indignity that is stranger than fiction. If a woman wants to be a mother *and* a master sergeant, the decision is hers to make. Then the service can hold her to its established performance standards, without invading her privacy first.

If these discriminatory practices are not eliminated, the military should begin asking men for affidavits of morality if they have fathered "illegitimate" children; and asking servicemen with working civilian wives (or divorced fathers and widowers), to prove to the top brass that they, too, have provided adequately for the care of their children.

Despite the negatives, everyone connected with the services mentions how fast things are changing for the better. Talking with the military representatives about the four women's branches is enough to send you double-timing it to the nearest recruiting office.

"Only five of our specialties are closed to women," says Col. Billie M. Bobbitt, the relaxed, witty Director of Women in the Air Forces, "and proportionately, we have more women in executive positions than there are in private industry." The Colonel is extremely proud that the

Air Force beat the Army to a historic "first." A WAF colonel, Norma Brown, became the first woman to boss an all-male unit of 2000 men at Ft. Meade, Maryland—and there's no sign of revolution, or even lowered morale.

The Air Force has opened up fifty-one foreign posts to enlisted women. And in September, 1973, Capt. Lorraine Potter was sworn in as the first female chaplain. Now the Air Force is eagerly seeking officer candidates who are scientists, mathematicians, space analysts, engineers and technicians.

Since so many male civilian pilots received their training and flight time in the Air Force, it seems only fair for women to get a similar occupational advantage—especially in peacetime, when they can fly without violating the no-combat law.

Col. Bobbitt answers: "We are still oriented to combat *readiness*. If we don't allow men limited duty, we can't create a special category of female non-combat pilots whose training could not be utilized in time of war."

What if the Equal Rights Amendment passes and women must be considered for pilot training?

"I'd love to see it," confessed Col. Bobbitt. "We'd attract hordes of qualified women!"

The Navy no longer has a counterpart to Col. Bobbitt or Brigadier General Mildred E. Bailey, Director of the Women's Army Corps (WACs), a 30-year career soldier—articulate, informed and remarkably unassuming. Now the Navy's women (WAVES) are integrated into overall duty assignments for all Naval personnel—male and female. This is no surprise, given the progressive attitude of Admiral E. R. Zumwalt, Jr., former Chief of Naval Operations. In a much publicized 1972 press statement, Admiral Zumwalt articulated sweeping goals for women. "I believe any man or woman should be permitted to serve his or her country in any capacity that he or she, as an individual, views as appropriate."

To put punch in this statement, there are developments to back it up. The Navy also accepts applications for women chaplains. Florence Dianna Pohlman, a Presbyterian from California, was the first chaplain sworn in by the Navy in July 1973. A group of women have been assigned to the crew of the converted hospital ship, *Sanctuary*. And eight women officers were accepted for flight training to become pilots of helicopters, transports and search planes. (These women met the same physical standard as all male candidates: minimum weight, 107 pounds; minimum height, 5 foot 4 inches.)

Speaking for the Marines, Lt. Col. Eric H. Weiler explains that while women officers do not compete with men for advancement, "in terms of years of service, our women have had as equitable promotions as our men."

Since the Marine Corps is essentially an elite assault force, it is understandable that women are excluded from 40 per cent of the available Marine specialties. (An MOS such as infantry, amphibians or artillery, for example, would be off-limits.) Also, according to regulations, a woman Marine may not command a male unit.

The Marines will accept officer candidates who are married, but enlistees must be single. Lt. Col. Weiler admitted that a small number of pregnant women had requested waivers but "the preponderance have been denied."

The Corps is in the business of making men "lean and mean" which doesn't necessarily sound like an image that would appeal to women. However, there *is* a fact sheet on women Marines that states: "Considerable emphasis is placed on good grooming . . . to present an attractive and feminine appearance in uniform." Perhaps this charm school approach is considered necessary to counteract the myth of the bitchy woman Marine. Whatever the rationale, it seems gratuitous, condescending to career-minded women, and not the sort of publicity that will attract the talented women that the Marine Corps claims it needs.

With the advent of an all-volunteer force, Uncle Sam *does* need you. But he'll have to set his house in order before women can really feel "gung-ho" about joining up.

Move Over, Dr. Welby!
(Women in White: Part II)

There are over 30,000 female physicians in this country but you could easily live a lifetime without meeting one of them. Women represent only seven per cent of those physicians who have direct contact with patients. Moreover, almost 60 percent of all active women doctors practice in seven states (New York, California, Pennsylvania, Illinois, Ohio, Massachusetts, and New Jersey), and they cluster in a relatively limited range of specialties. Psychiatry, anesthesiology, public health, general practice, internal medicine and pathology attract large numbers of women M.D.'s but nearly one woman in every four becomes a pediatrician. (By comparison, one man in four chooses surgery, the most prestigious and well-paid of the specialties.)

What sort of woman chooses medicine and how different is her life from yours or mine?

Barbara Logan, M.D., has been a practicing gynecologist and obstetrician for nearly thirty years. In 1945, she became the first woman ever to perform surgery in the operating room at New York's Roosevelt Hospital. During her early career, she delivered two hundred babies a year, but she now limits her obstetrical practice to high-risk pregnancies and cases of infertility.

Because of her single-minded devotion to medicine, Dr. Logan did not marry until she was over forty. She has no children but her desktop is covered with pictures of babies brought into the world by her own hands.

On a typical morning, Dr. Logan rises at 6:15, performs surgery from 7:30 to 10 A.M. and spends the rest of the day seeing patients in her office. "I'm doing exactly what I want to do," she says of her life, "and it's so gratifying that I feel guilty."

Lyn Howard, M.D., an internist, is assistant professor of clinical nutrition at Albany Medical College. Although she says it's been a "terribly long pull," she *has* managed to adjust her professional schedule to her personal life. When she married, she took off three months during her internship, stretched her residency from three years to four to accommodate her pregnancies, and worked part-time when her two children were preschoolers. Now that they're ages seven and five, she doesn't get home until about 7 P.M. by which time her husband, Burtis, an engineer, has dinner well underway. "He has no hang-ups about keeping the home scene going," explains Dr. Howard. "I do the heavy housecleaning on weekends; he keeps things ship-shape all week."

Julia T. Apter, M.D., is a rare combination: a physician and a social-political activist. An ophthalmologist by training, she is professor of surgery and director of the laboratory of biomechanics at Presbyterian–St. Lukes Hospital in Chicago. She married her husband, a psychiatrist, during her second year of medical school and *he* followed *her* to Johns Hopkins in Baltimore, where she interned. She took off four years to care for her two children. Then, when she had to spend many long days at the dentist's for her own severe teeth problems, she discovered that her husband was perfectly capable of "parenting." Thereafter, she worked part-time and shared child care with him.

When the children were in high school, Dr. Apter earned a Ph.D. in mathematical biology. She is the author of many books and articles as well as a tireless fighter for the rights of women in the profession. "Men think women don't need good salaries, status or equal opportunity," she says heatedly. "I didn't used to fight this attitude, but now I've stopped being a coward!"

Seventy-five-year-old Helen B. Taussig, M.D., professor emeritus of pediatrics at Johns Hopkins, went to medical school in the days when some professors didn't allow "ladies" in their anatomy classes. The inventor of the "blue baby" operation to alleviate defective circulation in infants, and one of America's foremost pediatric cardiologists, she has received innumerable awards, including the French Legion of Honor.

Explaining why she never married, Dr. Taussig says: "Almost *anything* is possible, but you can't do *everything*."

Estelle Ramey, M.D., is among the two per cent of full professors at U.S. medical schools who are women. An endocrinologist and professor of physiology and biophysics at Georgetown, and a strong feminist, Dr. Ramey is often quoted for her studies on the male monthly cycle and on the ability of the female of every species to tolerate stress better than the male.

"I have the utmost respect for the survival power of women," she says. "Women physicians particularly suffer inferior self-image, small recognition and the belief that they must be the female Albert Schweitzer, or else stay home with the kids. And with all their burdens, women can do anything!" Dr. Ramey is a wife and mother of two grown children.

Jane Ferber, M.D., supervising psychiatrist at Bronx State Hospital, and clinical instructor at the Albert Einstein College of Medicine, and a specialist in family crisis therapy, is married to a psychiatrist and has two children, ages seven and nine. Though she took off five years while her kids were small, she credits a fabulous housekeeper with being the secret of her success.

With their diverse backgrounds and specialties, these six women bring into focus both the problems and pleasures of a career in medicine.

Motivation

While a scientific boy is encouraged to become a doctor, a scientific girl is told to *marry* a doctor and channel her interests into a more "feminine" occupation. Social pressure is intense; her medical career aspirations are met with disbelief, resistance, loss of popularity and even ridicule. It takes great determination, perserverance and a supportive family to produce a woman doctor today.

If they have no sons, male physicians are more likely to nurture a daughter's medical bent. One who followed in her father's tracks is Jane C. Wright, M.D., assistant dean of the New York Medical College, a respected cancer researcher and one of the few doctors who is both female and black.

Another chip off the old Doc is Tenley Albright, M.D., the former Olympic ice skater who practices surgery with her father in Boston. Helen Taussig's grandfather was a doctor, as was Lyn Howard's uncle. The healing instinct seems to run in the family.

If a doctor father sets an example for a young girl, having a female role model is better still. Jane Ferber is a remarkable case in point: both her mother and aunt are internists and her female cousin is a neurologist. Barbara Logan, the obstetrician, was herself delivered by a woman doctor. She remembers too, that her mother and grandmother always had as the family doctors women physicians with great charisma.

Julia Apter says: "My mother approved of my career plan even when I was a child. She even refused to let me learn to cook so I wouldn't become a housewife." In Dr. Apter's situation, as in countless others, money was a special deterrent to the young woman in the family. When there was only enough to put one child through college, Dr. Apter's family paid to send her brother. However, Julia was so highly motivated that she won not one but five scholarships.

Training

In 1970, after a seven-year survey of American medical schools, Dr. Harold I. Kaplan concluded that "a significant number of schools were very negative about single or married women in medicine," some refused to admit women with children, and many schools had strict quotas.

Then in 1971, a new law prohibited discrimination on the basis of sex under the Public Health Service Act. At the same time, the feminist movement began to affect admissions policies as well as women's own perceptions of their role in life and the options they could exercise. Since then, according to Ms. W.F. Dubé of the Association of American Medical Colleges, women's enrollment has nearly doubled, and a nationwide census of 1974 medical school classes indicates that nearly one in every five freshmen is a "freshwoman." (The medical school drop-out rate for men and women is about the same—five per cent.)

But statistics don't tell the whole story. Prejudice against women students is not uncommon among male classmates and professors. Women often must be exceptional medical scholars to be taken seriously at all. Few medical schools make provisions for the needs of students who are pregnant or who have small children. Maternity leave, make-up exams, special child care loans and flexible schedules extending the M.D. study program are all vitally needed.

In most states, an M.D. candidate must attend at least three years of college, four years of medical school, serve one year as a hospital intern and then pass a state licensing exam. Specialists must pass more board examinations, which require two to five years of advanced hospital training as residents. Dr. Glen Leymaster, Director of Undergraduate Medical Education at the American Medical Association, says the average medical student will spend $6,000 a year on schooling. When she interns she will work a fifty- or sixty-hour week for approximately $10,000 annual salary. In her residency she'll be able to expect a $1,000 raise beyond that for each year in service.

Taking into account this immensely costly training period and early post-graduate years at relatively low pay, it is important to note that 91 per cent of all licensed female physicians practice medicine continually, full- or part-time throughout their lives. So much for the myth that women waste their medical educations!

Family-career conflicts

Sociologist Alice Rossi reports that most college women consider medicine "too demanding to combine with family responsibilities." However, once her training is complete, a doctor's life can be as flexible or structured as she wishes, depending on her choice of specialty. A psychiatrist can maintain a private practice in her own house and set office hours around her children's schedules. An anesthesiologist might work a regular hospital shift—and never be on call during the night. There are round-the-clock jobs (midnight appendectomies, pre-dawn Caesarian sections), but there are also part-time opportunities in research, public health or feminist self-health clinics, partnerships and group practice plans. The American Medical Women's Association (1740 Broadway, New York, N.Y. 10019) has several pamphlets, films and tapes that describe all the possibilities open to licensed physicians; they also administer scholarship, grant and loan programs.

Shared residencies, extended residencies and part-time residencies are becoming more readily available—and they are especially attractive to the woman with a young family. With new choices and relaxed timetables, there is no reason to find excuses to avoid a medical career, if you want one.

Carol Lopate points out in her book, *Women in Medicine,* that three-quarters of all women physicians are married and most of them have children. Half of their husbands are also doctors and the other half are mostly highly successful professionals. This makes sense because men with less prestigious jobs are known to demand traditional ranking at home and to put too many domestic demands on their wives for them to be apt to pursue medical careers.

There is a slightly higher rate of divorce among women doctors than among other American women, but this has not been attributed to marital competitiveness or the demands of the wife's career. On the contrary—the independent professional woman seems to feel self-sufficient enough to jettison a bad marriage and seek fulfillment in her work or in a more satisfactory love relationship.

As with the rest of us, child care arrangements are a primary problem for the woman doctor. In this crazy world, a doctor's car expenses are tax deductible business expenditures but her child care expenses are not—though some doctors need *both* car and babysitter in order to get out and see patients.

Society has a real investment in fostering an abundance of females in the medical fields. If mother-physicians take time off to rear their children, statistics prove that the time is well made up in later years. While only fifteen per cent of male physicians are active at age sixty, half of all women over sixty are still practicing medicine.

The impact of the women's movement

Lyn Howard claims feminism isn't her issue, yet she remembers that when she did neurosurgery she was at a disadvantage because nurses enjoy playing sexist flirtation games with male attendants in the operating theatre. She often felt that her presence deprived the nurses of this outlet for tension, and that there was occasional resentment from nurses who aren't accustomed to assisting a surgeon of their own sex.

In the hospital parking lot, Dr. Howard still gets challenged by the attendant when she drives her car into a "Doctors Only" parking space.

Julia Apter feels that the success of the movement in advancing women physicians has caused a backlash. She says there are cases where women don't get academic promotions and top job appointments because their biographical sheets are systematically condensed to appear less impressive. Dr. Apter has also seen statistics trumped up when a medical school wants to claim fair representation of women among its staff. (They include secretaries and maids under "female medical staff.") She believes these are early warning signs that the male establishment is starting to feel the squeeze from tough, competent female competition.

Barbara Logan reports that she has been besieged by women patients who have a new feminist consciousness. "Whereas women used to *prefer* male doctors, they now feel more comfortable with a woman gynecologist, and in fact many don't *trust* men. Male doctors have made a great mistake in treating women like dim-witted children," says Dr. Logan. "Women are capable of understanding what is wrong with them. And they deserve to know what the doctor plans to do about it."

Jane Ferber is grateful to the Women's Movement for relieving her guilt about being a doctor and a mother: "I no longer feel like a second-class man in my profession or a second-class woman in my home."

Estelle Ramey puts it all together this way: "The feminist movement has brought about the most difficult change of all—it has changed women's attitudes about themselves."

The Tight Blue Collar

Though there are about four and a half million blue collar women in the work force, it seems that no one speaks *to* her or *for* her. Like it or not, the men have their Archie Bunker. But for women, his "dingbat" wife, Edith, doesn't even come close as a comic representation.

In reality, America's working class women are more like the following examples:

- Jessica Lowery, a "hard hat" who works on construction of the Washington, D.C. Metro subway.
- Mary Lewis, mother of five, who rides a helicopter to service and repair Xerox equipment aboard the oil rigs in the Gulf of Mexico.
- Suzanne Wirtz, a garbage collector who drives a ten-wheeled, 50,000 pound truck, calling her job "a lot easier than the farm work I did out in Oklahoma."
- Katie Alderson of Cleveland, Virginia, who tried to get work as a coal miner, because $40 a day from a union mine buys a lot more groceries than $2.10 an hour in a non-union garment factory.
- Ida Phillips, a Florida assembly line worker who took a huge corporation to the U.S. Supreme Court because she was denied work on the grounds that she had preschool children—and won her case!
- Anita Baird, a San Francisco plumber's apprentice who (with support of male co-workers) is fighting the union for her right to work.

• Mary Joe Hamlin, the first woman truck driver in the Michigan Bell Telephone organization; or Debbie Vase, a flatbed truck driver (and teamster member) from Rock Springs, Wyoming.

• Gloria Dossett, a twenty-seven-year-old mother of four, who works five days a week from nine to four pumping gas at the Turnpike Texaco Station in Orlando, Florida.

• Paula Andrews, former model and medical secretary, who is the first woman admitted to a construction union in Los Angeles.

Today's blue collar woman is one of these wage-earners or she's any one of a number of factory workers, machine operators, cashiers, waitresses, saleswomen, assemblers and the like. For lack of an official designation, let's just say she's someone who uses her strength, works with her hands or stands on her feet in a far different world from that of the office worker.

She primarily works for hard cash, not for "fulfilment" or other emotional needs. Perhaps the *most* money-oriented blue-collar women are those who also serve as heads of households in 43 per cent of America's low-income families. Next in order of economic urgency are those working women whose wages are *vital* supplements to their husbands' inadequate incomes; and single women who have no one else's income to fall back on.

For these women, work is not a "pin money" proposition. It's not the difference between hamburger and steak; it's the difference between dry cereal and tuna casserole.

Blue collar wages vary widely depending again on geography, industry and unionization. You earn barely above the federal minimum wage of $1.60 if you're a dental lab worker in the South. As a skilled worker in a union shop you might average $4 a hour in the large urban centers of the East or West coasts. The 1970 Census reports over half a million women in the skilled trades, including such traditionally male vocations as carpenters, machinists, mechanics and electricians. There are even rising female enrollments in apprentice programs for welders, pipefitters, crane operators and glass blowers. Before any of us protest that these jobs are unsuitable for a woman, we should keep in mind the fact that these "unladylike" blue collar

specialties pay up to $20,000 a year! At those rates, over-
alls can feel pretty elegant.

Despite occasional breakthroughs into more lucrative
trades, most blue collar women are unskilled operatives
working where there are still frequent pockets of resistance.
For example, in 1974 the Equal Employment Opportunity
Commission charged General Motors, Ford, General
Electric and Sears-Roebuck with job discrimination "on
a national scale" including sex and race bias in wages,
benefits, promotion, training, layoffs, testing, seniority
and union representation.

Last year General Motors agreed to hire women for at
least 20 per cent of all assembly line openings at its St.
Louis plant after the EEOC found that GM's unnecessary
height and weight requirements for line workers tended
automatically to eliminate most women.

At a General Electric plant, a woman group leader who
works with twenty to thirty people gets the same pay as a
janitor; in fact, 90 per cent of female employees work at
or below the wages paid to a sweeper.

These companies are not isolated offenders; they're
sadly typical. To this workplace frustration, add all of the
pressures from her personal life, and you get a clearer picture of the blue collar woman's raw deal. After a boring,
dizzying day of drilling, capping, soldering, inserting,
punching or wrapping, she may come home to a husband
who deeply resents her working and who feels ashamed
that his own wages aren't enough to maintain the family.
She herself was probably reared to be a wife and mother.
Her education was relatively limited. She never learned to
seek personal gratification outside the home. Although her
job puts her in touch with new friends, the work she must
do can hardly be called liberating. More than likely, this
woman would consider liberation to be the freedom to become a full-time housewife.

It's important for the larger community of working
women to understand not only what we share in common
with one another, but what is important about our differences. In the case of the blue collar woman, the needs are
perhaps more basic and the discontent more desperate
because she has fewer choices.

In her excellent report, "Absent from the Majority:
Working Class Women in America," Nancy Seifer of the
National Project on Ethnic America, offers the following

commonsense recommendations for social change that would benefit our blue collar sisters: subsidized day care facilities in the community and at work; more generous tax deductions for child care; more flexible work schedules; neighborhood job banks and referral services; psychological counseling to overcome insecurities; mid-career or new career training centers; leadership training programs for women union members to learn to become officers; legal assistance both for work- and family-related problems; an end to separate seniority lists; fringe benefits for temporary and part-time workers; consciousness-raising to help male employees, bosses and husbands to change attitudes and general treatment of women.

These recommendations are not so different from the demands made by women everywhere—regardless of the color of their collars. Among the working class, however, there is a groundwork to build from previous battles. There are ethnic caucuses, now there will be women's caucuses. Working women can seek support from established neighborhood, union, religious and civic groups to work in coalition for new solutions. Women in the black community can borrow tactics and facilities from the black liberation leadership. And the feminist movement is now beginning to reach out to blue collar women. All these resources should be tapped, but at the bottom line, the best antidote to the blue collar blues is a red-hot organizer with some bright ideas and a lot of help from her sisters.

Pistol Packin' Mamas

The first policewoman in the United States was Lola Baldwin, who was recruited to protect young women at the Lewis and Clark Exposition in Portland, Oregon, in 1905. Los Angeles appointed women to its police force in 1911, but again their role was limited to protecting women, finding runaway girls or preventing the sale of liquor to minors.

In the ensuing years, policewomen's duties were always narrowly defined: they were matrons for women prisoners, they worked with juvenile offenders, or performed clerical jobs.

Research on police department sex discrimination conducted by Catherine H. Milton, assistant director of The Police Foundation, shows that while many police departments have trouble recruiting male personnel, they have turned away qualified women.

Now, in response to laws prohibiting sex discrimination, there are major breakthroughs and signs of permanent change in policy. In 1969, two policewomen in Indianapolis were assigned to Car 47 for limited patrol duty. In 1971, Peoria, Illinois, put women on *regular* patrol on the same basis as men. In May 1972, fifteen of New York City's 322 policewomen joined their fellow officers as "equal in every sense of the word on a radio motor patrol."

Lt. Lucy Acerra, who is in command of NYC's Policewoman's Section, describes this experiment as "an unqualified success." The women were assigned to two medium and one high crime area. "Whether because of its shock value or cultural factors, the public has responded beautifully," says Lt. Acerra. "The women seem to defuse violence by their presence, and people with problems seem to bypass males and go to females with their complaints. The public expects more understanding from policewomen on patrol."

New York's women ride in male-female squad car teams or as two-women partners. The two-sex teams have proven more effective in family disputes (which account for a large percentage of violence) because men and women seem to respond to same-sex allies in a tense situation.

New York has changed its promotion policies too. In March 1972, Sgt. Margaret Powers became the first woman desk sergeant. (She had made over three hundred arrests during her nine years in plain clothes. Once she dressed in a nun's habit to catch an extortionist.)

In April 1974, Deputy Inspector Gertrude Schimmel, the highest ranking woman in the Police Department, was named commanding officer of the department's Public Information Division. Inspector Schimmel, 55, has carved out several "firsts" in her thirty-three years on the New York City force. She was the first woman sergeant, lieutenant, captain and deputy inspector in the department's history. A Phi Beta Kappa (and mother of two sons), Inspector Schimmel clearly has earned her $31,600 salary!

In 1973, when nearly half of New York City's new recruits were women, former Police Commissioner Donald F. Cawley said: "Never before in this department or in the nation have so many women been sworn into police work at one time. This is a moment in history."

Other cities are making history of their own by expanding both the complement of women in their forces and the role of the policewoman. In Washington, D.C., a woman is on the Homicide Squad; Miami has women in investigation; Indianapolis assigns women to narcotics investigation; and Philadephia uses policewomen in its Civil Disobedience Unit. Many departments have found that plainclotheswomen can better merge with a crowd or be overlooked by a criminal because, at this time, a woman officer is still so unexpected.

One of The Police Foundation's most fascinating projects was the $300,000 study evaluating the experience of one hundred women on uniformed patrol in Washington, D.C. Among other things it was learned that women didn't take as many sick days as men, didn't issue as many traffice violations (although NYC found that women can be trained to take a tougher approach), had less driving accidents (though they didn't do as well on the actual driving test), and used force slightly less often in troublesome "incidents." The public seemed to find women as acceptable as men. One indication that the public was indeed receptive is the fact that women officers perceived citizens to be cooperative fifty per cent more frequently than did male officers in the same research control group. (Copies of the report *Women In Policing* are available for $3 from The Police Foundation, 1015 18th St. N.W., Washington, D.C. 20036.)

While Washington policewomen tended to be slightly less competent at handling disorderly males, Lt. Acerra reported that in the New York experiment, women managed to subdue a violent male psychotic with little problem.

In both Washington and New York, the attitudes of -

male officers has been the only persistent stumbling block. Men expressed resistance on the grounds that it's not "appropriate" work for a woman. Some feared promotional favoritism. A few claimed their wives would object to their having a woman partner in the squad car (and some police wives have protested). Despite these objections, the men have been required to accommodate themselves. Somehow, when personal adjustments are ordered from on high, the objections decrease and the problems vanish. In Washington, as a result of good experience on this project, the department has decided to hire women on an absolutely equal basis with men.

One new area of specialization has emerged for policewomen in some cities. In rape cases, where the victim is unusually distraught as well as physically violated, investigation and interrogation by male officers had been found to exacerbate the woman's feelings of shame. Policewomen with special sensitivity training—and with a natural sense of female identification—have been extremely effective in comforting and reassuring the rape victim, while also extracting the necessary details of the assault.

State police

In 1971, the Pennsylvania State Police began recruiting women. By July 1972, twelve were sworn in and assigned to regular patrol work and investigation of drug abuse and prostitution. Pennsylvania State Police Commissioner, Col. James Barger says: "We've had no drop-outs from that first class and they've all done outstanding work. In July 1973, we had thirteen more women troopers, among them, a black woman. And they all had to undergo the same training as men do—they have to clean the stables too. The women are doing excellent work."

Lt. Doris M. Hughes is the first woman who has ever held rank in the Connecticut State Police and the first to command male subordinates. Lt. Hughes was a registered nurse before she entered police work in 1956. "It was good preparation for working with people under stress," she remarks.

Until spring, 1973, Connecticut law limited the quota of women state police officers to twelve. "Now the barrier has been removed," says Lt. Hughes. "Different age, height and educational requirements for the sexes were also lifted. Now the department can hire its authorized complement of 825 *persons* without caring about the sex of a good officer."

To further equalize the Connecticut candidates, agility tests are given out in advance so that applicants can practice getting into shape to do fifteen push-ups, fifteen sit-ups, a 6 foot 2 inch long jump, run a mile in under nine minutes, jump over a 2 foot 6 inch bar, and lift a 125-pound dummy body. (Give yourself the test to see whether you would qualify.) "Women are holding their own in these tests," reports Lt. Hughes with a hint of pride.

As a general indication of state police wages, Connecticut pays its trainees about $9,000; officers, $11,500; detectives, $12,500; and sergeants, $13,500.

Federal Bureau of Investigation

In July 1972, the first two women "graduated" from the fourteen-week FBI training course and were sworn in as agents. (Starting salary: $13,379; with overtime $16,723.)

When interviewed in 1974, Jack Herington, of the office of legal counsel, reported that there were twenty-seven female FBI agents in the field, five more in training and two more scheduled to begin the course. He stressed that similar requirements apply to both sexes: a college degree, a legal education or accounting major, good knowledge of foreign languages and three years' experience in an administrative or advanced investigative position. There are age (over 23, under 36), height (minimum 5'7") and other physical requirements and you must be willing to travel.

Though the FBI is a brand new career area for women, Mr. Herington claimed that the Bureau is entirely pleased with the women's work records and "there are absolutely no restrictions on where or how women agents operate."

The U.S. Secret Service

Of 1,220 Special Agents employed in 1974, only nine are women. While this may not be an impressive figure, Jack Warner, assistant to the Director, points out that "nine is a long way from zero, which we had in 1971." (And they had zero women for 106 years before that.)

Mr. Warner adds that the nine women in the ranks are "well-accepted because they're doing the job they were hired to do and they're doing it well."

A Special Agent's training is the same regardless of sex. First, there's the Treasury Department's basic law enforcement officer's course in constitutional law, use of firearms, collecting evidence, fingerprinting, photography, laws of arrest, etc. In the second phase, the Agent goes through Secret Service Training School to learn the Bureau's specialties: protection of the President of the United States, the Vice President, widows of former presidents and visiting heads of states; and investigative work in the areas of counterfeiting and forgery. Each course takes six weeks. A Secret Service Special Agent can go from $8,700 annual salary to $17,600 in four years.

The Executive Protective Service

This uniformed security force is made up of foot and car patrols and stationary posts, all of whom guard the White House, the First Family, executive office buildings and foreign diplomatic missions in Washington, D.C. After forty-eight years, this agency just began employing women in 1973.

Private security companies

Pinkerton, the nation's oldest (1850) and largest (105 offices, 36,000 employees, $162 million in revenues) counts about 4,000 women among its guards and detectives.

Private security companies furnish guards to banks, stores and businesses. Since airport security has been tightened, personnel are needed to do personal searches—and nearly half of them must be women. A guard earns about $3 an hour. Detectives, who must have higher skills and more education, get about $5.

Using the law to get a law enforcement job

In some cases, complaint and litigation has been the only route to equality. Seven women filed suit because they were not allowed to take the qualifying test for the California Highway Patrol. In another case, the Civil Service Commission ruled that the U.S. Park Police had to give its next available job to a woman who had been turned down because she didn't come up to the minimum height and weight standards. The Commission found that being 5'8" and 145 pounds was an irrelevant requirement for officers who make traffic arrests on American park roads.

Another frontier was opened for women when the New York State Division on Human Rights ordered Nassau County to admit women to its exclusively male police cadet training program, which leads to the position of police patrol-officer. The case was brought by the New York Civil Liberties Union on behalf of Eileen Brennan, the daughter of a retired police sergeant.

In February 1974 the Maryland State Police signed a landmark agreement to substantially increase the number of women and blacks on the force—as a result of a Justice Department suit. Where women have been accepted, they have proven themselves not only equal but exceptional. When a class of 120 men and four women graduated from a 1974 New York State Trooper course, it was a woman, Regina M. Robbins who walked away with graduate honors as first in her class.

But the battle continues on all fronts. In a Cleveland Federal courtroom a 5'2" female ju-jitsu expert tossed a 200-pound male around the room to demonstrate that training and skill can make a formidable police officer out of women as well as men. Discriminatory height and weight requirements in cities in Oregon, California, Washington, New Jersey and Arizona are being systematically challenged by women who want to enter law enforcement careers. In Chicago and Buffalo, New York—as in other places—sex and race discrimination have been found to go hand in hand.

The outlook

The Bureau of Labor Statistics expects about 17,000 openings every year in local police departments and about 3,000 annual vacancies for State Police officers through 1980. No estimates are available for private or federal police needs, but it seems evident that for women interested in law enforcement the closed doors are beginning to open. And for each of us, the fuller utilization of female resources means the better protection of all citizens.

Equal Rites for
Women of the Cloth

Whatever your sect—and whether or not you choose to preach—the widespread exclusion of womankind from leadership and policy-making positions in organized religion affects you as it does all of us. About five per cent of all Protestant ministers are women, only one female Rabbi is ordained (in the Reform wing of Judaism), and women are as remote as ever from the Catholic priesthood. More and more women want to be ministers, priests and rabbis, pastors, deacons and cantors on an equal basis with their brothers. They want more women on church boards in decision-making roles; and equal job and pay opportunities for clerics. But a brief survey of the representative denominations suggests that it is easier for a camel to go through the eye of a needle, than for a woman to enter into the service of God.

Protestant

Although most sects now allow women to be ordained, female ministers are commonly relegated to subordinate jobs as assistant pastors or teachers in church schools. Women ministers who *do* have their own parishes report that the resistance doesn't come from lay people, but from church officials themselves—and often from male ministers.

There was no community negativism when Rev. Margaret Howland won an appointment to the Woodside Presbyterian Church in Troy, New York, by a vote of 199–1. Rev. Howland insists that the ministry is not masculine or feminine, "it's personal."

While smaller cities have welcomed women, it is almost impossible to be voted into a large or urban parish where "man-style" politics and high-level community relations are considered as important as in pastoral counseling, preaching or officiating at weddings. Given general prejudices against women, different denominations show different kinds of progress.

Women's status in the 3.4 million member *Episcopal* Church was set back by defeat of the resolution to admit women to the priesthood. The vote, taken at the National Episcopal General Convention in Louisville, Kentucky, in October 1973, means Episcopal women are still to be restricted to service on local church vestries, to vote at conventions and to be ordained as deacons (who can perform all the functions of a priest except marriages, consecration of holy communion and pronouncing absolution). At this writing, ony two women are deacons. The women who made headlines in 1974 with their rebellious act of ordination have yet to be officially recognized.

The Rev. Gary E. Maier, Rector of All Saints Episcopal Church in Great Neck, New York, acknowledges that ordination into the priesthood is only the beginning of women's battle for justice in the church. "We must rethink every aspect of our spiritual life—from our use of the masculine pronoun for God; to 'The Churching of Women' (a prayer of thanksgiving following childbirth), whose unfortunate imagery suggests that women must be cleansed; to the practice of making all angels female, and all shepherds male, in the kids' Christmas pageant."

The *Lutheran* Church began ordaining women in 1970. Its first female minister with her own parish is Judith Hird of Toms River, New Jersey, a woman who feels that her sex is a distinct advantage in her work. "People are very interested in the fact that I am a woman," says the minister who is addressed by her flock as Pastor Judy. "And for that reason they are more apt to listen to me than to someone to whom they're accustomed."

The *United Methodist* Church, which claims ten million members, began to ordain women in 1956. However, by the early Seventies only three hundred of its 40,000 ministers were female.

At its 1972 General Conference in Atlanta, the Methodists eliminated all sexist language from their book of church law, *The Discipline of the United Methodist Church*. A Commission on the Status and Role of Women in the Church was also established for the quadrennium of 1973–1976. This body was charged with "the responsibility of fostering an awareness of problems and issues related to status and role of women with special reference to full participation in the total life of the Church."

Proportionately, the *United Presbyterian* Church is no more progressive. Of its 13,000 ministers, only 107 are women—though, at this writing, more than fifty women are in the seminaries preparing for pastorates. Also encouraging is the three-year program, "Women in Leadership," funded by United Presbyterian Women to develop local projects that enhance women's role in church and society.

Ordination of women is not new to the *Unitarian Universalist* Church. It began in 1863, when Olympia Brown was a minister with full ecclesiastical authority. But with the rise of church school programs, women were directed into education, rather than parish ministry. Now, there are only fifteen active women ministers and just four of these have full-time pulpits.

Nonetheless, there are feminist rumblings. In 1973, the Women's Caucus of the Arlington Street Unitarian Universalist Church in Boston presented a feminist church service at the General Assembly in Toronto. About forty women became involved in this presentation which included personal statements about women's life experiences, music, dance and audience participation.

In 1974 a pamphlet entitled "Feminism from the Pulpit" became available from Unitarian Universalist Church (740 Main Street, Santa Paula, California 93060. Price: $2.50). This collection of thirteen sermons by Rev. Marjorie Newlin Leaming seems to go a long way toward assuring women a vital place in any congregation.

While the *United Church of Christ* (two million members) numbers less than three hundred women among its nine thousand ministers, notable efforts are being made in other areas. In 1973, Washington, D.C., Judge Margaret A. Harwood was elected moderator, the first black woman to become a church leader in a biracial denomination.

On October 29, 1972, to commemorate Reformation Sunday, the Woman's Task Force of the United Church of

Christ took a cue from Martin Luther's Ninety-Five Theses. Task Force members in Pasadena, California, nailed "Feminist Theses" to the door of Church headquarters. They petitioned that God be genderless, that all Protestant denominations ordain women and that the concept of sin (Eve as temptress), be redefined in the interests of justice toward women.

At its 1973 Synod in St. Louis, the United Church of Christ eliminated all sexist language from its constitution—changing "chairman" to "chairperson" and so on. In the secular arena, the Church has urged the securities industry to end sex and race discrimination in its employment practices. Such activism is an exemplary use of church power and influence.

Roman Catholic

Mary Daly, Associate Professor of Theology at Boston College, has been an outspoken critic of the Church, calling it patriarchal and sexist. After she delivered the first sermon ever given by a woman at the Harvard Memorial Church, Dr. Daly led a protest walkout. Asked whether she had left the Catholic Church, she replied: "The Church has left the modern woman." In her book, *Beyond God the Father*, Dr. Daly postulates a new theology that brings an end to "phallic morality" and that forges a new imagery to replace the Virgin Mother—an impossible role for today's women.

One needn't espouse Dr. Daly's radicalism in order to agree that there is little to rejoice about in terms of women's progress toward the Catholic priesthood. In the fall of 1972, Pope Paul reiterated a highly restrictive role for women in church services. Yet, in January 1974, the Vatican was quite embarrassed about all the attention lavished on Licia Dinisio, an Italian woman who had been giving Communion in a Roman Catholic church in Pescara, Italy. Ms. Dinisio had been assigned to her pastoral tasks by the bishop, under a policy that permits lay people to serve as "extraordinary ministers" to relieve overworked priests. Newspapers called Ms. Dinisio "the first deaconess in Italy, maybe in all Europe." The Vatican was not pleased with the publicity.

Teresa D. Marciano, who teaches the sociology of religion at Fairleigh Dickinson University, put the problem bluntly in a *New York Times* article: "Women can bear priests; they cannot *be* priests."

In present Catholicism, women cannot be deacons either, despite Ms. Dinisio's brief moment of glory. Lay women must fulfill the dictates of their bishops, of course. But their extended role must never be formalized. That is church dictum.

The National Coalition of American Nuns has attacked the United States Bishops' study on the Ordination of Women, calling it "self-defeating," "retrogressive," and "anti-ecumenical." The sisters suggest that the bishops take courses on the theology of women. They warn that if the Church is not responsive to change, Catholic women will begin to seek other Christian churches where they are not systematically alienated and rejected.

Another nuns' organization, the National Assembly of Women Religious (with 2,300 members nationwide) echoed this concern for the alienation of Catholic womanhood, at their 1973 conference on the changing role of women.

Addressing the Pope's persistent neglect of women's demands, Dr. Marciano wrote: "A hand extended in charity must not be a hand that also denies equality. For no Christian truth was pronounced by the Pope [when he restricted women's role]. He simply confirmed an organizational assertion of sexual privilege and preference. Jesus loved a prostitute and rescued her from death . . . Can the Pope not love the woman of proven virtue who wishes to celebrate the Mass, in love and in joy, with her fellow Christians?"

Perhaps there is hope. Since the Pope ruled in the Spring of 1973 that both laywomen and nuns may distribute communion in church or take it to the sick—which is how Licia Dinisio received the directive from her bishop—he went so far as to name a study commission to examine the role of women in society and the Church. For further information on the work of this commission, contact National Catholic Office for Information, 1312 Massachusetts Avenue, N.W., Washington, D.C. 20005.

Jewish

In 1972, Sally Preisand became the first woman rabbi in the world. Ordained by a Reform seminary, Rabbi Preisand became assistant spiritual leader at the Stephen Wise

Free Synagogue in New York City—where the liturgy has been changed so that "men" are now "people" and "fathers" are now "ancestors," whenever these words come up in the service.

On the West Coast, across the continent from Rabbi Preisand, is the world's first woman cantor, Perryne Aisenman, who is assistant cantor at Stephen Wise Synagogue in Bel Air, California. At least two more young women are soon to complete the courses that lead to a Bachelor of Sacred Music degree, a professional qualification for cantors. (A cantor co-officiates with a rabbi at Jewish services, weddings and funerals; supervises the choir and the school music program, and prepares young people for Bar Mitzvah and Bas Mitzvah confirmations.)

Both of these remarkable developments have occurred in the million-member Reform Jewish community, which is the most liberal branch of Judaism. Orthodox Jews (a million followers; 2,500 rabbis) still interpret Jewish law strictly; that includes segregated seating for women in the synagogue and the exemption of women from most prayers and rituals. Between the two extremes of Reform and Orthodoxy is Conservative Judaism (two million members; 1,100 rabbis) where mixed-set seating is permitted, women are counted in the quorum required for public worship and identical religious educations are provided for boys and girls—three inroads that could lead to eventual equality of employment for male and female clergy as well. But conservatives have yet to authorize ordination of women.

Until there is "room at the inn" for all women who seek it, you may want to join the National Organization for Women Task Force on Sexism in Religion. This group has issued resolutions on women's role, holds "Sister-celebration" church services, studies scriptural bias against women, recommends reasonable changes in the liturgy, and organizes "zap" actions to dramatize women's charges through leafleting, picketing and rapping with male clergy.

Read Mary Daly's mind-blowing, soul-satisfying book, *Beyond God the Father* and get a copy of *The Lady Was a Bishop* by Joan Morris. With these two volumes, Christian women will be armed with theological arguments as well as historical support for the involvement of women in ecclesiastical life.

Celebrate Women's Suffrage Day (August 26) in your

church by preparing a feminist service and reading from *The Women's Bible* which was written by nineteenth-century suffragist, Elizabeth Cady Stanton.

Jewish women who have no interest in becoming rabbis or cantors may nonetheless opt for a greater voice in the daily operations of their temple or synagogue. Rather than be relegated to "the ladies' auxiliary," you can run for a post on the temple executive board, or mount a vigorous campaign for the temple presidency. Lillian Maltzer, past president of a six-hundred-family synagogue in Detroit, says: "I suspect the reason women are elected is because they are doing much of the work." Unfortunately, not every community reacts with such simple logic and fairmindedness.

Dr. Harvey Cox, Professor of Divinity at Harvard, makes an eloquent plea that should be read at every Sabbath service: "What I long for is an 'ecumenical' unity which will reconcile not so much the churches as the scattered segments of the human family, which will bring together not divided denominations but the 'separated brothers and sisters' who reside deep within each one of us. This means we can no longer ignore the three-fourths of the race who are not Christians, nor the 51 per cent who are not men. And the moment of reckoning is here."

Amen, Dr. Cox. Amen.

New Graduates:
The Longest Journey Begins with a Single Step

There is no "perfect" profession and there is no company with an unblemished record as regards sex discrimination in employment. Because sexism is so pervasive in this country, none of us ever entirely escapes its effects. Even the woman boss, the Queen Bee and the token vice president are not immune. Tokenism is the price injustice pays to the corporate conscience—but it doesn't buy anyone's honor, least of all the woman who is supposedly a credit to her sex. Somewhere along the way, the Queen Bee and the file clerk each discover that femaleness cuts across class lines; that a woman can only go so far before being reminded that as a woman, she can go no further.

For all the superficial differences—in the size of our paychecks or the style of our work clothes—none of us can really claim our situation is special. Whether seeking a seat on the board of directors or a seat on the union hall dais, someone is bound to say "Don't worry your pretty little head about such serious matters." They would rather give up a seat on the bus to a "lady"—than give up a seat of power to a woman.

Where does it all end? Perhaps, at the beginning—at the point when a young woman goes from school to her very first job. If you are starting out now, without a history of personal defeats and private indignities, the lessons learned from other women can be your armor. Knowing the worst, you can demand the best.

For the new graduate, this chapter should be considered the commencement address society forgets to deliver to young women who may be embarking upon a lifetime of struggle in the world of work.

In the good old days, some events followed the calendar. When the month of June rolled around, we could count on an influx in both the wedding chapels and the personnel agencies. It was a time of fresh starts for both love and labor.

While nuptials are still with us (though the couple may be barefoot and the vows spoken to hard rock accompaniment), the job market's welcome to graduating seniors is no longer so predictable.

Widespread unemployment is a fact of life. Corporate economy measures have caused staff cut-backs and the energy crisis has knocked the stuffing out of entire industries. The end of the draft coupled with the influx of women and minority men have created a more competitive employment atmosphere. Because the baby boom is over, there are less students and a surplus of teachers. In some cities $40,000 a year executives are driving taxis and philosophy professors are waiting on tables.

Enter new graduates eager to put the American dream to the test. What are your job prospects? As the last to enter the labor market, must you be the first to be pushed aside in favor of your elders? And as a female graduate, are you doubly doomed—once by your youth and inexperience and again by the fact of being a woman in a job market that can't even absorb able-bodied men?

The answer depends on several very specific factors, some of which *are* within your control. While you are powerless to control the energy crisis or the depressed economy in your city you *can* move to a place where there is more demand for your skills and specialties. You *can* be willing to take further training. You *can* learn to analyze whether your salary expectations are realistic or too high or low. You *can* learn to spot the entry level jobs with the best growth potential. You *can* become familiar with all the work alternatives in your field or declare your willingness to change fields in response to a good opportunity. You *can* familiarize yourself with all your rights and feel confident enough to assert them or else to take legal remedies. And you *can* get lucky and be savvy enough to know the right job when it happens to you.

Graduates of colleges, universities and postgraduate schools

At a recent conference of college career counselors, the experts agreed on these items of basic advice to graduates:

1. Your expectations should be realistic, not pessimistic.
2. Don't feel locked into your first job. Unless it meets your needs, use it as a look-out post for a better opening.
3. Seek professional help in jobhunting, career planning and even writing resumés.

One of the real professionals is Frank S. Endicott, Director Emeritus of Placement at Northwestern University, who has made a survey of employment trends in business and industry every year since 1946. The most remarkable finding in the 1974 Endicott Report is that 140 companies reported they were planning to offer 54 per cent *more* jobs to women than they did in the previous year. If these intentions are honorable, it would mean that one woman would be offered a job for every four men.

Five years ago, women got only one offer for every ten jobs men were offered.

In 1974, companies were looking hardest for women with degrees either in accounting, general business, data processing, math or engineering. To a lesser extent they expected to hire some marketing and retailing graduates. The fewest entry level jobs called for a liberal arts major.

Rather than being doubly-doomed, women graduates seem doubly-blessed. Women are being sought and courted by companies who have federal affirmative action plans to fulfill in order to correct past patterns of sex bias. But the courtship is not without its indiscretions in the salary area.

From the Endicott Report, here's a sampling of average monthly salaries being offered 1974 graduates in various fields:

Field	Salary Offered Women	Salary Offered Men
Engineering	$952	$963
General science (lab, research)	878	890
Accounting	868	920
Data processing/ Math	836	848
Marketing/Retailing	823	822
General business	775	756
Liberal Arts (sales management, personnel work, banking jobs)	752	741

Notice a few curious points. In general business and liberal arts—the lowest paid fields—women's starting salaries are higher than men's; in marketing women have a $1 edge, but the offers are substantially equal. However, in the top-paying four job categories, equal pay for equal work is far from true. Men out-earn women by up to $52 per month.

If you had read the Endicott Report in 1974, you'd have discovered other pertinent information that may have helped you find a job even before your cap and gown ceremonies. For example:

• Many companies are interested in hiring women students for summer jobs and for internship programs.

• More women were offered jobs as a result of contact made on campus with job recruiters, than through mail and other contacts.

• More companies are providing on-the-job-training, rather than lengthy training programs in a classroom.

• Liberal arts graduates will continue to be passed over as long as students with business and technical degrees are available. If you want a long-term career in business or industry, change your major to one of the demand areas if there's still time—or take postgraduate work in their priority areas. An M.B.A. is a strong plus. Failing these rescue operations, get practical business experience on a lower level first, then come back to the big companies for more advanced professional placement. Part-time and summer jobs do count. Learn about business on your own—through books, research, attending career conferences, getting help from the college employment counselor.

• Sell yourself more aggressively in job interviews. Companies are looking for go-getters of both sexes.

• A woman with an engineering degree is like a baseball pitcher who can hit home runs. Everyone wants her on the team. She can look around and choose the best offer.

In another survey of eighty major manufacturing and service organizations, one-third of the firms indicated that candidates must be willing to relocate. If you are a married woman graduating and taking interviews this year, be sure to discuss with your husband whether he's prepared to follow you to wherever the best offer takes you. No one should any longer assume that women—single or married—cannot accept jobs requiring travel or relocation.

College Placement Council surveyed 697 employers in December 1973, before the impact of the energy crisis could be assessed. At that time they found that the employer groups with *decreased* hiring plans were automotive and mechanical equipment manufacturers, banking, finance and insurance firms, research and consulting organizations, non-profit and educational insititutions and local and state governments.

Overall, employer groups expected to hire five per cent

more people with Master's degrees than with Bachelor's. The demand for Ph.D.'s is the lowest of all.

According to the Bureau of Labor Statistics, only one half of all college graduates find work directly related to their major field of study. Humanities and social science majors continue to experience the toughest time finding a good job after graduation—and that means women with B.A.'s in these fields will probably be consigned to the secretarial route as usual. In the popular area of social work, welfare casework and youth and drug problems, funds are short so hiring is down.

Even the old faithful, Civil Service, is cutting back. In New York, for example, a liberal arts graduate has to score 95 or better on the Federal Service Entrance Exam in order to be considered for a job in personnel, budgeting or social security administration. (Annual salary: from $8,055 to $9,969 as of mid-1974.) On the other hand, accountants, auditors and engineers (salary: $9,663 to $11,297) are keenly sought, and no written test is required. These candidates need only submit an application, resumé of experience and academic records. For the gifted college graduate, a prestigious on-the-job-training program called the Management Intern Option, which used to be available with a $12,000 salary, was discontinued on March 1, 1974. By the time you read this, the Option may be reinstated, so check it out.

On the bright side, Robert J. Gallione, Jr., student job counselor at Columbia University, feels the economy is bottoming out and future years will see an upward trend in opportunities for young graduates. Mr. Gallione also finds an increased sensitivity toward the employment of women.

"During the school year, we sent men to interview for Gal Friday jobs and women to fill calls for furniture movers," he recalls. "Even the school bulletin, which used to list 'Placement services available to students and their wives' now reads 'students and their spouses.' Women are being considered by virtually every employer that lists a job with us—except for the company that calls us for sperm donors needed for artificial insemination."

Athena Constantine, placement director for both Columbia and Barnard graduates, explains that the heavy 1970–71 layoffs of engineers had discouraged students from majoring in engineering. Now employers are feeling the effects of that gap and there are too few engineers to fill the jobs that recruiters have to offer. "From the students' viewpoint the crisis is really happening in higher education," says Ms. Constantine. "English, philosophy and language majors who are oriented to become college teachers have nothing but dismal prospects ahead for the next ten years. They'll just have to change their plans."

· Given this spotty labor outlook, a new graduate would do well to heed the hard-nosed advice offered by the veteran observer, Frank Endicott: "Be sure to get professional counsel before you turn down any job in this market. Use the application method that eighty per cent of our surveyed companies prefer—the résumé accompanied by a covering letter explaining why you want to work for that firm. And if you haven't heard in a reasonable time, check back with the company. Timing is half the battle and you may be lucky the second time around. Most important, don't consider yourself turned down until you actually hear the word 'No!' "

From the U.S. Department of Labor, advice for college graduates comes in the form of a prediction: They forecast "excellent" opportunities for accountants and market researchers; a "favorable outlook" for personnel specialists; "a shortage" of rehabilitation counselors; "rapid growth" for engineers; and "very good opportunities" for dentists, dieticians and health administrators.

High school graduates

Of the three million youngsters who graduated from high school in 1972, more than half did not go on to college—the lowest proportion since 1967.

By the October after graduation, 1.2 million of these three million graduates were either still looking for work or else holding down jobs. (The rest had become part of the discouraged unemployed discussed in Chapter 15.) Most of the young men had taken blue collar jobs, while the young women had been hired to do clerical work.

If you haven't learned to type, take stenography, do bookkeeping, fix a car or a TV set, or perform some other kind of skilled work, your high school diploma alone will not get you very far. That is the opinion expressed by most career counselors at the secondary school level.

While barriers against women have been breaking down, specialization has been increasing. This puts you in a possible double jeopardy situation. Whether you want to be a photo engraver or a beauty operator, skill will separate the girls from the boys, if sex doesn't do it first. If you missed such technical or vocational preparation in your high school curriculum, your best bet would be to enroll in a training school after graduation and before you start your job search.

"Unskilled high school graduates may find work as gardeners, janitors, or waitresses," says Leroy Hill, job placement director at Palo Alto High School in California. "But jobs with built-in advancement possibilities require further education." Mr. Hill names nursing, sales, dental assistant, illustrator, machinist and secretary as those positions which do not require a bachelor's degree but *do* call for extra training.

Emory Williams, supervisor of vocational services at Evanston High School in Illinois, believes that success in finding a job is often a question of attitude: "Unless you can accept responsibility, respect authority, get along with other human beings and learn the way business works, you have no right to believe the world owes you a living." Mr. Emory also encourages "next-step" education for the unskilled. He is especially enthusiastic about job prospects for students who gained vocational experience through work-study programs during their high school years. Mr. Emory's basic tip to young graduates of both sexes is: "If you take a job, take it seriously."

As one who was weaned on the work ethic, I tend to agree with Mr. Emory's bromide. I have frequently praised the notion of taking the most ambitious summer job you can find during those vacations between the end of one school term and the start of another. It may be effortless to find work as a camp counselor, but if you have a white collar career in mind, two months of pottery and potato races won't add vitamins to your resumé. The best way to demystify the business world is to get in there during July and August to see what goes on. Use your various summer jobs as trial runs in different industries to see which appeals to you most. If you like a particular office or organization, try to make a deal that guarantees you good summer positions in return for your commitment to put in at least one year in the company after you graduate.

A few years ago, Abington High School, just outside

Philadelphia, faced a typical tense situation where high
school graduates were in direct competition with out-of-
work adults. Today, there are enough jobs to go around as
long as the jobhunter knows where the action is. For example, steel fabrication plants are operating to the hilt and
are desperate for workers; but Bell Telephone still isn't
hiring operators. A new industrial park in the Abington
area has brought in many firms who require clerical help
and who will take high school students for part-time jobs
during the school year and full-time work after graduation.
Young women who are alert to the influx of retail es-
tablishments or fast food chains can infer that job opportunities lurk behind all that development in their community.

John Althouse, director of guidance at Abington, sees
some fascinating new trends. There has been a ten per
cent drop in the number of graduates going on to four-
year colleges and a concomitant increase in students who
choose one- and two-year technical training schools. Mr.
Althouse also notes a rise in the number of boys who have
gone into nursing and clerical work and the increase of
girls in accounting and general business. The most marked
shift has occurred among those graduates who would have
gone into teaching, but have switched to health careers.
"The trend toward nursing, medical and hospital technicians and X-ray technology is simply astonishing," says
Mr. Althouse. "Our kids are responsive to employment realities. They know that in this part of the country there
are too many cosmetologists and not enough data pro-
cessors. They're going on to junior colleges or business
schools. They're taking special courses in police work, library science or broadcasting. They are truly sophisticated
jobhunters!"

From all the evidence and informed testimony, the job
outlook for graduates in the Seventies resembles the
weather report: cloudy with bright patches. There *are*
good jobs to be had for those who satisfy the requirements
and who know where to match their supply of talent with
the labor market's demand.

Best of all, we seem to be moving into the era of the
woman worker, at last. Perhaps women in the Class of '75
and those that follow, will be the first job seekers in recent
history who will be spared that most devastating of all re-
jections: "Sorry, we're looking for a man."

Where to Get Help
—And Inspiration

We can share experiences, learn from one another, ask advice, enlarge our perspective, work together, admire one another and be inspired. Remember:

1. It isn't necessary to reinvent the wheel.
2. You aren't the first to reshape your life.
3. You aren't alone.

Breakthroughs

Here are America's real First Ladies, the women who broke the sex barrier in their fields during the last five years. If they are to have impact as trailblazers, they must not become tokens. One female vice president in a large company or one woman partner in an all-male law firm is not a cause for celebration but simply a sign that doors are opening that should never have been closed in the first place.

Margie Tabankin was the first female president of the National Student Association.

Joan Brown was Bethlehem Steel's first woman civil engineer.

Gaylene Snow was the first woman trained to become a "brakeman" on the Southern Pacific Railroad. There are 12,000 brake*men*.

Dr. Nancy Doyle was the first woman to receive the highest award granted by the University of California Medical School to the person who exemplified the "true physician."

Sister Taddea Kelly was the first woman to hold a senior Vatican post in Rome.

Gail Scott of WMAL-TV was the first television news anchorwoman in Washington, D.C.

Betty Diener was the first female president of the Doctoral Association at the Harvard Business School.

Marsha Lane was Schenley Industry's first woman vice president.

Alene B. Duerk was the Navy's first woman admiral.

Sharon Roswell was the first telephone linewoman in the history of General Telephone and Electronics.

Yvonne Knight was the first American Indian woman to receive a law degree.

Bernice Sandler was the first woman on the professional staff of the Association of American Colleges.

Carol Polis was the first woman ever licensed as a professional boxing judge in the state of Pennsylvania.

Emily Howell was the first female pilot in commercial airline history.

Dixie Lee Ray was the first woman named to chair the U.S. Atomic Energy Commission.

Marion McAllister was the first woman to train to become a "motorman" on the New York City subways.

Helen Thomas was the first woman ever selected to the Executive Committee of the White House Correspondents' Association.

Sally Priesand was the first woman rabbi and *Barbara Ostfeld* and *Sheila Cline* were the first female cantors in American Judaism.

Barbara McClintock was the first woman to receive the Medal of Science, the nation's top award for scientific achievement.

Julie Price, Paulette Dessel and *Ellen McConnel* were the first female pages on the floor of Congress.

Mary Joe Hamlin was the first woman truck driver at Michigan Bell Telephone.

Jane W. Currie and *Janene E. Gordon* were the first women inspectors ever hired by the U.S. Postal Service.

Lois Harkrider Stair was the first woman to serve as spiritual leader of the three-million member United Presbyterian Church.

Barbara Thompson was the first woman elected Superintendent of Public Instruction in the 125-year history of the state of Wisconsin.

Chien Shiung Wu, a nuclear physicist and Columbia University professor, was the first female president of the American Physical Society.

Millie Johnson, who works for the Chicago White Sox, was the first woman ticket manager in major league baseball.

Eloise Jaeger, at the University of Minnesota, and *Joni E. Barnett*, at Yale University were the first women to work as directors of physical education in a coeducational school.

Eleanor Riger was ABC-TV's first sports show producer who was not male.

Pamela R. Chelgren, an engineer, was the first woman commissioned officer in the National Oceanic and Atmospheric Administration.

Cheryl White was the first jockey in horseracing who was both female and black.

Carolyn K. Buttolph was the first woman to be employed by the Internal Revenue Service as a district director.

Bri Murphy was Hollywood's first female director of photography, and *Dede Allen* was the industry's first woman film editor.

Marjorie M. Murtagh was the first woman ever admitted to the Naval Architecture Program of the Maritime College of New York.

Jeanne Holm was the first woman to hold the rank of two-star general in the U.S. Air Force.

Carmel C. Marr was the first woman and the first black person to serve as a member of the New York State Public Service Commission.

Lin Bolen, vice president for daytime programs at NBC, was the first woman to hold such a high position at a television network.

Dorothy W. Nelson, University of Southern California, and *Soia Mentschikoff,* University of Miami, were the first females to serve as law school deans. Prof. Mentschikoff is also the first woman president of the Association of American Law Schools.

Rosemary A. Judge, president of Mobil Foundation, was the first woman to head a major corporate foundation.

Harriet Henry was the first woman judge on a state court in Maine.

Barbara Allen was the Navy's first woman pilot.

Mary Estill Buchanan was Colorado's first female secretary of state.

Betty Southard Murphy was the first woman to head the U.S. Labor Department's Wage and Hour Division, which administers the minimum wage and equal pay laws.

Alice Sherman and *Louise Wilson* are the first women to be assigned as mounted police officers in the New York City Police Department.

Career Aids:
Counseling, Courses,
Employment Assistance

Talent book for all management levels—register with Long Island Chapter, NATIONAL ORGANIZATION FOR WOMEN, Box 176, Merrick, N.Y. 11566.

Counseling, testing, job leads, nationwide professional and managerial placement—a professional staff will help you define your goals, reorder personal priorities and explore work opportunities. *OPTIONS FOR WOMEN*, 8419 Germantown Avenue, Philadelphia, Pa. 19118.

Skills registry—ready-to-work, qualified applicants seeking part-time or flexi-time jobs should contact *FLEXIBLE CAREERS*, YWCA, 37 S. Wabash, Chicago, Ill.

Job referrals—when you fill out the information sheet, your qualifications are fed into a computerized data bank which coughs up your card when a matching job opening arises. Your identity is kept confidential until you decide the job interests you. Get information sheet from *INDIVIDUAL RESOURCES*, Box 5346, Grand Central Station, New York, New York 10017.

Career solutions for federally employed women—periodic two-day courses for women in government jobs. Special emphasis on civil service regulations, influencing male managers and bonding effectively with other women colleagues. Information from *BETSY HOGAN ASSOCIATES*, 222 Rawson Road, Brookline, Mass. 02146.

Communications and self-assertiveness course—a national training program designed to assist women's career mobility by developing self-awareness, speaking and problem-solving skills. Request details about "Breaking Barriers Through Speech" from *WOMEN'S TRAINING AND RESOURCES CORPORATION,* 142 High Street, Portland, Me. 04101.

Back-to-work seminars—vocational counseling and career workshops are available at many of the nation's YWCA branches. For specifics contact Dr. Aurelia Toyer, *YWCA,* 600 Lexington Avenue, New York, N.Y. 10022.

Life planning for career objectives—individual and group counseling leading to total reassessment and career change. Follow-up until client achieves career self-management. *CAREER MANAGEMENT ASSOCIATES,* 101 Park Street, Montclair, New Jersey 07042.

Shortened work schedule—if you live in the greater New York area and you want to or have to be home when your children return from school, a 9:30 to 3 job may be available through *NEWTIME AGENCY,* 2 West 45 Street, New York, N.Y. 10020.

Job exchange, counseling—full program of employment assistance including leadership training, workshops and testing. *WOMEN'S OPPORTUNITY RESEARCH CENTER,* Middlesex Community College, Springs Road, Bedford, Mass. 10730.

Career advice for young people—The "Career Awareness Project" assists schools and community groups in helping young people explore career alternatives. Information and a project guide may be ordered for $2.50 from *BUSINESS AND PROFESSIONAL WOMEN'S FOUNDATION,* 2012 Massachusetts Avenue, N.W., Washington, D.C. 20036.

Counseling workshop—eight-week course of three hour sessions, each session limited to eight women who hammer out career hang-ups, assess opportunities and define objectives. *CAREER COUNSELING FOR WOMEN,* 755 New York Avenue, Huntington, New York 11743.

College teaching positions—those seeking teaching or administrative jobs in higher education can send their curriculum vitae (resumé) plus $4 and get referrals collected by the *WOMEN'S EQUITY ACTION LEAGUE,* c/o Ruth Russell Gray, 517 Central Avenue, Plainfield, New Jersey 07060.

Talent bank—The State of New Jersey maintains listings of full- and part-time jobs to match up with qualified applicants. Request application from the Commissioner, *DEPARTMENT OF COMMUNITY AFFAIRS*, 363 West State St., Trenton, New Jersey 08625.

Law school for busy women—Interested in part-time, day-time law school? Write The Women's Committee, *NEW ENGLAND SCHOOL OF LAW*, 126 Newbury Street, Boston, Mass.

Vocational testing and counseling—job search assistance starting with analysis of your skills and life values. Take your choice from private counseling or group self-discovery sessions. *INDIVIDUAL DEVELOPMENT CENTER*, 310 15th Street East, Seattle, Wash. 98122.

Drop-in counseling service in seven cities—Atlanta, Richmond, Washington, D.C., Baltimore, Boston, Providence and White River Junction, Vt. have branch offices of this supportive, upbeat, and *free* peer group counseling service conducted by trained volunteers. Get help preparing your resumé, priming for job interviews, finding good job leads. For information about all seven cities write *WASHINGTON OPPORTUNITIES FOR WOMEN*, 1111 20th Street, N.W., Washington, D.C.

Career change specialists—task oriented program specializing in redesign of self-image, self-actualization, mastery of "the creative conversation," establishing a network of helpful job contacts and launching a full-scale career change campaign. *MAINSTREAM ASSOCIATES*, 343 Madison Avenue, New York, New York 10017.

Train for executive jobs—learn fundamental office systems and procedures, personnel functions, financial planning, business writing, marketing and sales, oral communication, managerial techniques and simulated on-the-job training. Entrance to course requires four years of college or four years of work experience or any combination of the two qualifications. Completion of eight one-semester courses wins you a Certificate of Management. Contact *MANAGEMENT FOR TODAY'S WOMAN PROGRAM*, Katharine Gibbs School, 200 Park Avenue, New York, N.Y. 10017.

Free educational and vocational counseling—women in Orange County, California, are welcome to use the reference library, apply under their scholarship program, discuss individual problems and goals. Write *WOMEN'S OP-*

PORTUNITIES CENTER, University of California, Irvine, Calif. 92664.

Employment agency for high level jobs—specializes in $10,000 to $30,000 openings for lawyers, engineers, financial analysts, auditors, publicists, architects, programmers and accountants. *TODAY'S WOMAN PLACEMENT SERVICE*, 21 Charles Street, Westport, Conn. 06880.

Feminist job counseling—problem-solving in the context of everyday work situations. Consciousness-raising sessions tackle sex role stereotypes on the job, working mothers' guilt, office relationships, and hardheaded how-to's. *OPTIONS: CAREER WORKSHOPS FOR WOMEN*, 333 Central Park West, New York, N.Y. 10025.

Director of feminist counseling services—listings of specialists in 15 states costs 50 cents from *THE ASSOCIATION OF FEMINIST CONSULTANTS*, 4 Canoe Brook Drive, Princeton Junction, New Jersey 08550.

Employment assistance for workers and management—this non-profit group aims to educate employers about the benefits of job sharing while at the same time matching first-rate people with the best possible jobs. *BOSTON PROJECT FOR CAREERS*, 83 Prospect Street, West Newton, Mass. 02165.

Continuing education courses at Michigan State—"Women: Potentials and Perspectives" is a course divided into three parts: Who is Woman (sex roles, the status of the female in society); Who Am I (personal assessment); Where Do I Go (back to school, career, volunteer work, politics). Catalog from *MICHIGAN STATE UNIVERSITY, EVENING COLLEGE*, 18 Kellogg Center, East Lansing, Mich. 48823.

Placement service for executive and professional women—full-time and shortened workweek openings for managerial candidates and other highly qualified specialists. *MANAGEMENT SERVICES*, 2 West 45th Street, New York, N.Y. 10022.

Career counseling at Penn State—"Life Work Planning" is a course that combines introspection with action. Students learn data gathering, management tools of organization and decision-making skills. *PENNSYLVANIA STATE UNIVERSITY, MCKEESPORT CAMPUS*, Pittsburgh, Pa. 15132.

$70,000 annual loan fund for graduate business education—thanks to Sears-Roebuck Foundation and the

Business and Professional Women's Foundation, women can borrow up to $2,000 a year to attend one of 110 participating graduate schools in business administration. The fund will be available between 1975 and 1980. Information from *BUSINESS AND PROFESSIONAL WOMEN'S FOUNDATION*, 2012 Massachusetts Avenue, N.W., Washington, D.C. 20036.

Summer sessions on organizing tactics—courses on unionization, affirmative action plans and coalition politics are supplemented by supervised fieldwork. A working woman's refresher course in radical activism. *THE MIDWEST ACADEMY*, c/o Heather Booth, 817 West George Street, Chicago, Ill. 60657.

Personal planning workshops—positive approaches to change, long-range career goals, time management, a personal five-year plan, how to handle conflicts. Registration information from *EFFECTIVE FEEDBACK INC.*, 840 Brookwood Place, Ann Arbor, Mich. 48104.

Career development—group counseling utilizing self-fulfilment concepts, career strategy, identification of resources and training programs and the dynamics of personal growth in a group work situation. *NEW ENVIRONMENTS FOR WOMEN*, 44 Bertwell Road, Lexington, Mass. 02173.

Career guidance for New Jersey women—group counseling is free; vocational aptitude tests and workshops on career choices and financial planning are available for a nominal cost. Reference library for do-it-yourself research. *EVE*, Kean College, Union, N.J. 07083.

Annual Career Fair in Los Angeles—a week-long program for high school and college students and for adults seeking re-entry. About a hundred booths are manned or womanned by representatives of business, industry, labor, government, the professions and educational institutions. Displays, resource materials and individual counseling in whatever field interests you. Details from *OFFICE OF LOS ANGELES SUPERINTENDENT OF SCHOOLS*, 155 West Washington Blvd., Los Angeles, California.

Financial aid—awards ranging from $50 to $350 are granted to women who need money for training courses, purchase of equipment needed for self-employment or rehabilitation. If you are widowed, disadvantaged, the sole support of your famliy or physically handicapped, you may qualify for this assistance. Apply to *FOUNDERS*

FUND VOCATIONAL AID, Altrusa International, 332 South Michigan Avenue, Chicago, Ill. 60604.

Get a diploma to qualify for better jobs—Your maturity and general life experience may have armed you with enough information to pass a high school equivalency test with little additional study. For addresses of testing centers write to *AMERICAN COUNCIL ON EDUCATION*, 1 Dupont Circle, N.W., Washington, D.C. 20036.

College credit without college classes—even if you haven't completed high school you may be able to get credit for college level achievement which would afford you advanced placement in fields such as nursing, foreign languages and professional education. For information about the College Proficiency Examination write Director, *COLLEGE PROFICIENCY PROGRAM*, State Education Department, Albany, New York 12224.

Computerized listings of job openings—the U.S. Employment Service maintains a Job Bank with daily computerized listings of job and training opportunities and a library of job search and guidance materials with full service in a hundred major metropolitan areas. Contact your local public employment office or request information about the "Job Information Service" from *U.S. DEPARTMENT OF LABOR*, U.S. Employment Service, Office of Technical Support, Washington, D.C. 20210.

Employment agency specializing in flexible schedule jobs—college-educated women seeking short-term assignments or permanent part-time work should register with *DISTAFFERS*, 1130 Western Savings Building, Philadelphia, Pa. 19107.

Career reorientation in two phases—phase one is assessment of off- and on-the-job skills, motivational patterns and goals; phase two is the job search campaign and discussion of options. Contact *MORE FOR WOMEN*, 2 Lexington Avenue, New York, N.Y. 10010.

Older women on the move—pre-employment counseling and training sessions for re-entry candidates of any age, educational level or financial profile. *CAREER CLINIC FOR MATURE WOMEN*, 628 Nicollet Mall, Room 331, Minneapolis, Minn. 55402.

Non-profit counseling service—information, referral, workshops, conferences sponsored by San Fernando Valley Branch of the American Association of University

Women. *CENTER FOR NEW DIRECTIONS,* 6950 Hayvenhurst Avenue, Van Nuys, Calif. 91406.

Learn to lead—teaches skills necessary to achieve career aims. *LEADERSHIP AND TRAINING TASK FORCE,* c/o Judith Greschwind, 2306 Greenery Lane, Silver Springs, Md. 20906.

Counseling project in Memphis—information and referral service for training and employment opportunities for women, young and older. *WOMEN AND GIRLS EMPLOYMENT ENABLING SERVICES,* 3485 Poplar Avenue, Suite 1, Memphis, Tenn. 38111.

Personal growth groups—consultations on group and individual change for more productive work and personal life; affirmative action counseling. *WELLS-CHRISTIE ASSOCIATES,* P.O. Box 3392, Beverly Hills, Calif. 90212.

Education for the jobhunt—non-credit courses and individual counseling for never-worked and return-to-work women. *JOB HORIZONS FOR WOMEN,* Broome Community College, Binghamton, N.Y. 13902.

Research and counseling for college students—checks out various career opportunities for women, runs workshops, provides private counseling. *DISTAFFERS RESEARCH AND COUNSELING CENTER,* 4625a 41 Street, N.W., Washington, D.C. 20016.

Vocational and educational workshop—helps you evaluate goals, aptitudes, etc. *CAREER HORIZONS FOR WOMEN,* Hofstra University, Hempstead, N.Y. 11050.

Better jobs with bigger potential—recruits women with high school educations for formal apprenticeship in non-traditional jobs. This information and referral service receives its funds from the U.S. Department of Labor, not your pocketbook. *BETTER JOBS FOR WOMEN,* 1545 Tremont Place, Denver, Colo. 80202.

Full-scale employment assistance—college-educated family women can receive counseling, referrals to jobs or educational opportunities, assessment of skills and strengths. Request forms to include your name and qualifications on their talent roster. *CATALYST,* 6 East 82 Street, New York, N.Y. 10028.

Recruitment and referral in Atlanta—minority women will be guided into training programs which in turn lead to white collar jobs with superior advancement possibilities. *BLACK WOMAN EMPLOYMENT PROGRAM,* Southern Regional Council, 52 Fairle Street, N.W., Atlanta, Ga. 30303.

Day or evening counseling classes—guidance, remedial education, special counseling. *SECOND CAREERS PROGRAM*, Tombrock College, P.O. Box 536, West Paterson, New Jersey.

Information lifeline in Philadelphia—for leads on child care, job openings, career counseling and continuing education; also check their job bank and resource library. *RESOURCES FOR WOMEN*, University of Pennsylvania Faculty Club, 200 South 36 Street, Philadelphia, Pa. 19104.

Women prepare for "man-size" jobs—instruction and training leading to well-paid skilled jobs in printing, manufacturing, construction and other trades. *WOMEN IN WISCONSIN APPRENTICESHIPS*, Department of Industry, Labor and Human Relations, Box 2209, Madison, Wis. 53702.

Counseling for careers in New Hampshire—paraprofessionals assist women in vocational, education and associated problems and choices. Eight local branches in the state. *WOMEN'S INFORMATION SERVICE (WISE)*, 19 South Main Street, Hanover, N.H. 03755.

Learn to recognize sex discrimination when it's committed against you—how to fight unequal treatment; which laws protect against what violation and who enforces them; how to file charges. Full counseling service from *EMPLOYMENT DISCRIMINATION COUNSELING PROJECT*, 1736 R. Street, N.W., Washington, D.C. 20009.

Financial, employment and credit counseling—this non-profit group assists women to become self-supporting; provides business development advice for entrepreneurs. *ADVOCATES FOR WOMEN*, 564 Market St., Room 218, San Francisco, Calif. 94104.

Non-traditional jobs for both sexes—placement assistance for jobhunters seeking jobs traditionally reserved for the opposite sex. *JOB SEARCH*, Women's Resource Center, YWCA, 1111 SW 10th Street, Portland, Oreg. 97205.

Measure yourself—aptitude tests for young people and adults of all ages, work-sample evaluation, assessment of your dexterity, memory, reasoning and the practical application of this evaluation to your place in the business world. *JOHNSON O'CONNOR RESEARCH FOUNDA-*

TION AND HUMAN ENGINEERING LABORATO-RIES, 11 East 62nd Street, New York, N.Y. 10021 (and 11 other locations in U.S. and Mexico).

Scholarships for college educations awarded to mature women—the first nation-wide undergraduate fund targeted to women over 35 has been established by Clairol, whose advertising motto is "You're not getting older, you're getting better." $50,000 will be split 50 ways among 4-year colleges who will enroll women in a full- or part-time degree program. *THE CLAIROL LOVING CARE SCHOLARSHIP PROGRAM*, 345 Park Avenue, New York, N.Y. 10022.

Looking for work in the $20,000 to $60,000 range? —an executive search and recruitment firm seeks qualified women to fill high level positions. Send resumé (fee paid by employer). *MANAGEMENT WOMAN, INC.,* The Plaza, Fifth Ave. at 59 Street, New York, N.Y. 10019.

Seminars for women—a full curriculum of meetings held in 10 major cities for businesswomen who lack formal instruction in finance. Courses such as "Fundamentals of Finance" and "Principles of Supervisory Management for the Newly-Promoted Woman" are offered by *THE DISTAFF GROUP,* Executive Enterprises, 10 Columbus Circle, New York, N.Y. 10019.

Under one roof in Los Angeles—galleries for women artists, art workshop, feminist bookstore, theater, associated Women's Press—full report for women in the arts. *WOMEN'S BUILDING,* 743 S. Grandview, Los Angeles, Calif. 90057.

Business skills for entrepreneurs—women who own their own businesses or want to start a company, service or store, will benefit from the conference called "How's Business?" offered by *PACT,* c/o Linda White, 635 Divisadero Street, San Francisco, California 94117.

Education for management—a two-year program of paid internship, supportive counseling and study leading to a Masters in Business Administration. If you have a liberal arts undergraduate degree, you may qualify. *GRADUATE MANAGEMENT PROGRAM FOR WOMEN,* Pace University, Pace Plaza, New York, N.Y. 10038.

Management development programs—helps businesswomen develop personal leadership qualities and related management skills. Programs available in New York, New

Jersey and Connecticut. *HUMAN RESOURCES DE-VELOPMENT*, 103 Gedney Street, Nyack, New York 10960.

Scholarships for mature students—if you want to resume your academic careers on a part-time basis, try to qualify for one of the scholarships available to mature women from *SCHOLARSHIP COMMITTEE, WOMEN'S RESOURCE CENTER*, 226 Bostwick, N.W. Grand Rapids, Michigan 49502.

Organizations and Services*

CAREER GROUPS

Accounting

AMERICAN SOCIETY OF WOMEN ACCOUNT-ANTS, 327 S. La Salle Street, Chicago Ill. 60604—career information for newcomers; professional cameraderie for practicing accountants.

Architecture

ASSOCIATION OF WOMEN IN ARCHITECTURE, P.O. Box 1, Clayton, Mo. 63105—shared concerns for the tiny minority of women architects; plus career information for those interested in entering the field.

Art

DISTRICT OF COLUMBIA REGISTRY OF WOMEN ARTISTS, 1023 Independence Avenue, S.E., Washington, D.C. 20003—a communications network for women artists; promotes them and their work.

* These are grouped under convenient headings. However, since there is considerable overlap of interests and activities, you may want to check the entire listing for organizations that may serve your needs.

Banking

NATIONAL ASSOCIATION OF BANK WOMEN, 111 East Wacker, Chicago, Ill. 60601—to learn how to prepare for bank management training programs, or to share experiences with other women in banking, join NABW.

Business and Professional

BUSINESS AND PROFESSIONAL WOMEN'S FOUN-DATION, 2012 Massachusetts Avenue, N.W., Washington, D.C.—research, bibliographies, scholarships, library, information on working women's problems and educational opportunities.

COALITION OF 100 BLACK WOMEN, c/o CTW, 1 Lincoln Plaza, New York, N.Y. 10023—a frankly elite, high-powered union of professional and activist black women to support specific projects and programs.

NATIONAL ASSOCIATION FOR FEMALE EXECU-TIVES, 10 East 40 Street, New York, N.Y. 10016—committed to economic parity (but disturbingly anti-feminist in its literature).

PROFESSIONAL WOMEN'S CAUCUS, Box 1057, Radio City Station, New York, N.Y. 10019—works to advance the status and welfare of women who are architects, scientists, engineers, lawyers, doctors and the like.

Domestic workers

DOMESTICS UNITED, 1222 Oaklawn Avenue, Charlotte, North Carolina 28206—presses for higher pay, benefits and better working conditions for household workers in the state of North Carolina.

NATIONAL COMMITTEE ON HOUSEHOLD EM-PLOYMENT, 8120 Fenton Street, Suite 300, Silver Springs, Md. 20910—get more information about how household workers want to be treated, what is fair or unfair, how to establish a respectful work relationship between employer and domestic. Also news about occasional conferences and organizing tactics.

PROGRESSIVE HOUSEHOLD TECHNICIANS, Room 601, 370 Lexington Ave., New York, N.Y. 10017—an activist group with branches in several states. Organizes for better pay and benefits; has created a suggested work contract outlining fair employment policies for domestics.

Engineering

SOCIETY OF WOMEN ENGINEERS, 345 East 47 Street, New York, N.Y. 10017—today, 90 per cent of engineering jobs are not done in mines or on construction sites, but in air conditioned offices. Learn more about an engineering career and job opportunities.

Federal service

FEDERALLY EMPLOYED WOMEN, 621 National Press Building, Washington, D.C. 20004—women's advocate group dedicated to eliminating sex discrimination in government jobs.

Mature women

GRAY PANTHERS, c/o Maggie Kuhn, Tabernacle Church, 3700 Chestnut Street, Philadelphia, Pa. 19104—a consultation service and support group for older adults. Write for branch addresses in Chicago, New York, Berkeley and Santa Fe, N. Mex.

INFORMATION CENTER ON THE MATURE WOMAN, 3 West 57 Street, New York, N.Y. 10019—information bank on psychological, medical and social realities of older women's lives; provides speakers; statistics, studies and other research findings; resource library.

OLDER WOMEN'S LIBERATION (OWL), c/o Peggy Fenley, 3711 Oakland Gravel Road, Columbia, Mo. 65211—send stamped envelope and get information on how to form a rap group (or join an existing group) where mature women can get help and encouragement from one another during mid-life adjustments, re-entry tremors and experience with age and sex bias.

Media

AMERICAN WOMEN IN RADIO AND TELEVISION, 1321 Connecticut Avenue, N.W., Washington, D.C. 20036—exchange of ideas among members, conferences, lunches, newsletter, career information on all aspects of broadcasting. Local chapters in several states.

MEDIA WOMEN, 320 Central Park West, New York, N.Y. 10025—activism, advocacy and consciousness-raising for women employed in the publishing industry; works for improved working conditions and upgrading of image of women in the media.

WOMEN IN COMMUNICATIONS, 8305-A Shoal Creek Boulevard, Austin, Texas 78758—serves and represents women journalists in all media. Publishes magazine and newsletter, honors journalistic excellence with various awards, runs career seminars, nationwide job search service.

Medicine

THE AMERICAN MEDICAL WOMEN'S ASSOCIATION, 1740 Broadway, New York, N.Y. 10019—provides statistics, lecturers, films, tapes and career materials. Also operates scholarship, grant and loan programs for aspiring women doctors.

Nursing

AMERICAN NURSES ASSOCIATION, 2420 Pershing Road, Kansas City, Mo. 64108—works for the professional and education progress of nurses in terms of economic improvement and increased funds for nurses' training. Career information available for high school, college and re-entry women. Refresher courses and demonstration of new equipment.

Office work

WOMEN OFFICE WORKERS (WOW), P.O. Box 439, Planetarium Station, New York, N.Y. 10024—clerical workers and secretaries meet for consciousness-raising and to discuss organizational strategy to fight for better working conditions, pay and benefits.

Politics

THE NATIONAL WOMEN'S POLITICAL CAUCUS, 1302 18th Street, N.W., Washington, D.C. 20036—a multi-partisan, national coalition of women—often with disparate views—seeking common grounds to encourage women's participation in every aspect of political life. Solid and informed advice on running for elective office, where the pay is not always the best but the emotional rewards are considerable.

Psychology

ASSOCIATION FOR WOMEN IN PSYCHOLOGY, M-101 McGraw, Cornell University, Ithaca, N.Y. 14850—counters the male supremacist bias of psychology and therapy, questions assumptions about what is "normal" for women, promotes research into women's problems and alternate life styles. Also works for equality of both sexes in the profession.

Religion

CHURCH EMPLOYED WOMEN, 830 Witherspoon Blding, Philadelphia, Pa. 19107—to promote and upgrade the status of women with jobs in the United Presbyterian Church structure.

INTERNATIONAL ASSOCIATION OF WOMEN MINISTERS, 1464 West 101 Street, Cleveland, Ohio 44102—promotes equal rights within the church; recruits women into the ministry.

Science

ASSOCIATION OF WOMEN IN SCIENCE, 1818 R. Street, N.W., Washington, D.C. 20009—organizing computerized data bank containing resumés of qualified women; promotes equal opportunities for scientifically inclined women; career development assistance.

Stewardesses

STEWARDESSES FOR WOMEN'S RIGHTS, 515 N. Washington, Alexandria, Va. 22314—fights for professionalism, upgrading of image and dignity of the job, encourages mobility ladder for advancement in airlines industry, publishes a newsletter.

Union women

COALITION OF LABOR UNION WOMEN (CLUW), c/o Addie Wyatt, Amalgamated Meat Cutters and Butchers International Union, 4859 South Wabash, Chicago, Ill. 60615—when it was founded in the spring of 1974, this group attracted 3,200 women from 58 unions. Their concerns are: securing affirmative action, organizing the unorganized, legislative and political action and participation of women in unions. All women covered by collective bargaining agreements are eligible for membership.

UNION WOMEN'S ALLIANCE TO GAIN EQUALITY, 2137 Oregon Street, Berkeley, Calif. 94705—this group, known as *Union W.A.G.E.*, is dedicated to all rights for women workers whether their adversary be the unions or the employers; encourages greater participation, leadership and organized unionism among women workers; promotes women's issues as valid negotiating demands at the bargaining table.

UNITED AUTO WORKERS WOMEN'S DEPARTMENT, 8000 E. Jefferson, Detroit, Mich. 48226—active proponents of all women's rights legislation, promotes unionization, informs and educates women on health and working condition demands for bargaining.

BROAD-BASED WOMEN'S GROUPS

ECONOMIC THINK TANK FOR WOMEN, c/o Center of Policy Research, 475 Riverside Drive, New York, N.Y. 10025—a catalytic discussion and policy-making group that will gauge effect on women of the energy crisis, recession, automation and other societal developments.

THE NATIONAL CONGRESS OF NEIGHBORHOOD WOMEN, Center for Urban Ethnic Affairs, 4408 8th Street, N.E., Washington, D.C.—an organization devoted to the problems of blue collar and other working class women.

NATIONAL ORGANIZATION FOR WOMEN, 5 South Wabash St., Suite 1615, Chicago, Ill. 60603—the grandmother of all the current women's rights groups. Task forces and subcommittees on all issues of interest to women from sexuality to education to employment. Request address of your local chapter and location of N.O.W. job discrimination counseling center nearest you.

NEW FEMINIST TALENT ASSOCIATES, 115 West 57 Street, New York, N.Y. 10019—furnishes lecturers able to discuss and advise women's groups or community organizations on job discrimination and related political and economic issues.

PROJECT ON THE STATUS AND EDUCATION OF WOMEN, Association of American Colleges, 1818 R.

Street, N.W., Washington, D.C. 20009—impressive research reports, newsletters, legislative analyses and technical assistance, all to advance women's place in education and employment.

WOMEN EMPLOYED, 37 South Wabash, Chicago, Ill. 60603—Chicago's working women have a functioning pressure group to publicize their plight, improve their status and police sex discrimination violations.

WOMEN'S EQUITY ACTION LEAGUE, 538 National Press Building, Washington, D.C. 20004—promotes economic progress for women, enforcement of antidiscrimination laws, gathers data on women's status in education and professions, government and private industry. Write for address of WEAL division in your state, or for reports from various subcommittees on "Money and Credit," "Legislation," "Want Ads," "Discrimination in Higher Education."

WOMEN FOR CHANGE, Zale Bldg, 3000 Diamond Park, Dallas, Tex. 75247—talent banks, referrals, speakers, day care, newsletter, library, task forces on employment, legal rights, politics.

WOMEN'S ORGANIZATIONS AND LEADERS DIRECTORY, published by Women Today, National Press Building, Washington, D.C. 20004. ($25) In 470 pages, 9,000 individuals and organizations are listed alphabetically, geographically and by subject. If it's not listed here, it's probably an all-male club.

JOB DISCRIMINATION AND WOMEN'S RIGHTS

AMERICAN JEWISH CONGRESS WOMEN'S DIVISION, 15 East 84th Street, New York, N.Y. 10028—initiated investigation of sexist practices of employment agencies and employers who file discriminatory job orders with personnel services. General commitment to women's rights.

CATHOLIC WOMEN FOR THE E.R.A.—a new lobbying group formed to promote ratification of the Equal Rights Amendment in those states that have yet to pass it. Contact Linda Redington, 5545 Dunning Place, Cincinnati, Ohio 45227.

THE CENTER FOR CONSTITUTIONAL RIGHTS, 588 Ninth Avenue, New York, N.Y. 10036—takes cases on job discrimination, maternity leaves and sexism in education. No fee.

CIVIL LIBERTIES LEGAL DEFENSE FUND, c/o Bliss Matteson, 67 Winthrop Street, Cambridge, Mass. 02138—takes women's rights cases in the Boston area.

HUMAN RIGHTS FOR WOMEN, 1128 National Press Building, Washington, D.C. 20004—provides free legal assistance in key sex bias cases, publishes educational materials and researches the legal, economic and social condition of women. To get on their mailing list, send a tax deductible contribution.

NEW WOMEN LAWYERS, c/o Mary Kelly, 382 Central Park West, New York, N.Y. 10025—litigates women's rights cases, plans conferences to educate women lawyers in specialties such as job discrimination.

WAGE AND HOUR DIVISION, United States Department of Labor, Washington, D.C. 20210—write for all the facts about The Equal Pay Act.

WOMEN'S CENTER LEGAL PROGRAM, 1027 South Crenshaw Blvd., Los Angeles, California—all-purpose legal aid for women.

WOMEN'S JOB RIGHTS, YWCA, 620 Sutter, Room 318, San Francisco, Calif. 94102—helps women organize, offers counsel on legal complaints, conducts job discrimination clinics.

WOMEN'S LAW FUND, Keith Building, Room 620, Cleveland, Ohio 44115—women lawyers, financed by a Ford grant, litigate complaints of sex bias in fringe benefits, promotions, insurance, housing and government benefits.

WOMEN'S LEGAL CENTER, 558 Capp Street, San Francisco, Calif. 94110—teaches legal skills to laywomen, refers cases to lawyers, initiates class action suits, provides legal counseling on employment problems.

WOMEN'S LEGAL DEFENSE FUND, c/o Gladys Kessler, 1910 N. Street, NW, Washington, D.C. 20036—handles women's tax, corporate and commercial problems. (Welcomes volunteer non-lawyers to help process forms, investigate cases and recruit both financial contributions and lawyers.)

THE WOMEN'S LOBBY, INC., 1345 G. Street, S.E., Washington, D.C. 20003—you have a friend on Capitol Hill. This group includes skilled lobbyists (veterans of the battle for congressional passage of the ERA) who are directing their efforts toward child care legislation and discrimination against women in employment, credit, insurance and social security among other issues.

WOMEN'S RIGHTS PROGRAM UNIT, U.S. Civil Rights Commission, 1121 Vermont Avenue, N.W., Washington, D.C. 20425—national clearinghouse on women's rights information. Send them copies of your discrimination complaints or lawsuits; let them know of legal progress in your area; ask them if you're not sure whether you have been denied equal protection under the Constitution.

THE WOMEN'S RIGHTS PROJECT, American Civil Liberties Union, 22 East 40th Street, New York, N.Y. 10017—has liaison people in 32 states who can advise you on legal problems that fall under protection of the U.S. Constitution.

I Wish I'd Said That...

Myths take on the weight of fact simply by being repeated often enough. When people can't handle the complex diversity of individual tastes and behavior, they often take refuge in facile generalizations. One effective method of destroying stereotypes is to cite facts that contradict them. Data gathered through studies, surveys and government statistics can be useful verbal ammunition during your battles with sexist adversaries.

THE NEXT TIME SOMEONE TELLS YOU "MOST WOMEN BELIEVE THEIR PLACE IS IN THE HOME," YOU TELL HIM:

• In a 1972 survey conducted by *The Youth Service,* 64 out of 100 college girls declared that they intend to combine marriage *and* a career. Of the high school girls interviewed, 57 out of 100 plan to have jobs and families simultaneously.

• When the *American Association of University Women* sounded out 7,000 men and women they discovered that 60 per cent of the men thought a woman's primary purpose was to be a wife and mother. But only 43 per cent of the women thought so. (A surprising sidelight result: Southern women were the *most* willing to give up "feminine" privileges in return for job equality.)

• "Even if they had enough money to live comfortably without working," most women would not quit their jobs. That is the clear finding of a study conducted by *Ohio State University* among 5,000 women.

• Wives of blue collar men say they would not choose homemaking as a career if they were 15 years old and had it to do over again. Today's blue collar wives want fewer children and much more independence. (From a study done by Social Research, Inc., Chicago, Illinois.)

• A Stanford University study found that barely one in 25 female college seniors plans to become a full-time homemaker after graduation.

• An extensive study of working and non-working women, conducted by the *Bureau of Advertising*, showed that 82 per cent of the working women agree "Working makes me a more interesting person." The Bureau found that in a given month it was the working women who were more likely to visit friends, shop, dine out, see a movie or show, attend club meetings or participate in sports. Which proves the old adage: the more you do, the more you find time to do.

• At a career symposium at the *University of Maryland*, Dr. Jessie Bernard reported two key findings of a 20-year study of 100 married women: wives who limited themselves to domestic duties suffered a higher incidence of emotional damage than working wives; and, relationships of married couples deteriorated when male and female functions were strictly specialized.

• A study made by the *U.S. Department of Labor and the University of Michigan Survey Research Center* has revealed that one-fifth of the women who have preschool children said they would work more hours in an outside job if child care centers were available.

• A nationwide survey of teenage *YWCA* leaders demonstrated that even young women in middle America have been affected by feminism. Sixty per cent of them want day care centers; 68 per cent believe women should play decision-making roles in society, 61 per cent believe men should help with the household chores; but only 39 per cent say that a working wife should feel comfortable about earning more than her husband.

• *The U.S. Department of Labor* tells us that its analysis of the 1970 Census indicates that nine out of ten women and girls in this country will work at jobs outside the home at some time during their lives.

THE NEXT TIME SOMEONE TELLS YOU THAT "ANY WOMAN WHO REALLY WORKS HARD AND IS QUALIFIED CAN EARN AS MUCH AS A MAN," YOU TELL HIM:

• *The Bureau of Census* reports that women overall earn only half as much as men who have the same education. Or to put it another way, men with less than one year of high school earn more than women with a college degree!

• In 1970, according to the *U.S. Department of Commerce*, 45 per cent of working women but only 14 per cent of working men earned less than $5,000 a year. The Department of Labor reports that in 1974 only 7 per cent of all employed women earned more than $10,000 a year, as opposed to 40 per cent of men.

• The earnings' gap between women and men has not closed, it has widened. According to *The Labor Department*, for every dollar that a man earned in 1955, a woman made 64 cents. In 1972, however, women were down to 59.4 cents for each dollar earned by men.

• *Chemical and Engineering News* did a study of chemists' salaries in 1970. They found that women with Ph.D.'s made less than men with only B.A.'s.

• *The Monthly Labor Review* reported that in 1969 the median earnings of women were lower than men's in *every* occupation except public school kindergarten teachers.

• *E.B. White* did an analysis of 10 years' worth of women and men graduates of a law school. The figures showed that one year after graduation the average man earned 20 per cent more than the woman lawyer. Ten years after graduation, the male lawyer earned 200 per cent more than his female counterpart.

THE NEXT TIME SOMEONE TELLS YOU "WORDS AND TITLES ARE TRIVIAL COMPLAINTS OF FEMINISTS," YOU TELL HIM:

• A *Texas court* found that women were paid far less than men for doing the same hospital work and the only difference was that the men were called "orderlies" and the women "nurses' aides."

• The *Census Bureau's Occupational Classifications System* has ordered a change in 52 sex-stereotyped job titles because they found that the old titles had a chilling effect on equal hiring policies. As a result craftsmen and clergymen have been replaced by crafts workers and clergy. Stewardesses are now flight attendants, firemen are fire fighters, newsboys are newspaper carriers and public relations men are now designated p.r. specialists.

• The U.S. Department of Labor considered exclusionary language important enough to change "Workman's Compensation" to "Workers' Compensation" as of July 1974.

Reading Is Believing:
Books, Pamphlets, Newsletters, Essays

It wasn't by way of threats, promises, crises, voices or flashes of light. No, I was converted to feminism through the printed word. For many months in 1969 and '70, I devoured essays on class and caste, underground newspapers reporting on sexism and sexual politics, position papers whose subjects ranged from housework, to job rights, to the myth of the vaginal orgasm.

Other women's research informed me. Other women's confessions and exhortations sounded the trumpets of recognition. Other women's efforts motivated me and helped me reorder priorities in my own life.

All this came via the supposedly passive act of reading. For me it was far from passive. While some are moved by eyeball-to-eyeball confrontation, and others by the tangible lessons of experience, those who, like me, can be galvanized by reading the right words at the right time may find all the help they need in one or another of the books and pamphlets listed here.

The personal is political

I'm Running Away from Home, But I'm Not Allowed to Cross the Street, by Gabrielle Burton. The ways in which the author and her husband reorganized their household, their five children and their work lives are provocative and relentlessly honest. ($3.75 from KNOW, P.O. Box 86031, Pittsburgh, Pa. 15221.)

Occupation: Housewife, by Helena Znaniecki Lopata. Scholarly style but challenging findings about the housewife and her role. ($9.50, Oxford University Press.)

The Male Machine, by Marc Feigen Fasteau. An incisive treatment of the "man problem"—why they are the way they are, how it hurts them (as well as us) and why they will have to change in order to survive. ($8.95, McGraw-Hill.)

The Liberated Man, by Warren Farrell. How to free men and their relationships with women. (Random House, $8.95.)

The Politics of Housework, by Pat Mainardi. The four-page essay that has become a mind-expanding classic on the oppressive nature of division of labor in the home. (10 cents from KNOW, P.O. Box 86031, Pittsburgh, Pa. 15221.)

Dual Careers, a progress report on the labor market experience of women, aged 20-44, living in two-career marriages. ($2.10 for Manpower Research Monograph #21, Superintendent of Documents, Government Printing Office, Washington, D.C. 20402.)

The Two-Career Family, by Lynda Lytle Holmstrom. An impeccably thorough overview of the problems and adjustments of couples who are both highly motivated career types. ($3.50, Schenkman, 3 Mt. Auburn, Cambridge, Mass. 02138.)

Dual Career Families, by Rhona & Robert Rapoport. Reports on five British professional couples. ($1.95, Penguin.)

The Dual Profession Family, by Margaret M. Poloma and T. Neal Garland. Summarizes interviews with 53 dual career families. (25 cents from Business and Professional Women's Foundation, 2012 Massachusetts Avenue, N.W., Washington, D.C. 20036.)

A Male Guide to Women's Liberation, by Gene Marine. Attempts to promote understanding between the sexes of the new roles, the "masculinism" of American society and the harmful stereotypes that warp our relationships at home and on the job. ($6.95, Holt, Rinehart and Winston; paperback edition, Avon Books.)

Male Chauvinism! How It Works, by Michael Korda. One executive's view of the damage done by male supremacy in work situations and how it is that authority, power, money and prestige remain in masculine hands. ($6.95, Random House.)

Man's World, Woman's Place, by Elizabeth Janeway. Perceptive, readable and persuasive assessment of women's role and what it does to us. ($8.95, William Morrow.)

Women and children first

The Working Mother, edited by S.D. Callahan. Sixteen women reflect on making it in motherhood and the marketplace. (95 cents, Paperback Lib.)

The Case for the Working Mother, by Dorothy Whyte Cotton (95 cents, Tower Books.)

The Working Mother's Guide to Her Home, Her Family and Herself, by Alice Skelsey ($6.95, Random House.)

How to Go to Work When Your Husband Is Against It, Your Children Aren't Old Enough, and There's Nothing Your Can Do Anyhow, by Felice N. Schwartz, Margaret H. Schiften and Susan S. Gillotti. ($2.95, Simon and Schuster.)

NOTE: None of the above books are radical or visionary. They are entirely apolitical, pragmatic guidebooks on managing work and family life. If you're looking for a blueprint for social change, don't look here.

Working Mothers Bibliography. List of books, periodicals and tapes dealing with the special problems and opportunities. (50 cents from BPW, 2012 Massachusetts Avenue, N.W., Washington, D.C. 20036.)

Day Care: How to Plan, Develop and Operate a Day Care Center, by E. Belle Evans, Beth Shub and Marlene Weinstein. A concise, complete guide covering budget, legal requirements, criteria for a site, selection and training of staff, classroom curricula, health and social services and fundraising, licensing, evaluation charts, costs. ($3.95 from Beacon Press, 25 Beacon Street, Boston, Mass. 02108.)

Industry Sponsored Day Care. Consolidates information on business and industry involvement in day care and states categorically that child care facilities aided businesses in "recruiting personnel, reducing absenteeism, increasing employee productivity and improving employer-employee relations." (25 cents, Bulletin #296, The Women's Bureau, U.S. Department of Labor, Government Printing Office, Washington, D.C. 20402.)

Federal Funds for Day Care Projects. Find out whether your local child care program is eligible for economic help from a government agency. ($1 for Women's Bureau Pamphlet #14, same address as above.)

Day Care Facts. Legislation, statistics, alternatives, tax information, resources, bibliography. A useful reference. (Free from The Women's Bureau, Pamphlet #16, same address as above.)

Various publications, bulletins, newsletters. Write for listing, 15 cents from Day Care and Child Development Council of America, 1401 K. Street, N.W., Washington, D.C. 20005. (Of special interest: "Do You Need Day Care," by Helen Matheson, 50 cents; "Getting It Together," $1.50.)

A Parent's Guide to Nursery Schools by Jean Curtis. Why to send your young child to nursery school, how to choose the best one, how to start your own. ($6.95, Random House.)

Doing Your Own School by The Great Atlantic and Pacific School Conspiracy (a writers' collective). A practical guide to starting and operating a community school. ($2.95, Beacon Press.)

Children in the Nursery School, by Harriet M. Johnson. Read this if you're not convinced that kids can flourish and benefit from a quality day-care facility. ($7.50, Agathon.)

To Start a School, by Margaret Skutch and Wilfrid G. Hamlin. The woman who started a school in Connecticut in 1964 tells how a good, private school can be created from scratch. ($5.95, Little, Brown.)

Storefront Day Care Centers: The Radical Berlin Experiment, translated by Catherine Lord and Renee Neu Watkins. An experiment in revolution child rearing in West Berlin. For counter-culture parents, not traditonalists. ($9.95, Beacon Press.)

Day Care for Infants, by E. Belle Evans and George E. Saia. Europeans have found "no significant developmental differences between infants in day care and those reared exclusively in the home." In fact, day care infants were found to have several advantages. This book makes the case for a controversial innovation in America: infant and toddler child care centers—and tells how to organize and operate one. ($6.95, Beacon Press.)

Women and Child Care in China, by Ruth Sidel. A stimulating account (from first-hand observation) of Chinese attitudes toward working women, multiple mothering, child care programs and other surprisingly advanced solutions to the work-home conflict. This cross-cultural report may give you some good ideas. ($6.95, Hill & Wang.)

How to Organize a Child Care Center. Instructions to help you establish a community-controlled center that reflects the diversity of your neighborhood and is free of sexism, racism and classism. Contains an 11-point program for health, funding, curriculum and staff recruitment. ($1 from Women's Action Alliance, 370 Lexington Avenue, New York, N.Y. 10017.)

Day Care: Who Needs It? Just the facts—and a useful persuasion tool for those with serious misconceptions. (35 cents from League of Women Voters, 1730 M. Street, N.W., Washington, D.C. 20036.)

The Day Care Book. A Canadian perspective on day care alternatives, financing and legislation. ($1.50 from The Women's Press, 280 Bloor Street, W., Ste. 305, Toronto, Ontario, Canada.)

Parents and Child Care, by Dr. Stevanne Auerbach-Fink. The report of a two-year study of parents who used child care centers and child care family homes in the San Francisco area. Contains parents' responses, problems, preferences and recommendations. ($5 from Parents and Child Care, 1855 Folson Street, San Francisco, Calif. 94103.)

Who's Minding the Children? The History and Politics of Day Care in America, by Margaret O'Brien Steinfels. Everything you always wanted to know about day care—or should have thought to ask. ($2.95, Simon and Schuster-Touchstone.)

Re-education, jobhunting and career planning

Continuing Education Programs and Services for Women. A free, 104-page booklet listing courses offered by educational institutions in 43 states. Many class schedules and accelerated degree programs are geared to the needs of adult women. Where listings are outdated, contact the institution anyway for current catalogs. (Request Pamphlet 10 from the Women's Bureau, Department of Labor, Washington, D.C. 20210.)

No Experience Necessary, by Sande Friedman and Lois C. Schwartz, is targeted to the female liberal arts graduate who has no idea of how to use her fine brain and unspecialized education in the labor market. Advertising, banking, TV, and public relations are some of the 14 career areas analyzed. ($1.25, Dell.)

Your Career Selection Guide, by Allan B. Goldenthal. 110 in-demand occupations and the personal and educational qualifications needed for each. ($1.95, Regents.)

Career Planning for College Women, by Renee Taft. A practical job counseling course between book covers. ($1.30 from Distaffers, 1130 Western Savings Building, Philadelphia, Pa. 19107.)

Moving Up: How to Get High Salaried Jobs, by Eli Djeddah ($5.95, Lippincott), and *How to Get a Better Job Quicker,* by Richard A. Payne ($5.95, Taplinger). Both books were not specifically written for women but you can learn good strategy from each of them in the areas of jobhunting, resumé writing and interview techniques.

Careers for Women in the Seventies. This free pamphlet states: "Careers for women should not be any different from careers for men," and goes on to discuss non-traditional occupations where opportunities are good for both sexes. (From The Women's Bureau, U.S. Department of Labor, Washington, D.C. 20210.)

Jobfinding Techniques for Mature Women. A dry run-through on resumé-writing, making applications, enduring and succeeding at interviews or finding training programs and career organizations for extra preparation. (Request Pamphlet 11, for 30 cents from U.S. Government Printing Office, Washington, D.C. 20402.)

Quaker Oats Company Job Interview Skit. This remarkable skit is based on a typical job interview but reverses the usual sex roles: a male biochemistry honors graduate is asked by a female personnel manager about his typing speed—and worse. You can use this consciousness-raising script as a guideline for your own pre-interview preparations and for employers' awareness education. (Free from Stanley Birstein, Quaker Oats, 345 Merchandise Mart, Chicago, Ill. 60654.)

Making the Most of Your Job Interview. A 26-page booklet targeted to young graduates but useful to women reentering the job market. (Send stamped, self-addressed business-size envelope to Terri Hilton, Yankee Trader, East Setauket, New York 11733.)

Private Employment Agencies Directory. Lists member agencies and their specialties. ($3 from National Employment Association, 2000 K. Street, N.W., Washington, D.C. 20009.)

Job Training Suggestions for Women and Girls. Not your favorite radical pamphlet, but simple facts on courses in-service training, home study, apprenticeships and Federal Manpower (Personpower) Programs leading to jobs that don't require a college degree. (15 cents for Leaflet #40. U.S. Government Printing Office, Washington, D.C. 20402.)

Creative Careers for Women, by Joan Scobey and Lee Parr McGrath. A how-to with offbeat job suggestions and a good section on "Starting Your Own Business." ($1, Essandess Special Edition.)

The Teenage Employment Guide by Allan B. Golderthal. Full-time, part-time and summer jobs for the 13- to 19-year-old student, graduate or drop-out. ($2.95, Regents.)

The Complete Job Hunting Guide by Ess Wein. The A to Z approach including a directory of nearly 1,000 employment agencies. ($1, Cornerstone.)

Occupational Outlook for College Graduates. 100 professional and related jobs, supply and demand imbalances, training requirements, earnings expectations, etc. ($2 from Bureau of Labor Statistics, Washington, D.C. 20212.)

Career Counseling: New Perspectives for Women and Girls. A selected bibliography of career guidance materials. (50 cents from Business and Professional Women's Foundation, 2012 Massachusetts Ave., N.W., Washington, D.C. 20036.)

Planning for Work (Booklet G-1) and *Your Job Campaign* (Booklet G-2) are two useful getting-started guides. ($1.25 each from Catalyst, 6 East 82 Street, New York, N.Y. 10028.)

Job discrimination, women's rights

Everything a Woman Needs to Know to Get Paid What She's Worth, by Caroline Bird. Quality first aid for emotional and economic workday wounds. ($8.95, McKay.)

Born Female, by Caroline Bird. Subtitled "The high cost of keeping women down," this is both bible and Baedecker for, to and about the 33 million women who work. ($1.25, Pocket Books.)

The Rights of Women, by Susan Ross, can save you many phone calls and fees to your lawyers. ($1.25, Avon.)

Survival in the Sexist Jungle, by Andrew J. DuBrin. A psychologist's program for combating job discrimination against women. ($1.50, Books for Better Living.)

A Working Woman's Guide to Her Job Rights. Sections include "Why Women Should Know Their Job Rights," "Getting the Job," "On the Job," "When You Retire," "Sources of Assistance," and cover problems in the areas of equal pay, maternity leave, overtime, minimum wage, child care, unemployment insurance, social security, pensions and unions. Updated to June 1974. (60 cents. Request Women's Bureau Leaflet 55 from The Superintendent of Documents, U.S. Government Printing Office, Washington, D.C. 20402.)

The Business and Industry Discrimination-Kit. What to expect in the way of employers' violations and how to file suits. ($3 for members of National Organization for Women, $5 for non-members. From NOW, 5 South Wabash, Suite 1615, Chicago, Ill. 60603.)

A Guide to Federal Laws Prohibiting Sex Discrimination. Ask for Clearinghouse Publication #46. ($1.40 from U.S. Government Printing Office, Washington, D.C. 20402.)

The Equal Rights Amendment—What It Will and Won't

- *Do.* A succinct analysis of the effects of ERA on our everyday lives. Answers for all the unfounded fears. (Free from the Citizens' Advisory Council on the Status of Women, U.S. Department of Labor, Room 4211, Washington, D.C. 20210.)

The Women's Advocate Corps. Guidelines. Illinois women can get legal counsel on sex bias in jobs and housing by sending 25 cents and a stamped, self-addressed envelope to Ginger Corrigan, 420 W. Eugenie, Chicago, Ill. 60614.

Women and the Law: A Collection of Reading Lists. This bibliography, compiled by four women attorneys, is exhaustive and practical. ($1 from KNOW, Box 86031, Pittsburgh, Pa. 15221.)

Tools to Eliminate Sex Discrimination in State and Local Government. Civil service employees are vulnerable without this booklet. ($2 from Women's Action Alliance, 370 Lexington, New York, N.Y. 10017.)

Washington State Laws Against Sex Discrimination. An interpretive guidebook that decodes the laws and tells you how to make them protect you. (Free from Washington State Human Rights Commission, 1411 Fourth Avenue, Seattle, Wash.)

Women Office Workers Organizing Kit. Literature on white collar unionization and how to mount a conference for office workers in your area. ($1.75 from WOW, Box 439, Planetarium Station, New York, N.Y. 10024.)

Academic Discrimination Kit, by Ann Scott. How to file sex discrimination complaints in academia ($1); and *Write On!*—how to write effective letters of suggestion, complaint, commendation, congratulations and political opinion. (50 cents both from NOW, 5 South Wabash, Suite 1615, Chicago, Ill. 60603.)

The Myth and the Reality. Posits stereotypical statements and counters them with facts and figures. Gives you answers to employers' comments, such as: "I can't take a chance on you because women are prone to absenteeism," or "You might get pregnant and quit like all the other women." (25 cents. From The Superintendent of Documents, Washington, D.C. 20402.)

Women and Credit. A 15-page booklet prepared by the San Francisco Chapter of NOW; describes the effect of credit discrimination and focuses on California law. Whether or not national credit protection laws are passed, this booklet is a valid course in self-protection and understanding of your rights. (55 cents from Michele D. Stratton, 546 Eleventh Avenue, San Francisco, Calif. 94118.)

The Legal Rights of Women, by Brian Richard Boylan. A state-by-state breakdown of the rights and laws affecting women. (95 cents, Award Books.)

The Sexual Barrier, by Marija Hughes. Bibliography of articles, books and publications dealing with sex bias in business and the professions. ($5, from the author at 2116 F. Street, N.W., Washington, D.C. 20037.)

Women and the Law, by Leo Kanowitz. This 1969 book could use factual updating but its principles and explanations are timeless. ($3.95, University of New Mexico Press Paperbacks.)

Sexist Justice, by Karen DeCrow. The author, an attorney and chief officer of the National Organization for Women, covers legalized sexism in jobs, credit, alimony, family life, wills and trust, etc. ($7.95, Random House.)

Sex in the Marketplace: American Women at Work, by Juanita Kreps. A comprehensive analytical work that plumbs the depths of working women's problematical status. ($1.95, Johns Hopkins Press.)

Affirmative Action for Women: A Practical Guide, by Dorothy Jongeward. How to make equal opportunity happen in the work place. Helps employers fulfill their federal compliance programs; helps employees know what to ask for and expect. ($8.95, Addison-Wesley.)

Women at Work, edited by William L. O'Neill. Two studies—one by a working woman in 1905, one by a telephone company worker in 1970—illuminate why "you've come a long way, baby" is a hollow slogan. ($2.95, Quadrangle.)

The Law and You, by Elinor Porter Swiger. A legal handbook for young people in which employment rights of minors is covered in one chapter, among other chapters about compulsory school attendance, parents' divorces and juvenile crimes. ($4.95, Bobbs-Merrill.)

Your Legal Rights: Making the Law Work for You, edited by Kenneth P. Norwick. Another young people's guide written by young lawyers on subjects ranging from employment to birth control, consumer fraud, student's rights and the draft. ($7.95, John Day.)

Women's Rights Law Reporter is a serious law review with a laser beam focus on women's rights. Intended for lawyers but useful for laypersons interested in keeping abreast of legal progress in employment and other areas affecting women. ($12 for four issues a year, from Women's Rights Law Reporter, 180 University Avenue, Newark, New Jersey 07102.)

The Woman Activist is a monthly action bulletin that polices women's rights bills in the Congress. Editor Flora Crater keeps track of legislators' voting records too. ($5, from Women Activist, 2310 Barbour Road, Falls Church, Va. 22043.)

ALERT, the Women's Legislative Review, covers federal and Connecticut state laws of interest to women, and serves as a central forum for job exchange, and news of local groups' efforts to combat job discrimination. ($4 for 15 issues, from ALERT, Box 437, Middletown, Conn. 06457.)

Womanpower: A Monthly Report on Fair Employment Practices for Women. This is intended for managers, employers and supervisors, but if you can afford the price it's a solid source of news on sex bias suits, affirmative action programs, court decisions. ($37 per year, from Betsy Hogan Associates, 222 Rawson Road, Brookline, Mass. 02146.)

Specialized career information

LAW

Wanted by the Law: WOMEN is the overall title of three booklets on the legal profession—and how to enter it even if you've been out of school for decades. Ask for the blue and purple booklets for general information ($1 for the two), and the red booklet, if you're interested in California law schools in particular. (50 cents. All three from the Boalt Hall Women's Association, School of Law, University of California, Berkeley, Calif. 94720.)

A Directory of Women Attorneys list over 5,000 practicing women lawyers throughout the U.S. Profits from the sale of this book will be used to promote legal rights for women. ($10 from Ford Associates, 701 S. Federal, Butler, Indiana 46721.)

What Can She Be? A Lawyer, by Gloria and Esther Goldreich. An inspiring, realistic story of an average day in the life of a woman attorney. For readers aged 5 to 10. ($3.95, Lothrop, Lee & Shepard.)

Sex Discrimination in the Legal Profession, by Beatrice Dinerman. Reprint from the American Bar Association Journal. Why women lawyers sometimes need a lawyer to protect their own rights. (25 cents from KNOW, Box 86031, Pittsburgh, Pa. 15221.)

Women in the Law: The Second Hundred Years, by Doris Sassower. The first woman was admitted to practice law in 1869. This article surveys what has happened since. (Request reprint from Volume 57, American Bar Association Journal, 1155 E. 60 St., Chicago, Ill. 60637.)

MEDICINE

The Fuller Utilization of the Woman Physician is a report of a 1968 conference but it hasn't lost its relevance. (Free from The Women's Bureau, Washington, D.C. 20210.)

Women in White, by Geoffrey Marks and William K. Beatty. A survey of women doctors throughout history, including Dr. "James Barry" who masqueraded as a man during her noteworthy 50-year medical career. ($6.95, Scribners.)

Ms.–M.D., by D.X. Fenten. Tells young readers the training requirements, available specialties, average workloads of a practicing doctor. ($4.95, Westminster.)

The Challenge to Become a Doctor, by Leah Lurie Heyn ($1.50, Feminist Press, SUNY, Box 334, Old Westbury, N.Y. 11568) and *The First Woman Doctor,* by Rachel Baker (50 cents, Scholastic Book Services). Both are young people's biographies of Elizabeth Blackwell who received her M.D. over 125 years ago.

Women in Medicine, by Carol Lopate. Statistics, sociology and good common sense. ($5.95, Johns Hopkins Press.)

Medicine ... A Woman's Career (50 cents) and *Career Choices for Women in Medicine.* Solid advice for aspiring physicians. ($2 for two volumes from The Ameri-

can Medical Women's Association, 1740 Broadway,
New York, N.Y. 10019.)

Why Would a Girl Go Into Medicine? by Margaret A.
Campbell, M.D. A survey of discrimination against
women in U.S. medical schools, written to inform and
encourage women medical students of the past, present
and future, and to promote radical change in medical
education and in the care of patients. ($3 from Ann
O'Shea, 320 West End Avenue, New York, N.Y.
10023.)

Women Physicians Directory lists all women doctors by
geographical location and medical specialty. ($10 from
American Medical Association, 535 North Dearborn,
Chicago, Ill. 60610.)

Accredited Institutions of Higher Education lists those colleges and universities that provide adequate pre-med
training. (Free from American Council on Education, 1
Dupont Circle, N.W., Washington, D.C. 20210.)

NURSING

*Scholarships and Loans for Beginning Education in Nurs-
ing.* Local, state and national programs of financial assistance to pay for training as a licensed practical nurse
or registered nurse. (50 cents from National League for
Nursing, 10 Columbus Circle, New York, N.Y. 10019.)

Making It in Nursing. A 14-page pamphlet that explains
how disadvantaged students can plan a nursing career.
(Free from U.S. Department of Health, Education, and
Welfare, Division of Nursing, 9000 Rickville Pike, Be-
thesda, Md. 20014.)

Nursing at the Crossroads, a special issue of *Nursing Outlook* magazine, discusses the question of expanded nursing roles, independent practitioners and legal aspects of
the new developments in nursing. (75 cents from American Journal of Nursing, 10 Columbus Circle, New
York, N.Y. 10019.)

Basic Facts About Nursing: Bulletin 1650 describes the
profession in its many forms and assesses the employment outlook for R.N.'s, L.P.N.'s and Hospital Attendants. (15 cents from Superintendent of Documents,
Washington, D.C. 20402.)

Publications Catalog offers nursing career advice and educational options gathered by the National League for Nursing. *Do You Want to Be a Nurse?* is a mini-brochure that asks key questions to check career commitment. (Both free from National League for Nursing, 10 Columbus Circle, New York, N.Y. 10019.)

BUSINESS: CLERICAL AND EXECUTIVE CAREERS

Directory of Women in Business is a Yellow Pages listing of businesswomen in the Detroit metropolitan area who consult, advise, own businesses or do business in the arts, education, industry, science and the professions. ($1.25 from Directory, 764 Channing, Ferndale, Mich. 48220.)

Careers for Women in Broadcasting, a practical booklet providing job classifications and descriptions, necessary training and schools that offer broadcasting courses. The pamphlet is divided into four job areas: Administration (program director, public relations, fashion director, etc.); Engineering (audio, camera, lighting); Sales (traffic manager, account executive, etc.); and Promotion (acting, announcing, music, etc.). (Free from American Women in Radio and Television, 1321 Connecticut Ave., N.W., Washington, D.C. 20036.)

The Secretarial Ghetto, by Mary Kathleen Benet. Over 60 per cent of America's office personnel are female. Without them, the economic gears would grind to a halt— yet they are virtually powerless as individuals. This book looks to the past, assesses the present white collar revolt and new feminist consciousness, and faces the future squarely. ($5.95, McGraw-Hill.)

The Executive Suite—Feminine Style, by Edith M. Lynch. The title is a giveaway; this is often couched in a "we-they" tone that suggests the woman's movement is just peripheral and that each woman can make it on her own. But there are enough sensible chapters to make it worth reading nonetheless. ($10.50, American Management Association.)

Breakthrough: Women Into Management, by Rosalind Loring and Theodora Wells. Why more managerial women will ensure greater productivity for business and industry; and how a responsible employer can recruit, train and promote women effectively. Read it first then pass it on to your boss. ($7.95, Van Nostrand.)

Corporate Lib: Women's Challenge to Management, edited by Eli Ginzberg and Alice M. Yohalem. Thirteen papers delivered to a recent conference on Women's Challenge to Management, each suggesting reasons and remedies for the double standard of success in business. ($6.50, Johns Hopkins University Press.)

Shortchanged: Women and Minorities in Banking is a 1972 report on the status of bank employees of 18 banks in six cities *vis-à-vis* race and sex discrimination—and the picture isn't pleasant. Order from Council on Economic Priorities, 456 Greenwich Street, New York, N.Y. 10013.)

Accounting. One of the career specialty booklets in the Career Opportunity Series which also includes pamphlets on *Advertising, Art, Banking, Communications, Data Processing, Finance, Insurance, Personnel, Public Relations, Publishing, Retailing, Travel Agent*—all of which offer executive and clerical opportunities. Ask for information about entire "C" series. (From Catalyst, 6 East 82 Street, New York, N.Y. 10028.)

The Status of Women in the Field of Computing, by Gerald H.F. Gardner. The whole truth about jobs and careers in data processing. (15 cents from KNOW, Box 86031, Pittsburgh, Pa. 15221.)

For Women, A Difficult Climb to the Top. This article about women executives in the August 2, 1969 issue of *Business Week* hasn't lost its punch. Get it from the periodicals section of your library if you can't get a reprint from Business Week, 1221 Avenue of the Americas, New York, N.Y. 10020.

The Executive Woman is a monthly newsletter of news and advice and an exchange for women who need or women who sell products and services. ($20 per year, Executive Woman, 747 Third Avenue, New York, N.Y. 10017.)

Women in Management: Strategy for Increase, is a lengthy excerpt from a speech by Dr. Hilda Kahne to the Advisory Committee on the Economic Role of Women, suggesting methods of promoting women into top jobs with good results. (50 cents from Business and Professional Women's Foundation, 2012 Massachusetts Ave., N.W., Washington, D.C. 20036.)

The Plight of Women in Industry, a special report on the status of California women in industry. (Free from California Industry magazine, 609 Mission Street, San Francisco, Calif. 94105.)

Media Report to Women. A monthly newsletter that provides facts, actions, ideas, philosophy, news of legal challenges, women's progress in journalism, radio, TV and other editorial jobs. ($10 a year from Media Report, 3306 Ross Place, N.W., Washington, D.C. 20008.)

Sex Stereotyping in the Executive Suite, by Benson Rosen and Thomas H. Jerdee. This article contains the painful truth about executives' sexist attitudes, many of which are completely unconscious. (Request reprint #74208. $3 from Harvard Business Review, Boston, Mass. 02163.)

HOUSEHOLD WORKERS

What's a Day's Work? ($3), a personnel fair-working-conditions guide; *Housekeeping Careers—A New Frontier* ($3), a manual to help groups or individuals start projects to upgrade household employment; *Thursday's People on the Move!* ($2.50), case histories of household employees' experiences; *Training Household Technicians* ($25), a comprehensive training program for community leaders, social workers, women's groups. (All publications may be ordered from Uvelia S.A. Bowen, 4131 North Broad Street, Philadelphia, Pa. 19140.)

Facts About Household Workers. Statistics, income information, legislative materials from National Committee on Household Employment, 8120 Fenton Street, Suite 300, Silver Springs, Md. 20910.

Thursdays and Every Other Sunday Off, by Verta Mae. Humorous but uncompromisingly honest discussion of domestic workers' experiences. ($5.95, Doubleday.)

JOBS OVERSEAS

How to Get a Job Overseas. Check if this has been updated and get price information. (From Research Associates, Box 889-MA, Belmont, Calif. 94002.)

Employment Abroad. (Free from the Council on International Educational Exchange, 777 U.N. Plaza, New York, N.Y. 10017.)

Federal Jobs Overseas. (10 cents. Order Pamphlet 29, from Superintendent of Documents, Washington, D.C. 20402.)

Opportunities Abroad for Teachers. (35 cents from Department of Health, Education, and Welfare, Washington, D.C.)

CIVIL SERVICE

Working for the U.S.A. explains what the Civil Service is, how to apply for a job, benefits and pay scales, addresses of Federal Job Information Centers. About 3 of every 10 federal employees are women, and only 10 per cent are working out of Washington, D.C. Mid-level jobs in your area may be opening up to women. (20 cents for Pamphlet 4, from Superintendent of Documents, U.S. Government Printing Office, Washington, D.C. 20402.)

Calling All Women in Federal Service. Female government employees are informed of their job rights and opportunities in this free Leaflet #53 from The Women's Bureau, U.S. Department of Labor, Washington, D.C. 20210.

Bulletin 1650-127—Employment Outlook: Government. A 1970–71 reprint from the Occupational Outlook Handbook. (15 cents from Superintendent of Documents, Washington, D.C. 20402.)

Study of Employment of Women in the Federal Government—1968. The status of women in white collar government jobs. ($2 from Superintendent of Documents, Washington, D.C. 20402.)

RELIGION

Women's Liberation and the Church, edited by Sarah Bentley Doely, is "must" reading for the thinking Protestant, male or female. Seven authors offer penetrating analyses of the historical, theological and traditional role of women. ($2.95, Association Press.)

Employment Outlook: Clergymen. Ignore the "men" in the text and read this leaflet for specific information about training, duties, salaries and career opportunities for clergy. (15 cents for Bulletin 1650-29, from Superintendent of Documents, Washington, D.C. 20402.)

The Lady Was a Bishop, by Joan Morris, tells the hidden history of ecclesiastical women who have been lost to posterity because of biased male scholars and keepers of the record. ($6.95, Macmillan.)

Lilith's Rib, the Jewish Women's Movement newsletter reports on women's progress in organized Judaism, conferences, new women's liturgy. (25 cents per copy from Maralee Gordon, 815 W. Wrightwood, Chicago, Ill. 60614.)

Women and the New Creation, a study course on identity of women in the 70's. (50 cents from Office of Women's Concerns, United Presbyterian Church, 730 Witherspoon Building, Philadelphia, Pa. 19107.)

Bibliography on the Jewish Woman, compiled by Aviva Canto Zuckoff. Valuable references to support the fight for enhanced roles for women. (25 cents from Network, 36 West 37 Street, New York, N.Y. 10018.)

The Discipline of the United Methodist Church, the book of church law, eliminated all sexist language from its pages in 1972. The study *Women: Over Half the Earth's People* reflects the Methodist concern for women. Information about both publications may be obtained from Women's Division, Board of Global Ministries. The United Methodist Church, 475 Riverside Drive, New York, N.Y. 10027.

Jesus Was a Feminist, by Leonard Swidler. A reprint from the January 1971 issue of Catholic World. (35 cents from KNOW, Box 86031, Pittsburgh, Pa. 15221.)

The Jewish Woman, An Anthology. 190-page paperback arising out of a national conference on Judaism and feminism. ($2 from Network, 36 West 37 Street, New York, N.Y. 10018.)

Speakout, the publication of the Unitarian Universalist Women's Federation, comes free with membership. ($5 per year, from UUWF, 25 Beacon Street, Boston, Mass. 02108.)

Feminism from the Pulpit: Thirteen Sermons on Sex, Etc., by The Rev. Ms. Marjorie Newlin Leaming. Mind-expanding sermons on "Motherhood and Sisterhood: Are They Incompatible," "Men's Lib," and other provocative issues. ($2.50 from Rev. Leaming at Unitarian Universalist Church, Santa Paula, Calif.)

The Christian Woman in the Working World, by Martha

Nelson. Tame advice and "inspiration" for the most traditional woman. ($3.50, Broadman.)

Beyond God the Father: Toward a Philosophy of Women's Liberation, by Mary Daly. A brave, radical and profoundly challenging work by one of the great theological scholars of our time. ($8.95, Beacon Press.)

MIXED-CAREER COLLECTIONS AND MISCELLANEOUS SPECIAL CAREER INTERESTS

From Tipi to Skyscraper, by Doris Cole. A totally fascinating history of women in architecture. ($8.95, I Press, Inc., 145 Hanover Street, Boston, Mass. 02108.)

The Professional Woman, by Athena Theodore. What are the effects of socialization on the female professional; how does she define her identity; how does she manage the career/marriage balance; what are her classic career patterns? These questions are answered with a focus on women in teaching, library work, science, social work, medicine, nursing, dentistry, college teaching, engineering, the clergy, architecture and the law. ($5.95, Schenkman.)

Woman's Place, by Cynthia Fuchs Epstein. Options and limits in professional careers such as law, medicine, science, engineering and university teaching. A straightforward and deeply affecting study. ($6.95, University of California Press.)

Young and Female, edited by Pat Ross. A young-adult book offering personal accounts of turning points in the lives of these eight American women: Shirley MacLaine, actress; Shirley Chisholm, congresswoman; Dorothy Day, crusading journalist; Emily Hahn, engineer; Margaret Sanger, early birth control advocate; Althea Gibson, gifted black athlete; Edna Ferber, author; Margaret Bourke-White, photographer. ($3.95, Random House.)

National Apprenticeship Program presents a brief explanation of the federal apprentice system and a list of apprenticeable occupations and trades. (Free from U.S. Department of Labor, Manpower Administration, Washington, D.C. 20210.)

Women Today is a newsletter containing small items of interest to women in various occupations and professions, as well as general news, legislative reports, conference and seminar notices, and special bulletins on books, organizations and lobbying. ($15 a year from Today Publications, National Press Building, Washington, D.C. 20004.)

Prime Time, a monthly newsletter with subscribers in every state and eight foreign countries, has been called a life-line for older women. It lists loans and scholarships, job openings, medical programs and relevant courses for the mature woman, plus news of OWL (Older Women's Liberation) groups forming in various localities. ($5 for a year's subscription, from Prime Time, 264 Piermont Ave., Piermont, N.Y. 10968.)

The Spokeswoman. Monthly news bulletin noted for superior coverage of women's issues: child care, affirmative action, career conferences, legislation, politics, unions, education. A Help Wanted Section is worth the price of a subscription. ($7, from The Spokeswoman, 5464 South Shore Drive, Chicago, Ill. 60615.)

What Women Have Done: A Photo Essay on the History of Working Women, pictures and facts tell the story most history books ignore. ($1.50, United Front Press, Box 40090, San Francisco. Calif. 94140.)

CHILDREN'S BOOKS THAT ESTABLISH CAREER OPTIONS EARLY IN LIFE

Firegirl, by Gibson Rich. As lawsuits are filed all over the country by women seeking jobs as firefighters, this book goes a long way toward liberating such secret desires from the soul of a small girl. ($1.95 from The Feminist Press, Box 334, Old Westbury, New York 11568.) Ages 4–8.

Girls Can Be Anything, by Norma Klein. A picture book that offers limitless horizons. ($4.50, E. P. Dutton Co.) Ages 4–7.

The Sheep Book, by Carmen Good-Year. A female farmer on her sheep ranch. ($1.25, from Lollipop Power, Box 1171, Chapel Hill, North Carolina 27514.) Ages 3–7.

Busy People, by Joe Kaufman. How people do their work—including people like Irma the telephone installer and Doris the doctor. ($3.95, Golden Press.) Ages 3–6.

Mothers Can Do Anything, by Joe Lasker. Modern women engaged in very real jobs—from folk singing to research to archeology. ($3.95, Albert Whitman & Company.) Ages 3–6.

Saturday's Child; 36 Women Talk About Their Jobs, interviews and photographs by Suzanne Seed. A female carpenter, pilot, biophysicist, policewoman and bank vice president, among others. ($4.95, J. Philip O'Hara.) For age 11 and up.

What to Be? by Meredith Powell and Gail Yokubinas. A little girl considers becoming a mathematician, pediatrician, politician or beautician, among other occupations. ($3.95, Children's Press.) Ages 3–6.

What Can She Be? A Veterinarian, by Gloria and Esther Goldreich. Photographs and text enliven the description of this attractive profession. ($3.95, Lothrop, Lee & Shepard.) Ages 4–10.

Great Women Athletes, by Martha Moffett. Sports can be as remunerative as they are personally rewarding. These mini-biographies of outstanding athletes provide ample inspiration in eight sports. ($3.95, Platt & Munk.) Ages 7–12.

Mommies at Work, by Eve Merriam; illustrations by Beni Montressor. All kinds of mothers doing all kinds of worthwhile work—and loving their children as much as any mommies anywhere doing anything else. ($4.95, Knopf.) Ages 3–6.

I Can Be Anything You Can Be, by Joel Rothman. Two friends fantasize about their anything-is-possible futures. ($4.95, Scroll Press.)

Catalogues of non-sexist children's books are available from several sources: feminist publishers, bookstores and media groups. For openers, try: *Lollipop Power,* Box 1171, Chapel Hill. N.C. 27514. *Feminist Press,* Box 334, Old Westbury, New York 11568, *Child's Play Bookstore,* 226 Atlantic Avenue, Brooklyn, N.Y. 11201. *The Woman's Store,* 4157 Adams Avenue, San Diego, California 92122. *Feminist Book Mart,* 162-11 Ninth Avenue, Whitestone, New York 11357. *New Seed Press,* 431 North Baldwin Street, Madison, Wisconsin 53703. *The Joyful World Press,* 468 Belvedere Street, San Francisco, Calif. 94117.

Changing attitudes and alternatives: new views of work schedules, job satisfaction and success

4 Days, 40 Hours, edited by Riva Poor, examines the

trend toward the four-day week and three-day week-end. ($5 from Bursk & Poor, 22 Hadley Street, Cam-bridge, Mass. 02138.)

Work When You Want to discusses the advantages of temporary jobs—but not the disadvantages of lacking fringe benefits, insurance and job security. (Free from Western Girl, 60 East 42 Street, New York, N.Y. 10017.)

The 8-Day Week, by John Ward Pearson. A blueprint for an almost unheard-of work pattern: four days' work followed by four days' leisure—and use of all the days of the week for ongoing business activity. ($6.95, Har-per and Row.)

The Job Revolution, by Judson Gooding ($1.95, Collier), and *Where Have All the Robots Gone?* by Harold L. Sheppard and Neal Q. Herrick ($3.95, Free Press). Both books grapple with the pursuit of a humanized work experience. The first title is more readable; the second more comprehensive, but heavily statistical.

The Successful Woman is a relatively new monthly newsletter, written in Norman Vincent Peale inspira-tional prose. The enthusiasm of this positive thinking just might be infectious; and besides, it's open-minded enough to publish many different definitions of success. ($5 a year from The Successful Woman, Box 160, Sun Prairie, Wis. 53590.)

A Practical Guide to Flexible Working Hours, by Stephen J. Baum, teaches management how to relax the old rigid schedules. ($15, Noyes Data Corporation.)

Youth and the Meaning of Work. Report of a 1972–73 study of college graduates' career aspirations, including some discouraging findings about young women's per-ceptions of themselves and their potential. ($6 for Re-port PB-217-360, from National Technical Information Service, 5285 Port Royal Road, Springfield, Va. 22151.)

The Nightmare of Success, by William J. Ruzicka, Ph.D. To understand what's wrong with the conventional male approach to career success and competition, read this and weep. ($6.95, from Peninsula Publications, Box 975, Los Altos, Calif. 94022.)

The Achievement Motive, by D.C. McClelland, J.W. At-kinson, R.A. Clark and E.L. Lowell. ($6.75, Appleton) and *A Theory of Achievement Motivation*, by J.W. At-kinson and N.T. Feather ($13, Wiley). Both afford readers a theoretical side-trip into the meaning of achievement.

Women's Motive to Avoid Success, by Matina Horner. The classic study of women's fear of success due to the "double bind." Must we always choose between "femininity" and achievement? (25 cents for reprint of the article that appeared in *Psychology Today,* November 1969 issue; from KNOW, Box 86031, Pittsburgh, Pa. 15221.)

Women and Success: The Anatomy of Achievement, edited by Ruth B. Kundsin. Thirty-seven essays by and about accomplished women. Note particularly: "Marriage with a Successful Woman" and "The Professional Woman as Mother"—two chapters to discuss with your family. ($7.95, William Morrow, Inc.)

Afterword:
One Man's Life with a Working Wife or, "How Does It Feel to Be the Husband Of . . . ?"

by Bertrand B. Pogrebin

At a recent political rally, I meet an old college classmate. Though we haven't seen each other for twenty years, his first words to me are, "How does it feel to be an Also? You were such a star in college—now all I read about is your wife."

After completing a Labor Board hearing, the opposing lawyer claps me on the back and says, "How come you're still practicing law? I thought you would have retired on your wife's money."

In the middle of a squash game (which I'm losing), I suddenly realize I've forgotten an appointment. As I rush off the court, my partner taunts me, "Going home to make dinner?"

It's funny how people react to you when your wife achieves some measure of success on her own. It's as though you had an affliction.

The comments started a couple of years ago when Letty wrote a book that was quite well-received. As she began appearing on TV talk shows, writing for magazines and getting press coverage, I began getting what I think of as The Question: How does it feel to be the husband of . . . ?

The Question may be phrased differently by different people, but the intent is always the same. It's a put-down. In one form it implies my slump in the Pogrebin League standings (How does it feel to be the Avis in the family?). The other common variation is a frontal attack on my status as a wage-earner (How does it feel to be supported by your wife?). The questioner's tone may range from genuine concern to an elbow-in-the-ribs chuckle. But whatever the person's style, his message is clearly that my wife's success reflects badly on my manhood. For what my challengers are really asking is, "How does it feel to be married to a woman who is something besides your wife? Isn't it embarrassing? Can't you control your woman? Aren't you man enough?"

Only when we reverse the sexes do we see the absurdity of this attitude. Imagine putting down a woman for having allowed her husband to become successful. Would anyone ask "How does it feel to be the wife of ... ?" unless the question were asked in admiring curiosity? We find it natural for a woman to gain status through the achievements of her husband. Yet a man somehow loses status through the achievements of his wife. Presumably, for a man to enjoy the full bloom of his manhood, his wife must be a wallflower.

The irony is that, prior to marriage, no one wants a wallflower. Consider a situation where bachelor Melvin Macho is offered the choice of a blind date with either of two women. One is Simone Success, well-known columnist and social activist. The other is Doris Drudge, noted for the neatness of her home, who had washed what was reputed to be the cleanest plate in the Western World and who spends her days at home polishing these talents.

Is there any doubt about the choice Macho would make? Or any man? If we all want to date success before marriage, why turn her into Drudge soon after marriage? And if a husband fails as Pygmalion—if his wife's own identity not only survives his hand but flourishes—then why should he suddenly feel that he has suffered a loss of self-esteem?

The same questions may be asked in the area of premarital and postmarital economic relations. Before marriage, relative earnings rarely figure in the male-female relationship. But after the wedding, it is crucial that the balance of payments weigh in favor of the male. Young husbands today seem to have abandoned the old "I don't want my wife working" routine for one that says she can work as long as she doesn't have a very prestigious job or make very much money. I vividly remember one man— free enough in his thinking to be working in child care ("so that kids can grow up with a male presence around")— who admitted that if his wife ever earned more than he did he wouldn't feel "like a man."

This seems to be a key symptom of the new virility anxiety. Supposedly, as the Women's Movement grows, so does male impotence. It's as if we could chart the rise in the stock of womankind inversely to the fall of the male organ. A sort of wedding of Dow-Jones to Masters and Johnson. First, no one has ever shown that one depends on the other. Second, even if it did, the fault more likely would be with the man's dependency on a false superiority and on his inability to relate to an equal, than with the change in women's status.

Also, The Question reveals something very basic about the prevailing masculine view of marriage itself. It is seen as the final refuge where the battered male ego can fatten up on the structured inferiority of his mate.

That's why "a man's home is his castle." Because inside that framework there is someone who is not doing anything as worthwhile and not earning as much money—the Little Woman. No matter how modest his achievement, she is always there, achieving less. And that's supposed to demonstrate manhood.

A friend of mine explained it to me like this (man-to-man, of course): "The only way marriage can work is if the man is dominant. Otherwise, how could you resolve the one-to-one situation? Somebody has to be Top Gun to break the impasses."

This version of marriage as a face-off with the same person always programmed for supremacy and the other one always charted to lose is not even a fair contest. What's so manly about winning when your opponent always *lets* you win? What's so satisfying about measuring success against a wife who has promised, in one way or another, *not* to be successful? What kind of man knowingly plays a rigged game—and enjoys it? What's more, why get married at all if the union is viewed as a series of confrontations and impasses? To live together as two clashing wills doesn't make sense, even if one is always guaranteed to prevail.

Because it's no fun living with a continuous loser, men should have jettisoned the man's-home-is-his-castle concept along with the divine right of kings.

So much for the hang-ups of the questioners. What's the answer to The Question: "How does it feel to be the husband of . . . ?"

In a word—terrific.

I could go on at this point with all the superlatives that describe the pleasures of living with someone who likes what she is doing and is recognized for doing it well. I could describe the people I've met and the places I've been because of her. Or the genuine interest and respect I have for her activities.

But the main and most terrific pleasure of this equal union is my freedom from guilt. I didn't obliterate her identity and she didn't sacrifice herself to mine. She continues to be her own person, with her own mind and her own ambitions.

In short, like the late Duke of Windsor, I gave up the throne for the woman I love. Call me a feminist dupe. I think it was the manly thing to do.

Index